TEXAS BED & BREAKFAST

COMPLETELY UPDATED 4TH EDITION

Discover the wonders of Texas with Texas Monthly® Guidebooks
from Gulf Publishing Company:

Austin
Dallas
El Paso
Hill Country
Houston
New Mexico
San Antonio
Texas
Texas Parks and Campgrounds
Texas Missions
West Texas and the Big Bend

TEXAS BED & BREAKFAST

COMPLETELY UPDATED 4TH EDITION

DISCOVER THE LONE STAR STATE'S BEST BED & BREAKFAST INNS

GAIL DRAGO, MARJIE MUGNO ACHESON,
AND LYN DUNSAVAGE

ILLUSTRATIONS BY ANTHONY DRAGO

Gulf Publishing Company
Houston, Texas

Gulf Publishing Company
Book Division
P.O. Box 2608 □ Houston, Texas 77252-2608

10 9 8 7 6 5 4 3 2 1

Library of Congress Cataloging-in-Publication Data
Drago, Gail, 1947–
    Texas bed & breakfast / Gail Drago, Marjie Mugno Acheson, and Lyn Dunsavage ; illustrations by Anthony Drago. — Completely updated 4th ed.
        p.   cm. (The Texas Monthly Guidebooks)
    Updated ed. of : Texas bed & breakfast / by Ann Ruff, Gail Drago, and Marjie Mugno Acheson. Completely rev. 3rd. ed. c1993.
    Includes index.
    ISBN 0-88415-868-3
    1. Bed and breakfast accommodations—Texas—Guidebooks. 2. Texas—Guidebooks. I. Mugno, Marjie. II. Dunsavage, Lyn. III. Ruff, Ann, 1930– Texas bed & breakfast. IV. Title.
TX907.3.T4D73   1997
647.94764'03—dc21   97-3974
                                                                  CIP

Printed in the United States of America.

Texas Monthly is a registered trademark of Mediatex Communications Corporation.

Dedication

To all whose hospitality and homes have made this book possible, as well as to those who are enjoying bed and breakfast in Texas—and our book. A fond salute also to our former co-author and legendary travel writer, the late Ann Ruff. Her spirit lives on.

—Gail, Lyn, and Marjie

CONTENTS

DALLAS, FORT WORTH, AND NORTHEAST TEXAS

THE PANHANDLE AND WEST TEXAS

ACKNOWLEDGMENTS

What a great experience this has been touring this past year searching for the best B&Bs in Texas! To the reservation service directors, especially Donna Mittel of Fredericksburg's Gastehaus Schmidt and Donna West and Brandy Davis of Bed and Breakfast Hosts of San Antonio, I send heartfelt gratitude for your assistance. As for the many hosts who opened their doors to me in spite of inconvenient timing, I learned from you the true meaning of Texas hospitality.

Laurels also go to Gulf Publishing editor, Joyce Alff, whose amazing patience, support, and literary expertise kept us free of panic. Also, thanks go to the artist of our visuals, my husband Anthony, who would rather take a backroad than the interstate, and my son and fellow traveler, Nick, who reads a map better than any teenager I know. Last, I wish to acknowledge Ann Marie Paradowski who drove for me while I compiled notes, and Alisa Paradowski, who, along with Nick, showed constant good humor spiced with touches of bravery as we ventured into the unknown. Because of you three, I now have memories enough to last a lifetime.

Gail Drago

Thanks to the bed and breakfast owners and innkeepers in North, Northeast Texas, Austin, Salado, and West Texas for being so cooperative and helpful when I reviewed their areas. I especially appreciated two B&B hosts, Dorothy Grant of Uncertain and Caddo Lake, and Ann Thornton of Canton, for each spending the better part of a day chauffeuring me around to outlying properties. Thanks also to input from some special people—Rosie and Ed Hughes, Ginger Hubbard, Pat Bradley, Candace Beesley, and most of all, my husband, Alex Acheson; and to Ruth Wilson, Bed & Breakfast Texas Style, and to Historic Accommodations of Texas, for their inspiration and help through the years.

Marjie Mugno Acheson

I couldn't have done this book without some excellent support. My daughter Jennifer, who has extraordinary organizational capabilities, packed up all her things in the last weeks of her graduating summer to accompany me. Jennifer kept track of what day it was, what town we were in, and where the B&Bs were located and also kept the files with the notes, which mysteriously crept about in the car, finding niches under the seat and other unlikely places. It was no easy task. When Jennifer had to register for her freshman year in Southwestern University, her sister Katrina took over. When the car no longer could make the trip, son Doug, whose job was to man the home front, offered up his 1978 Chevrolet pick-up truck to finish the job, creating an effect a little like the Joads making their way through the hills of Texas sixty years after their California trek. This book, truly, is a family accomplishment.

Texas Co-op writer/editor Joel Horton stepped in with his B&B expertise. He's visited many B&Bs on his journeys and provided some valuable insights. If it hadn't been for the lovely hosts and hostesses who took us in, gave us the most comfortable beds, and fed us wonderful breakfasts to fortify us so we could go forth the following day, we definitely couldn't have accomplished this feat. There have been so many wonderful places and people and so little space, "thank you" is too meager a term, but it has to be said again. Thank you.

Lyn Dunsavage

INTRODUCTION

Bed and breakfast in Texas has an entirely new face—one drawn from the industry's dramatic growth during the last twelve years. Our first edition of this guidebook, published in 1985, is testimony, in fact, to that change. We find it amusing that in those early days we had to dig deep to uncover a grand total of 133 accommodations, most of which were simply "host homes," private residences where guests stayed in a spare bedroom and had breakfast with the host family in the morning.

Today, B&B in the Lone Star State is big business. Host homes have given way to grand mansions, posh beach houses, historic cottages, and working cattle ranches with guest quarters sure to turn any city slicker into a seasoned cowboy. And, no longer did we have to search. Scores of hosts around the state found *us*. When word leaked that we were updating the guide, our phones never stopped ringing, with one lead yielding ten others. Our master list took on a life of its own, growing daily in spite of our efforts to finalize it. When the total reached an astounding one thousand, fear gripped us. How could we possibly visit all these B&Bs and meet our deadline scheduled for six short months away? But with our names already scrawled on the contract's dotted line, there was no turning back. With alarm in control, we jumped into our cars and took off in three different directions through the second largest state in the union. It was a whirlwind tour that has changed us forever. Our motto is now "Give us liberty and the B&B!"

As we traveled, it also grew very apparent that our old criteria for the "best" B&Bs needed a facelift. Over a decade before, private bath facilities ensured an accommodation a high rating. Today, private baths are givens, and amenities stretch the gamut from Web site access to massage sessions to private lake tours and carriage rides. As for variety, guests can now choose from a cozy country experience far from the "maddening crowd" to elegance in the city where high tea marks a pleasant afternoon.

As for locations, we found pockets of unhosted B&Bs in such quaint towns as Fredericksburg, to hordes of ranches in West Texas where "buffalo roam and the deer and the antelope play," to urban cities such as Dallas and San Antonio. Also on our list is an old historic Brenham office building converted to an exquisite B&B along with an impressive number of stately mansions, as well as a list of stagecoach inns that whisper tales of affluent Texans long gone down that final dusty trail. Our favorites, though, were those accommodations, grand or not, that were managed by enthusiastic, upbeat hosts who knew the true meaning of professional attitude and hospitality. What proved to be true wherever we went was that if the hosts loved their B&Bs, their guests quickly caught the emotion.

New on the horizon are a large number of "unhosted" B&Bs, completely furnished guest houses or country cottages where you are totally alone. An invisible host stocks the refrigerator with a self-serve breakfast that ranges from continental fare of orange juice, cheese, and croissants, to a full country breakfast of farm fresh bacon, fresh yard eggs, gourmet coffee, and local fruit. Homemade jams and jellies grace some tables. Some B&B hosts also give discount or complimentary tickets for guests to breakfast at a local restaurant. Our favorites, though, were the true B&Bs where hosts prepared and served their guests and even joined them at the table if invited. As far as we know, no listing here sports itself as a B&B, yet leaves refrigerators totally empty.

Rates vary, depending upon location. Bigger cities tend to be more pricey, but that's not true everywhere.

B&B goers enjoy! We would like your input and encourage any of you to write us through Gulf Publishing with comments, compliments, and complaints.

HOW TO USE THIS BOOK

Making Contact

Although each independently operated listing has its own phone number and address, we have included a list of the Texas reservation services. Some B&B hosts prefer to have all their paperwork and guest screening done for them, and some may find it more convenient to book through them as well. Others, however, book themselves and are also listed with a service just on a referral basis. For the guest, using a service means access to other accommodations if the first choice is already booked. Fredericksburg, for example, now has over 100 B&Bs, most unhosted, because it has become a very popular tourist town. Jefferson runs second in Texas while Wimberley is third. For the less adventurous, a reservation service can find just the right B&B for just the right price. Whichever way you handle reservations, book early. You will be amazed how fast the B&Bs are booked on any weekend, anywhere, all year.

RESERVATION SERVICES

AAA Reservations
Jimmie Ruth Ford
Box 310
Jefferson 75657
(800) 299-1593 (903) 665-3692
Fax (903) 665-1331

A&L Reservations
Angela Fyffe, Lynette Morris
603 Elizabeth St.
Jefferson 75657
(903) 665-1017

Be My Guest
Bed & Breakfast Homes
Elizabeth Barclay, Reservations Manger
8014 W. Woodway Dr., Suite 2092
Waco, Texas 76712
(817) 776-6708
Fax (817) 776-0934

Bed & Breakfast of Fredericksburg
Kathy Kopp, Director
619 West Main
Fredericksburg, Texas 78624
(210) 997-4712

Bed and Breakfast Hosts of San Antonio
Douglas and Donna West
P.O. Box 831203
San Antonio, Texas 78283
800-356-1605
(210) 824-8036
Fax (210) 226-7136

Bed & Breakfast Texas Style
Ruth Wilson, Director
4224 W. Red Bird Lane
Dallas 75237
(972) 298-8586 or (800) 899-4538
Fax (972) 298-7118
E-Mail address: BDTXStyle1@aol.com

Book-A-Bed-Ahead
Alma Anne & Joseph Parker
Box 723
Jefferson 75657
(800) 468-2627 (903) 665-3956
Fax (903) 665-8551

East Texas Reservation Service
Gayle Irby, Reservations
c/o Sweet Creek Farm
Rt. 3, Box 94 WW
Canton, Texas 75103
(888) 327-8839 or (903) 479-4052
Fax (903) 479-3158

Gastehaus Schmidt Reservation Service
Donna Mittel, Director
231 West Main
Fredericksburg, Texas 78624
(210) 997-5612 Fax (210) 997-8484

Jefferson Reservation Service
124 West Austin
Jefferson 75657
(800) 833-6758

Rio Frio Bed N Breakfast
LeAnn and Anthony Sharp, Directors
Ranch Road 1120
Rio Frio, Texas 78879
(210) 232-6633

Sand Dollar Hospitality
Pat Hirshbrunner, Director
3605 Mendenhall
Corpus Christi, Texas 78415
(512) 853-1222

Wimberley Lodging
Nancie Austin, Director
P.O. Box 1807
Wimberley, Texas 78676
(512) 847-3909
800-460-3909

For Information Only:
Historic Accommodations of Texas
Box 1399
Fredericksburg 78624
(800) HAT (428)-0368

Our System of Labels

This guide is divided into territories. See Table of Contents for boundaries. The B&Bs are listed in alphabetical order under each city or town. The description for each B&B is preceded by basic information that upon quick glance gives you name, address, phone and fax numbers, "hosted" or "unhosted," type of breakfast served, rates, restrictions, number of guest accommodations, and method of payment required.

So that you'll know ahead of time the kind of morning fare to expect, we have labeled breakfasts as follows:

- Continental breakfast: rolls, juice, coffee or tea.
- Continental plus breakfast: several choices of rolls or muffins, juices, fresh fruit, coffee or tea (may even include cereal).
- Full breakfast: fruit, juice, eggs, meat, coffee or tea. Or fruit, pancakes or waffles or omelets and meat, coffee or teas.
- Gourmet: Eggs Benedict, casseroles, smoked fish, breakfast steaks, lox and bagels, champagne, imported coffees or teas.
- OYO (on your own): fixings left in refrigerator for you to prepare. Supplies vary.

As for rates, we used the old favorite "$" with a price range. Though some here seem pricey, we think the money is well spent. Our price ranges, however, do not include the state and local motel/hotel tax that the B&B must add, so budget accordingly. Also, these rates are subject to change:

xviii

$—Under $60
$$—$61–$80
$$$—$81–$100
$$$$—over $100

Credit cards accepted are listed as follows:

AE—American Express
D—Discover
MC—MasterCard
V—Visa
DC—Diners Club
No cr—cash only
All cr—all credit cards

The reservation services usually take credit cards.

Area Code Alert

An increasing number of area codes around the state have been changed or are in the process of being changed, so if you have trouble reaching a bed and breakfast, check to see whether its area code has changed.

AUSTIN, SAN ANTONIO, AND THE HILL COUNTRY

AUSTIN

You can get just about anywhere in no time at all in this Central Texas town, which now has as fine an array of B&Bs as anywhere in the state. (More B&Bs here even have the welcome mat out to children—pets, too—than anywhere in the state, it seems, despite the elegance of their decor.)

Blessed with unending charm and proximity to the Highland Lakes, where the wildflowers really put on a spectacular show each spring, Austin is a town for all seasons. Town Lake, where you can hike and bike in the shadow of the city skyline, go canoeing or take a narrated ride on an excursion boat; scenic Lake Austin, Barton Springs (some brave the chilly water even in winter), and so much more, make Austin one of the state's most popular destinations.

Austin's Wildflower Inn

Host: Kay Jackson, 1200 W. 22½ Street, Austin 78705,
(512) 477-9639, fax (512) 474-4188, 4 guest rooms, 3 baths,
full breakfast, $–$$, children welcome, but no smoking inside
or pets, MC, V, AE

Built in the early 1930s and on a quiet, tree-lined street, this two-story frame home has original oak hardwood floors, antique furniture, and handmade quilts. A shaded stone patio under a Texas oak on one side, a bi-level wood deck in back, and porch in front add to the charm of Austin's Wildflower Inn, which has four inviting rooms with double beds (two share a bath).

The Country Room has its own private upstairs entrance and a sitting porch. Three rooms are named for members of Kay's family, including the David G. Burnet Canopy Room. Burnet was president of the Republic of Texas. Homemade breads will be among your hearty breakfast treats.

The Wildflower Inn is minutes away not only from the State Capitol and Governor's Mansion downtown and The University of Texas, but also recreational landmarks such as Caswell Tennis Courts and the Shoal Creek Hike and Bike Trail, which parallels Lamar Boulevard.

Kay Jackson, by the way, belongs to the **Greater Austin Bed & Breakfast Association,** which has a well-organized in-town inspection and vacancy referral service. If the Wildflower Inn or B&B of your choice can't accommodate you when you wish, ask to be referred to the association member on duty that week.

Bremond House

Host: Connie Burton, 404 West 7th, Austin 78701,
(512) 482-0411, fax (512) 479-0789, 4 rooms, 2 private baths,
1 shared, gourmet breakfast, $$–$$$, no pets, smoking on porch or
grounds only, MC, V

Now a Historic District, the Bremond Block long has been a treasured part of Austin's charm, with three majestic tree-shaded turn-of-the-century homes, imposingly elevated on a hill a few blocks from the State Capitol. It's exciting that the Bremond House—the showpiece of the impressive block with a grand wraparound screened porch and 14-foot ceilings—is now accessible to the public as a B&B. The lower level has been converted into Cafe Bremond, where offerings ranging from musical entertainment to literary readings are held several times a week. B&B guests are given a complimentary ticket to the cabaret. (Little sound can be heard in the guest rooms above, if a good night's sleep is what you have in mind.) Art exhibits, weddings, and other social and business functions are often held at the Bremond House as well.

Two of the handsomely furnished, first-floor guest rooms have king beds and sitting areas, and one a queen-sized bed. The fourth includes a full bed, screened porch, and table. Each guest room is equipped with a telephone/modem line; just ask if you need a fax or copier.

Enjoy the inviting common areas, too, including the parlor (ask to see the window that is really a door). A Cordon Bleu culinary artist presides over Bremond breakfasts as well as special events. A buffet breakfast is served in the dining room, but some prefer eating in their rooms or on the porches.

Connie, a former children's book publisher, adds that children are welcome at the historic Bremond House.

The Brook House

Host: Barbara Love, 609 W. 33rd, Austin 78705, (512) 459-0534, 6 guest rooms, 6 baths, full breakfast, $–$$, smoking on porches and grounds, all cr

Around the corner from the McCallum House is another long-time, picturesque B&B, The Brook House. The beautifully restored and furnished home, built in 1922, has a shaded backyard, garden, and tin-roofed gazebo. While there is an antique pine king-sized bed in one guest room, the other two in the house, as well as in the Upper and Lower Carriage House suites and the Cottage, all have queen-sized beds. Children and pets are welcome guests in the latter, which also has a trundle and daybed.

Amenities in each room include TV and a phone, but the special charms of the Brook House are all the porches and decks—and a yellow lab named Ernie.

Carrington's Bluff and The Governor's Inn

Hosts: Lisa and Ed Mugford, 1900 David Street, Austin 78705, (512) 479-0638 or (800) 871-8908, fax (512) 476-4769, 8 rooms, 7 private baths, 1 shared, the Writers' Cottage, full breakfast, $-$$, children and (well-behaved) pets are welcome, but smoking outside only, all cr

The spacious, sloping grounds—which include a garden, gazebo, and a 500-year-old oak—gives Carrington's Bluff's main house special appeal. Though a busy thoroughfare (Lamar Boulevard) is down below, you wouldn't know it because the wooded setting is so serene. It's tucked away on a tree-covered bluff on an easy-to-miss street just minutes from UT Austin or downtown.

Built in 1877 on land that was once part of a 22-acre dairy farm, the house itself is picturesque, with a full-length veranda in front and five guest rooms. Carrington's Bluff is cozy and comfortable with a fireplace, player piano, and lace cloths on the tables in the dining room where breakfast is served.

The hospitable hosts' three bedroom, three bath Writers' Cottage across the street includes a kitchen. Two rooms have queen-sized beds, and the third a king and twins. It is especially suited for those in town on business—or writers, of course.

The Governor's Inn, 611 W. 22nd, and only two blocks from UT, is another one of the Mugford's acclaimed B&B properties. Built in 1897, this inviting B&B has ten elegantly furnished rooms with private baths, all appropriately named for former Texas governors. The Sam Houston Room has its own porch. The Governor Ma and Pa Ferguson Suite on the third floor has a king and daybed with a trundle. This neoclassical Victorian is also a favorite for weddings and other business and social functions, which the hosts are happy to help you plan.

Cable TV and private phones lines are among amenities in all three B&Bs. A fax machine is available in the office.

Casa Loma

Hosts: Ron and Sharon Hillhouse, 5512 Cuesta Verde, Austin 78746, (800) 222-0248 or (512) 327-7189, fax (512) 327-9150, 1 suite, 2 guest rooms, all private baths, full breakfast, $$$-$$$$, no children, pets, or smoking, all cr

Seeing is believing! Incredible Casa Loma—a gorgeous, 10,000-square-foot Mediterranean villa with a red tile roof perched on the edge of a hilltop in Austin's affluent Westlake Hills—brings to mind the majesty of Monaco or romance of the Riviera. From the verandas that wrap around three sides of the palatial home on two levels, you'll have panoramic views that will be etched in your memory: Lake Austin and its acclaimed arched bridge, the Austin Country Club fairways, the Austin skyline—even the UT Tower—and of course, the exquisite Hill Country sunsets. Floor-to-ceiling windows permit commanding vistas even from inside the exclusive retreat.

An expansive gate buttressed by curving limestone walls adorned with heavy iron coach lamps is the impressive entry to Casa Loma. The first, or ground level, has a swimming pool at one end adjoining a fitness room, which you're welcome to use. Other amenities include a dry sauna, and the hosts can arrange on-site massages and spa treatments—even tee-times, since you're minutes away from several great golf courses.

The three handsome guest rooms are on the lower level. Each has its own private parking area and entrance, phone, TV—and magnificent view. The Burgundy Room has a queen mahogany four poster (and art by the world-renowned Jack White), while the Rose Room and Fairway Suite, king beds.

Casa Loma, incidentally, means house on the hill. Since the hosts' last name is Hillhouse, Casa Loma seemed like a name that was meant to be.

Amid all the world-class luxury, you'll still feel right at home because of the personable couple's joy in sharing all that is there, whether your stay is for business or pleasure. Casa Loma...their home is your home.

Chequered Shade (Lake Austin)

Host: Millie Scott, 2530 Pearce Road, Austin 78730, (800) 577-5786 or (512) 346-8318, 3 rooms, 2 baths, full breakfast, $$, no pets or children under 12, smoking outside only, MC, V, AE

Framed by hilly terrain, Lake Austin surely is one of the most scenic lakes in the state! And if relaxing at a water getaway has appeal, you'll enjoy your stay at the Chequered Shade even more, for it's in a rural neighborhood right across from Lake Austin. At the end

of Pearce Road is the quaint Ski Shores Restaurant—a waterfront fix-
ture for 50 years—where you can sit at wooden tables outside year
round and enjoy the view, whether you go for lunch, dinner, or whenever. You also can dock your boat there or charter one for a spin
around the lake.

Nearby Emma Long Park has boating, swimming, and picnicking
facilities, too, and you're only 15 minutes from some great lakeside
restaurants and resorts where you can golf or play tennis. Austin is 30
minutes away.

Watching deer is a special treat from the patio in back of the B&B.
It is not unusual for 10 or 15 deer at a time to come down the brush-
covered rocky hill to eat, unconcerned about being watched. In fact,
they even graze on the lawn in front!

The patio is just off the downstairs guest room, which has a private
bath. The two rooms upstairs have a connecting bath, and are ideal for
a family or friends; otherwise, only one room is booked so the guest
also will have a private bath. Amenities include private phone lines
and a fax. Millie is not only a gracious host, but a gourmet cook, so
you'll enjoy breakfast as much as the scenery at the Chequered Shade.

Millie advises guests, "When you leave our lovely area, expect some
difficulty in readjusting to everyday life!"

Citiview

**Host: Carol Hayden, 1405 E. Riverside Drive, Austin 78741,
(512) 441-2606 or (800) BST-VIEW, fax (512) 441-2949,
3 rooms, 3 baths, full breakfast, $$$, no smoking indoors,
MC, V, AE**

If you love animals, this two-acre, exotic bird and animal sanctu-
ary south of Town Lake is for you. Your pet is welcome, too, which
is not surprising since Carol, who founded the Fur Ball in Dallas in
1992, now the largest fund-raiser in the state, and her husband, an attor-
ney who is on the S.P.C.A. board in Dallas, have an amazing menagerie
that includes three great danes, a cat, about 100 exotic birds and, of
course, Charlie Girl. The blue and gold Macaw's phone repertoire
includes, "Citiview, may I help you?" (She even can wave good-
bye.) Phantom, the llama, peacocks, Nigerian dwarf goats, rabbits, and
ducks are part of their petting zoo. Usually penned up, occasionally
they are allowed to roam around to the delight of young and old.

With a cascading waterfall that dramatically drops five feet into a Koi pond and a Japanese Zen garden, the tree-covered grounds are a beautiful backdrop for any social or business occasion. A pool, gazebo, 600-square-foot domed English conservatory, plus patio and terrace areas for dining and dancing—even dinner for two, if you ask in advance—contribute to the ambience.

Built in 1951 in a style reminiscent of Frank Lloyd Wright, the stunning house has hardwood floors, high beam ceilings, picture windows, and European art deco furnishings imported from Paris. On a secluded street just off a busy boulevard, Citiview sits serenely atop a steep incline. Your view of Austin landmarks like the capitol dome and Town Lake is the "best view," according to a local newspaper poll.

The couple have three spacious guest rooms with private baths and phone lines. An in-house chef prepares a healthy gourmet breakfast; often the organic produce comes from their garden. Services such as manicures and massages can be arranged in the privacy of your room. The exciting pulse of the city beats right outside Citiview's door—but you'll be in a peaceful world of your own in this unique B&B.

Fairview

Hosts: Duke and Nancy Waggoner, 1304 Newning Avenue, Austin 78704, (512) 444-4746 or (800) 310-4746, 4 rooms, 4 baths, 2 suites in the Carriage House, full breakfast, $$–$$$$, no pets or smoking, children in Carriage House only, all cr

This majestic B&B sits on a knoll surrounded by ancient oaks and lovely gardens, just south of the Congress Avenue Bridge in an older neighborhood that is being revived. Built around 1910 and an excellent example of Texas Colonial Revival Architecture, Fairview was divided into nine apartments during the '50s. Beautifully restored by the Waggoners, it is an Austin landmark. The four spacious, antique-filled guest rooms have a TV and phone; some even have screened porches that reach out into the trees.

Especially suited to business meetings as well as overnight lodging, the Governor's Suite includes an enclosed sun porch with a small conference table as well as a double sofa bed. It also has a massive king Victorian Renaissance bed and a bathroom with a separate dressing/sitting room. Another guest room is named the Back Room, which seems appropriate since Austin is a political center. (The couple has a neat story about the full Eastlake half-tester bed in the Ambassador's Room.) Your "to-die-for" breakfast is served in the impressive Great Room, as are light refreshments each afternoon.

The cozy Carriage House in back has two suites with different, but delightful decors. The first-floor Garden Cottage and four-room Sunday House upstairs have queen beds, full kitchens, and private baths.

Duke says Nancy deserves most of the credit for the lavishly landscaped backyard, which includes a rose garden. You can stop and smell the roses here!

The Gardens on Duval

Hosts: Dorothy Sloan, 3210 Duval, Austin 78705, (512) 477-9200, fax (512) 477-4220, 2 suites, full breakfast, $$, no children under 12, pets, or indoor smoking, MC, V

Another B&B in a quiet neighborhood near UT and the fabulous LBJ Library is The Gardens on Duval. Dorothy Sloan's spacious, two-story stucco home, which has two comfortable suites, is aptly named because of the grounds, which abound with magnificent trees, a formal herb garden, and over 200 varieties of antique roses. Fresh flowers fill the restored home, built in 1919. Enjoy the view from the patios and porches.

One suite has a king-sized sleigh bed, private bath, sitting room/study, and sun room; the other, a queen canopy bed with a sitting room/study, and bath with claw-foot tub and shower. Both have TV, a phone, and access to a fax. Let Dorothy know your dietary needs when she fixes breakfast. Everything will be coming up roses if you stay at The Gardens of Duval, which can also accommodate weddings and small meetings.

The Inn at Pearl Street

Host: Jill Bickford, 809 West Martin Luther King at Pearl Street, Austin 78701, (800) 494-2203 or (512) 477-2233, fax (512) 795-0592, 5 guest rooms, private baths, continental breakfasts OYO weekdays, full on Saturday, champagne brunch on Sunday, $$$–$$$$, no children, pets, or smoking, all cr

Showcased by the Austin Symphony League as the Designer Showhouse in 1995, The Inn at Pearl Street is another exceptional B&B. Look here, look there, look everywhere, and something will catch your eye at this luxurious inn, which abounds with old-world charm and class, art, and collectibles. Many of the fine furnishings or pieces of art were collected on Jill's numerous jaunts abroad, and she has lots of stories to tell.

Located a little beyond the steep incline on a very busy street, just five blocks from UT, The Inn at Pearl Street has a different decor in each well-appointed guest room. For a romantic rendezvous, choose The Gothic Suite, which includes a cathedral bed and gold and marble shower/Jacuzzi. And ask about the Celebration Package, which includes a five-course candlelight dinner served in your room.

All the guest rooms have private baths and balconies, phones with answering machines ready for modem hookup, and cable TV. Amenities also include a morning paper with breakfast, turndown service, plush bathrobes, complimentary wine, and snacks. And service with a smile!

The Inn at Pearl Street caters to business travelers, too. It has a conference room and table for up to 25, plus a library with lighted study tables and a fax machine. (Books and games are also available in the library.)

Built near the turn of the century, and used as a Hollywood movie set in the mid-1980s, the Greek Revival home was purchased in 1993 by Jill, who, with her family, spent two years on restoration of this architecturally interesting, three-story gem before opening it to guests. The enterprising young woman also has big B&B plans for the mammoth white mansion next door, which she also owns and is renovating. As if she didn't have enough to do, Jill also has a full-time business, lining up fully furnished apartment homes for executives.

Lake Travis Bed and Breakfast

Hosts: Judy and Vic Dwyer, 4446 Eck Lane, Austin 78734, (512) 266-3386, 3 bedrooms, 3 baths, full breakfast, $$$$, no city hotel tax, no children, pets, or smoking inside, MC, V, AE

On a cliff overlooking the blue waters of Lake Travis, this luxurious 6,500-square-foot house has 7 levels and 12 decks! You can see for 75 miles from just about every spot in this fantastic B&B—and the sunsets are incredible. Once an oil company's retreat, it is only 20 minutes from downtown Austin.

Each exquisitely furnished guest room, which has a king bed and a private deck facing the lake, is on a different level. You'll be served an imaginative breakfast in bed if you wish or eat on your deck. Judy's artistic culinary creations include cantaloupe shaped like a hummingbird and longhorn steers made from crescent rolls.

You'll be pampered with turndown service, perfumed sheets (satin sheets are extra), chocolate truffles, and bathrobes. A theater/library/study where you can watch videos or shoot a few rounds of pool, a swimming pool where you can sit at tables in the water and play cards, a 26-jet therapeutic spa, and a fitness area are among other amenities. A massage and spa treatments can be arranged. Live the life of Riley here!

What else is there to do? A winery is within walking distance, and The Oasis Restaurant, known for its nachos and view, is only five minutes away. (Lake Travis has come of age with about 22 restaurants now!) Steps lead down to the hosts' private floating dock, which has a kitchen, bar, and dining area. Tie your own boat up or charter their Catalina. Fishing and snorkeling gear is available. The Dwyers even will be happy to take you sailing at this mini-resort. Talk about a perfect B&B!

McCallum House

Hosts: Nancy and Roger Danley, 613 W. 32nd, Austin 78705, phone/fax (512) 451-6744, 3 guest rooms, 3 baths, 2 suites in Garden Apartment, full breakfast, $–$$$, no pets, but children over 11 are welcome, smoking on porches or grounds, MC, V

In business since 1983, the McCallum House is like a good bottle of wine: the B&B keeps getting better with age. Credit the entertaining hosts and their warm hospitality with perpetuating the McCallum mystique (you might ask about their recent bicycle trip through France). Only a few blocks north of UT, the three-story Princess Anne Victorian has worlds of charm, too. You'll feel right at home, whether you come for a romantic getaway (special packages are available) or on business.

Lovingly restored with both a Texas historical marker and designation as an Austin landmark, it was built in 1907 by A. N. and Jane McCallum. He was superintendent of Austin schools for 39 years, while Jane, the only person ever to serve two governors as secretary of state, was a leader in the Texas Woman Suffrage Movement.

Private baths, individual phone lines and even answering machines are in all the rooms, along with mini-kitchens or kitchenettes and sitting areas, porches, or verandas. On the second floor are the Blue and Rose Rooms with queen beds and porches and the Green Room, which has its own entrance and twin beds. An elegant suite on the third floor, Jane's Loft, has a queen and two twins. Built in the 1920s, the spacious Garden Apartment in back has a queen bed and two twins.

You'll usually find an interesting assortment of visitors at the breakfast table in the beautiful period dining room, but you can order a tray for your room. The Danleys also have corporate suites for those in town on business, by the way.

Southard-House

Hosts: Jerry and Rejina Southard, 908 Blanco, Austin 78703, (512) 474-4731, 4 rooms, 4 baths, 1 suite, 2 cottages, continental breakfast weekdays, full breakfast weekends with 3 seatings, $$–$$$, no pets, children, or smoking, all cr

Filled with antiques and artwork, Italian marble fireplaces, pine floors and crown mouldings, the Southard-House is located just west of the Texas Capitol in what was once the residential heart of Austin. This 1890 Greek Revival home is a short stroll from four-star restaurants, antique shops, art galleries and offbeat clubs on 6th Street. In 1910, the entire house was raised and an identical first floor was built under it.

The Treaty Oak Suite includes a queen white-iron bed and a parlor with a fireplace, queen sleeper sofa, desk, TV, and small refrigerator. There are queen or double beds in all the rooms, not only in the Southard-House, but in their two guest cottages nearby.

The Lone Star Inn, a single-story bungalow built in the 1920s, has a pool and three rooms and a suite—all named for colorful characters like Lillie Langtry, Ma Ferguson, Pancho Villa, and Judge Roy Bean. All the rooms here as well as in the **The Republic,** which is next door, have phones, private entrances, and baths.

Built in 1890, The Republic has two luxurious, amenity- and antique-filled rooms and three suites, with either small refrigerators or kitchenettes. The John C. Hayes Suite (named for the first Texas

Ranger) has a fully equipped kitchen and large skylight over a small Jacuzzi tub.

Like many of the properties in Austin, the three are geared not only to guests in town on business, but pleasure as well.

Woodburn House

Hosts: Herb and Sandra Dickson, 4401 Avenue D, Austin 78751, (512) 458-4335, 4 rooms, 4 baths, full breakfast, $$, children 9 and up, smoking on porches only, no pets, MC, V, AE

In the memory book at the Woodburn House, departing guests often write about feeling "more like honored guests than paying customers." And you will, too, at this Austin landmark in Hyde Park, which is listed in the National Register of Historic Places. Built in 1909, the Woodburn Home more recently has been recognized in the Register as a contributing structure to the historic area.

The home—and one of the four upstairs guest rooms—bear the name of Bettie Hamilton Woodburn, who bought it in 1920. Her father, Andrew Jackson Hamilton, was the provisional governor of Texas. A former Hyde Park resident, Texana artist George Boutwell, purchased the house in 1979 to save it from demolition and moved it to this site, then helped with its restoration. The Dicksons have added their own special touches.

The Woodburn House has wraparound porches on the first and second floors where guests sip their morning coffee or relax at the end of the day. Many of the Dicksons' American antique furnishings and handmade quilts have been in Herb's family since before the turn of the century.

Two of the inviting guest rooms have queen beds, one a king, and the fourth, a queen and twin beds. All include a rocking chair, desk, and phone with a private line. Complimentary toiletries are in the hall if you've forgotten something. Herb whips up those delicious gourmet breakfast dishes you'll enjoy in the formal dining room.

Easily accessible from IH 35 and the airport and just north of UT, the Woodburn House is ideal for University and business travelers as well as tourists.

Save time for the Elizabeth Ney Museum a block or so away and the self-guided walking tour of Historic Hyde Park. The Hyde Park

Bar and Grill has an interesting ambience, good food, and late night service. Asks the Dicksons for directions to the City Market, too, or about other B&Bs you might want to visit.

Ziller House

Hosts: Sam and Wendy Kindred, 800 Edgecliff Terrace, Austin 78704, (800) 949-5446 or (512) 462-0100, fax (512) 462-9166, 3 rooms, private baths, 1 suite, Carriage House, full or continental breakfast OYO, $$–$$$, children welcome with prior approval, no pets, smoking on terraces only, MC, V, AE

Dennis Quaid and Meg Ryan, Lyle Lovett and Julia Roberts, and other Hollywood notables have had romantic rendezvous at the secluded Ziller House—another sophisticated Austin B&B with an incredible setting, fine furnishings, and art. On a rocky bluff overlooking Town Lake, the home's elegant ambience surely equals any found in Tinseltown. You'll feel at home nonetheless.

Enhanced by natural foliage as well as landscaping, the Ziller House is a gated, three-story, 8,000-square-foot Mediterranean-style estate at the end of a cul-de-sac. You'll especially enjoy the water below and Austin skyline beyond while relaxing on the multi-level patios. A huge limestone and fossil fireplace and dramatic screen are focal points of the living room.

Up to 15 can be accommodated in the Main House and Carriage House. A private phone line, portable phone, cable TV, small refrigerator, microwave, and coffee/tea maker are in each room's service cabinet in the main house as well as the Carriage House nearby. Choose between a full or continental breakfast, which is refrigerated in your room so you can reheat it whenever you wish in the morning. (Sam is the gourmet chef.) Being able to eat and run has special appeal for those in town on business. A cliffside Jacuzzi spa and a gazebo are among amenities. Hiking or biking along Town Lake is a special treat.

As you'd expect, the Ziller House is in demand for business and social functions. The Italianate mansion, surprisingly enough, was the headquarters for the Austin Humane Society when built in 1938. Animals, supposedly, were allowed free access to all the rooms! B&B guests ahead of their time!

BANDERA

Tallichet's Serendipity

Hosts: Jan and Julian Tallichet, P.O. Box 2069, Bandera 78003, (210) 460-8343, fax (210) 283-3029, e-mail: oceangre@hctc.net, 1 suite, full breakfast, $$, smoking allowed, pets accepted, no children, no cr

A rarity in B&Bs, the Tallichets accept smokers and—given they have a silky, a shepherd, and three poodles, as well as several cats—they accept pets (obviously, yours needs to be friendly). The Tallichets (who retired from the travel business) have been just about everywhere, which is reflected in the eclectic, rich fabric of their decor, with Oriental art and furniture, African spears and masks, ornate silver and crystal, and historic children's and Civil War literature mixed with stuffed furniture (from which it's difficult to escape). Your two-room suite overlooks the gardens, the terrace of which has a hot tub (just over from the fish pond), all of which overlooks Bandera Creek. Jan prides herself on her breakfast, which she'll serve outside, in the formal dining room or in your own room, whatever your preference.

BASTROP

Buttonwood Row

Host: Susan B. Long, 1402 Hill Street (on the corner of Buttonwood and Hill), Bastrop 78602, (512) 303-5664, 1 suite with private bath, continental plus, $$$, no children, no pets, smoking allowed on terrace, no cr

The Buttonwood Row B&B sits on almost an acre of beautiful old trees, including elms, pecans, and magnolias. The Greek Revival-style home is filled with Victorian antiques, some of which date back to the 1700s. When you arrive, Susan attempts to have freshly baked chocolate chip cookies ready for you. You have your own private ivy-covered terrace, with lanterns lighting your private entrance into the solarium and sitting room in front of the large bedroom suite (with king bed) and private bath off of the hall. Breakfast includes a fresh fruit compote and freshly baked hot breads (including jalapeño cheese) served on fine china and crystal. Susan focuses on privacy for her guests and emphasizes making special arrangements for them, if they want, so they can "be allowed to cut their engines off." From a golf package to a catered dinner on the terrace with horse-drawn carriage, she will put together special packages for you.

The Crossing, Cabins on the Colorado

Hosts: Judi and Tommy Hoover, 601 Chestnut, Bastrop 78602, (512) 321-7002, 4 small homes with private baths and kitchens, continental plus, $$–$$$, no TV or telephones, smoking in designated areas, kids accepted, fishing, canoe livery (from 4 hours to overnights), all cr

The Crossing is a collection of authentic small old homes in a village of shops and restaurants nestled alongside the Colorado River under the Old Iron Bridge. There's a windmill, an old Model A truck, porches and decks with swings and rocking chairs to watch the river flow by so you can experience what life was really like "way back when," although headboards made from old picket fences and other cute decorating touches (bubble bath by your bath) are reflective of modern touches. Breakfast at The Crossing is as unique as its setting; guests are given a $10 credit at the Yacht Club Restaurant or at breakfast shops on the premises, in which you can have either dinner or breakfast on your hosts. The Yacht Club doesn't open until 11 on Sunday, however. Make sure you stop by Judi's Naturally Country Clothing shop (where clothes hang on old saw blades, for an instant grin), because her selection will exceed almost anything you find in the city. If you want to do something other than water activities, eating, or shopping in one of the best little towns in Texas, the "family entertainment" productions at the Opera two blocks behind you are year-round.

Pecan Street Inn

Hosts: Shawn and Bill Pletsch, 1010 Pecan, Bastrop 78602, (512) 321-3315, 4 rooms with private baths, two fireplaces (one in master bedroom), welcomes family reunions and weddings (will accommodate up to 12, when whole house is leased), full breakfast, $$–$$$, smoking in designated areas, accommodates children, pets in carriers (or in utility room), cats outside in residence, no cr

The house, built in 1903, is a Queen Anne carpenter Gothic Victorian (seven colors make it the "Painted Lady" of Bastrop). Considered one of Bastop's finest homes, constructed entirely of native loblolly pine, it was the home of the county judge who was "LBJ's main man" for 30 years, so it is sprinkled with portraits of former residents and friends, including LBJ and Lady Bird, and some of the nine children who were born in the house. Although it contains Victorian antiques, Shawn points out it's a "friendly Victorian," not full of knickknacks. Bill, a gourmet cook, prepares homemade breads and pecan waffles with Grand Marnier sauce and strawberries, a "typical" breakfast that can be served in your room, if you prefer. He will also prepare a dinner you'd definitely remember and will include a horse-drawn carriage around Bastrop after your meal (by prior arrangement). Shawn is an unabashed Bastropian enthusiast, who will tell you its history or design personal tours for you if you'd like. The second oldest town in Texas, Bastrop—then called Mina—was founded before Texas was a state. It was the Colorado crossing point into the wilderness. In 1862, a fire destroyed all the Spanish mission architecture, so it was entirely rebuilt at that time, which is the reason it contains so many Victorians on the National Register today. Bastrop State Park has a magnificent stand of loblolly pines that don't exist anywhere else in central Texas, which is a whole other story Shawn can tell you if you want to know how they got there.

Pfeiffer House

Host: Marilyn Whites, 1802 Main Street, Bastrop 78602, (512) 321-2100, 3 bedrooms with 1 shared full bath, full breakfast, $–$$, no pets, no children, smoking in restricted areas, no cr

On a large, tree-shaded lot in the residential end of Main Street, Marilyn Whites oversees her carpenter Gothic home, filled with lifetime collections (the pewter, linen, and beautiful cut glass caught my eye) and Victorian bric-a-brac in every nook and cranny. The Whites' home, named for the original builder, Joseph Pfeiffer, who built it in 1901, is like Grandmother's, with fresh-baked smells always coming from the kitchen and a huge breakfast even other B&B owners in town say is the biggest and the best. The Pfeiffer House is a warm, comfortable B&B, a little worn in a place or two—something you'd expect when you come home for the weekend. The side porch with wicker, overlooking the large tree-filled lot and gardens, is worth the visit alone. If you want a glitzy showplace, the Pfeiffer House is not for you. If you want to meet a delightful, charming hostess who wants to make you feel at home (down comforters in cool rooms, year round!) or, if you want total privacy upstairs, she will make it happen, the Pfeiffer House is the place.

BELTON

The Belle of Belton

Hosts: Ron and Krissie Lastovica, 1019 N. Main, Belton 76513, (817) 939-6478, 4 rooms, 2 baths, full breakfast weekends, continental plus weekdays, $$, no pets, no children, no smoking, no cr

Belton, the home of Mary Hardin Baylor, which is directly across from the Belle of Belton B&B, offers this beautifully restored Victorian, built in 1893 as the home of Ele Baggett, a prominent citizen in Bell County. The four upstairs guest rooms are named after the seasons, with each decorated in lovely colors and period antiques that fit the season. Fall has its own bath, and the other three share a hall bath. As in all Queen Anne Victorian homes, rooms are huge with high ceilings and decorative moldings. Belle even has a music room complete with harpsichord in case you would like to trill a few Bach fugues. In the hallway are the portraits of past owners who obviously cared for the house, since it's much the same as it was when it was built, except for modern conveniences such as central air and heat.

BLANCO

Amenthal

Hosts: Bill and Mary Godden, 819 River Road, Blanco 78606, (210) 833-5438, 1 room (west bedroom upstairs), continental plus upstairs, $$, open only between October and May (excluding Christmas) because there is no air conditioning, smoking accepted, no cr

Amenthal (pronounced Ament Hall) is not your typical B&B for many reasons, not the least of which is that its hosts accept smokers. To stay at Amenthal is a rare treat, because Bill, a retired colonel in the Air Force, and his wife Mary don't really believe in air conditioning, which is the reason Amenthal is open only between October and May. Amenthal is the maiden name of Lyndon B. Johnson's maternal great-grandmother, whose family purchased the house in 1887. Rebekah Baines Johnson, LBJ's mother, spent her formative years in this house, situated on the Blanco River. This impressive "rubble stone" house is open for tour at Christmas, but guests are always given a booklet that describes in detail the restoration process (a constant since 1983 when the Goddens purchased it). B&B guests stay in the west bedroom upstairs, which opens out onto the huge porch where a breakfast of fruit, sausage rolls, muffins, and scrambled eggs (if Mary feels up to eggs) is brought to guests, should the weather permit. Caution: People were smaller in years past and the stairs are original. That means the risers are taller and narrower than modern standards. Watch your head so you can relish the excitement of sleeping in LBJ's mother's home.

Chandler Inn Bed and Breakfast and Restaurant

Hosts: Kip and Lee Munz, 1031 Chandler Street, Blanco 78606, (210) 833-4117, 2 rooms with private baths, 1 fireplace in king bedroom, full breakfast, $$–$$$, smoking on veranda, accommodates children and pets, cat and dog on premise

This turn-of-the-century farmhouse, built in the late 1890s on the far side of the Blanco River, is attractive and enticing, with its Texas and American flags billowing from the huge pillars out front. But it's the food that draws people from as far as Austin and San Antonio. They come for the dinner on the weekends because their host, Kip, is a Cordon Bleu chef who knows the art of cooking! Guests smart enough to recognize they will drink the fine wine (from their extensive wine list), eat the incredible food (the entrées change all the time, so you'll just have to trust you'll find something fabulous), and will not want to budge from the spot, can arrange to stay the night over the restaurant, which is the downstairs of Kip and Lee's house. Their bonus? Breakfast fixed by the same chef! What more could you ask, if you're really into the culinary experience?

Creekwood Country Inn

Host: Charlotte Dorsey, P.O. Box 1357, Blanco 78606, (210) 833-2248, 2 rooms with private baths and porches, gourmet breakfast, $, no pets, smoking in restricted areas, no cr

Creekwood Country Inn is billed as a "peaceful oasis," an apt description for guest cottages tucked away in the heart of the Texas Hill Country (five miles north of Blanco, nine miles south of Johnson City). A spring-fed creek is just down the hill from the large shaded porch outside your French doors. The rooms are a tasteful blend of antiques and hand-crafted furniture, creating an atmosphere of comfort and elegance. Pastures of wildflowers create the entrance to the place, but the simple wood buildings are somewhat deceptive because the creek behind the B&B rooms define its atmosphere, as do the deer and other wildlife. Because Charlotte collects bird houses, she has a bird-lovers' paradise, with painted buntings, country jays, cardinals, titmice, wrens, wild turkeys, and roadrunners common sights. She is flexible about almost everything—check-in, check-out, time of breakfast, special dietary needs, and she's a gourmet cook to boot. She routinely fixes an egg, cheese, peppers, sausage strata ("If it's puffy, it's soufflé; otherwise, it's strata") for breakfast, including fresh apple muffins and homemade bread. No wonder her guests rave! Charlotte loves the Blanco country, so don't fail to ask about its various attractions, including the gift shops in town (one sells dinosaur tracks). Blanco is advertised as a "nice, little Texas Hill Country town" where there "is no fast lane." They're right, so enjoy.

My Little Guest House

Host: Doris Cox. Contact Bed and Breakfast Hosts of San Antonio, (800) 356-1605, (800) 577-5264, 1 guest cottage, breakfast OYO, $, no pets, no smoking, cr

My Little Guest House is practically at water's edge at one of the best swimming holes in Texas at Blanco State Park. Blanco (pronounced Blank-O, which the Merchant's Association admits "sends shivers up the spine of anyone who knows the correct Spanish pronunciation") was named for the white limestone bottom and outcroppings of the river (it's Spanish for "white"). Typical of the laidback attitude in Blanco, the Chamber of Commerce admits "the name is one of the few things not perfect here." If you like beautiful, quiet Texas Heartland, they're correct. Doris has furnished her Little Guest House in tasteful antiques and stocks the fridge for breakfast. Some of her guests were so impressed with Doris's idea of a well-stocked refrigerator, they took a picture of it. You can sit a spell on the porch and catch a cool breeze or take a brief stroll to town, just a few blocks away, where you can see the finest example of a Second Empire-style building in Texas in their courthouse. Blanco is also home to the second-largest live oak tree in the country. It has a circumference of 17 feet 6 inches and a canopy of 150 feet. The best guess is that it was around about the time of Columbus.

BOERNE

Settled by German immigrants in the 1840s, Boerne is home not only to descendants of its founders but also for the growing numbers of resident commuters who work in San Antonio. It's a town of quiet streets and country trails that cut through trees that in their younger days shaded early pioneers. With a population of just over 4,000, Boerne, however, is sporting two new feathers to wear on its Bavarian hat. They are two bed-and-breakfast accommodations, opposite in appearance and atmosphere, yet both offering a unique overnight experience for Hill Country travelers.

Boerne Lake Lodge Bed and Breakfast Resort

Hosts: Leah Glast and Alan Schuminsky, 310 Lakeview Drive, Boerne 78006, (210) 816-6060 or (800) 809-5050, also listed with Bed and Breakfast Hosts of San Antonio (800) 356-1605, 3 separate accommodations, continental and full breakfast, $$$$, no cr

A drive through the stone gates and a first glance at the main house can cause envy in even the most humble heart. Newly constructed and an architectural wonder, this breathtaking estate, headquarters of Leah Glast and Alan Schuminsky, fronts the 200-acre crystal Boerne Lake and sports approximately three miles of shoreline that connects with that of the meandering emerald Cibolo Creek. To experience the water firsthand, guests walk down to the private dock to use the resort's electric-powered bass, paddle, or sailboats, or they can take a short tour of the waterways with Alan on his barge. Untouched by pollution, the water is so clear here it's the town's drinking water supply. If you swim, floats are at hand. Land lovers will enjoy great hiking and bicycling excursions.

The estate's three accommodations sit among herb, rock, rose gardens, and rustic walkways that dip through woods with beds of ivy. The 2,000-square-foot Sweet Cibolo has 20-foot ceilings, a loft, and gracious arched windows that complement elegant bleached furnishings and shiny wood floors that whisper of good taste. All furnishings on the estate, in fact, sport clean lines that are accented by fine linens, down comforters, and antique quilts. Room enough for up to seven people, the two-bedroom house with two baths is also furnished with two additional beds. The smaller Sunday House, a mere 1,000 square feet, accommodates four people, while the Boerne Lake Lodge has two elegantly furnished bedrooms with private baths, a media room, library, and stainless steel island kitchen with a panoramic view of the stretching landscape.

A continental breakfast is served to one-night-only guests. Those staying longer become guests of the hosts for a full country breakfast buffet at Boerne's Bear Moon Bakery. Glast and Schuminsky are health-minded. No smoking, but body massages arranged. Two-night-minimum stays on weekends. Special rates for longer stays and weekends.

Oldfather Inn Bed and Breakfast

Host: Valerie Oldfather, 120 Old San Antonio Rd., Boerne 78009, (210) 249-8908, also listed with Bed and Breakfast Hosts of San Antonio (800) 356-1605, 2 cottages, OYO full breakfast, $$$–$$$$, no pets, smoking in designated areas, children 10 and over, MC, V, AE, DC

If God needed a rest, he would certainly spend at least one night at the Oldfather Inn. After spending an evening on the swing that hangs from ancient boughs and watching the host of deer as they feed, the "Old Father" would probably come away once again with the belief that as far as His creations were concerned, "All's [still] right with the world."

A big part of the charm of this B&B is hostess Valerie Oldfather. In fact, what Valerie knows—old-fashioned "set-your-guests-at ease" hospitality—you just can't teach. Her two rustic little cottages sit behind the main house. Tastefully decorated with country antiques, and accented by such touches as denim curtains and patchwork quilts, this B&B could make the pages of *Country Living.* In the winter, wood burning fireplaces keep you warm, while Valerie's homemade nut bread comes first before thoughts of dieting.

This one is a must for families with kids 10 and over. The basketball goal hung from a grand old crooked oak, a pristine swimming pool, and a nearby nature walk give parents a perfect setting to relax and bond. Patches and Ellie May, resident pot-bellied pigs, love to be fed by visitors who head their direction on their way to the creatively constructed chicken coop, its architecture cherished by the cluster of cluckers.

As for creatures of the human variety, Valerie has a chilled bottle of champagne waiting for adults, while kids can't get enough from the bowl of area fruit from peaches to grapes. The refrigerator is stocked with cook-it-yourself breakfast fixings from eggs fresh from the coop to local bacon to homemade bread. Hershey kisses are here for chocolate lovers.

Outside, bird houses sit among impatiens, irises, crepe myrtle, rosemary, and basil that flourish under 300-year-old boughs. Some of Valerie's plants are very old. Forget phones, traffic, and deadlines here. The hostess has a businessman husband and two little boys who respect guests' privacy. This one is a personal favorite.

BURNET

Airy Mount

Hosts: Charles and Roseanne Hayman, Route 3, Box 280, Burnet 78611, (512) 756-4149, 3 bedrooms, 3 baths, TV/VCR, full breakfast, $$, no pets, no smoking, MC, V

Perhaps there is no more spectacular view in the Hill Country than Charles and Roseanne Hayman's Airy Mount, a historic B&B that is perched on top of a hill on the outskirts of Burnet. The barn, which was actually the homesite of Confederate General Adam Johnson, is composed of the original stone and mortar walls. Downstairs, a cozy room encourages guests to relax by the Franklin stove, and the modern kitchen is stocked with a few yummies for nibbling. Upstairs are two delightful bedrooms with antique accents and old-fashioned ambience with private baths. Roseanne worked for the Melrose Hotel in Dallas a number of years, and Charles prides himself on his gourmet cooking, so any meal at Airy Mount, particularly breakfast, is not to be missed. Burnet is the place to catch the Vanishing Texas River Cruise up the Colorado River for eagle watching or, if you're a land lover, the drives overlooking Lake LBJ and Inks Lake just down the road from Kingsland are perhaps some of the most fabulous vistas in Texas. Not to be missed!

CANYON LAKE

Aunt Nora's

Hosts: Alton and Iralee Haley, 120 Naked Indian Trail, Canyon Lake 78132, (210) 905-3989, 1 guest room, 1 bath, 4 cottages, full breakfast weekends, continental weekdays, $$–$$$$, smoking on porches and patios, children over 14 welcome, pets in carrier ok, no cr

You're really in tune with nature here! From the front porch swing, chances are you'll see a deer, a raccoon or a rabbit, and the country air is wonderful! Roam around the four-acre homesite to your heart's content amid naked Indian, oak, and cedar trees. A scenic walk takes

Airy Mount

you to a spot where you can view Canyon Lake. Then, refresh your-self in the hot tub on the patio.

Inside your country cottage, you'll find handmade furnishings, antiques, paintings, lacy crafts, a wood stove, and natural wood floors. Breakfast is served in the country kitchen. And remember to take home a jar of Aunt Nora's jam or jelly as a memento.

CASTROVILLE

Landmark Inn Bed and Breakfast and State Historical Park

Host: June Secrest, Park Superintendent, 402 Florence, Castroville 78009, (512) 389-8900, Web page http://www/TPWD.state.tx.us, 4 rooms with baths, 4 rooms with shared baths, continental plus, $, children welcome, no pets, smoking in restricted areas, V, MC

Located in the Alsatian settlement of Castroville just west of San Antonio, this 19th-century stage stop and hotel was built near an old ford of the Medina River. Decorated with furnishings ranging from 19th-century Texas-made furniture, including feather beds, to the 1940s, its charm is more in the gardens, the spacious veranda on the second floor, and the incredible programs routinely offered on early Texas, from soap-making to tatting to making homemade root beer (it's really great!). Fresh-ground coffee and pastry from Katy's Bakery and fresh fruit, including locally grown figs, begin your day in the 1849 kitchen (warmed by a fireplace on cold winter mornings). You can bicy-cle (a knowledgeable cyclist manages the inn), hike trails, catch huge fish (the place is legendary!), poke around the historic gristmill, dam, old bathhouse, and cotton gin, or shop in a charming town just blocks away. Landmark offers special packages (you can take over the entire place for a family reunion or meeting for next-to-nothing). It's the best buy in historic preservation in Texas for families.

COMFORT

Brinkmann House Bed and Breakfast

Hosts: Melinda and John McCurdy, 714 Main Street, Comfort 78013, (210) 995-3141, 2 cottages with private baths, gourmet breakfast, $$, no pets, no children (with exceptions), smoking in restricted areas, phone in house, no cr

Melinda and John McCurdy win the "Most Charming Hosts of Comfort" award, with their restoration cottages and their herb and perennial gardens. On the street behind the Comfort Common, they have restored two picturesque Texas German cottages, nestled in their gardens that blaze with color. Their concept of their responsibility "to improve and not to change" creates small delights such as a TV hidden in a pie safe or an old smoking room transformed into a contemporary bathroom. You can relax in an atmosphere that echoes the elements of the outdoors—twig, wicker, wrought iron, and natural fabrics such as homespun quilts. The seclusion of the cottage is not interrupted by breakfast, which is brought to your door. But what a breakfast! Baked eggs, homemade pecan Belgian waffles with sauteed peaches, homemade muffins, and something like a puffed-up taco or a cross between a pancake and a cake called Dutch Babies with a blackberry sauce. If you enjoy Southwestern, they can whip up a stuffed Poblano pepper or a Southwest casserole. Each morning brings something new, but they always take advantage of the seasonal harvests from their herb and vegetable garden. Do we need to tell you they both love to cook? If you visit their home in front of the cottages, you can understand why they spend time in their kitchen. Since Comfort is known for attracting antique collectors, most B&B guests would agree that the McCurdy kitchen is a dream kitchen, filled with antiques from Melinda's days as a dealer (and now a collector). You can salivate over more than food at the Brinkmann House. The house's name, by the way, comes from its original owner, Otto Brinkmann, a prominent merchant, who built it in 1894.

Comfort Common

Hosts: Jim Lord and Bobby Dent, P.O. Box 539, Comfort 78013, (210) 995-3030, 5 rooms (ask about baths), 2 suites, 2 cottages (one a log cabin), unique breakfast arrangements, $$–$$$, TV in rooms, no children, smoking in restricted areas, all cr

Said to have one of the most original business districts in Texas, Comfort has obtained the distinction of being one of Texas' best little getaway towns in the Hill Country. When you stay at the Comfort Common, you not only understand that nomenclature, you are literally surrounded by antiques, including the 1880 building itself. Not only are the downstairs and the picturesque grounds stashed with shops, the rooms are decorator-perfect, each one reflecting the eclectic (and sometimes funky) taste of its owners. Many of the items are for sale. One room is Victorian, another English, another primitive, so you might browse for future visits, which are almost guaranteed because everything is done so well. Because the Comfort Common has no space for dining, you are given a card for a special breakfast Thursday through Sunday at the cafe next door. During the early part of the week, fresh muffins, yogurt, fruit, and pigs-in-a-blanket are delivered in a basket to your door. The Comfort Common has captured the quiet essence of its town's name.

The Meyer Bed and Breakfast on Cypress Creek

Dorcas Mussett, Innkeeper, 845 High Street, P.O. Box 1117, Comfort 78013, (800) 364-2138, or (210) 995-2304, 9 suites with private baths, full breakfast, $$, cable TV, smoking outside, no pets, AE, MC, V

Frederick Christian Meyer managed the Stage Stop depot (1857), which was the last stop before the stage crossed the Guadalupe River going toward San Antonio on the Old Spanish Trail. The depot, now a gift shop, forms the cornerstone of a complex of bed and breakfast buildings. These include Mrs. Meyer's "midwife's house" (built in 1872); the Meyer home (1869) built of locally quarried, handfaced limestone; a cottage (1872) overlooking the creek (which unfolds the scenic beauty behind the complex); the White House Hotel (1887), which was built when the railroad came to Comfort; and the Meyer

Hotel four-plex stucco (1920), a hotel operated by the Meyer's daughter until 1956. The summer kitchen, which overlooks the grounds, is used in cooler weather for the huge breakfast of quiche, German-fried potatoes, rolls, sausage biscuits, and sweet breads only the Germans know how to fix. Old bathroom fixtures, hardwood floors, old pictures, and other details round out the preservation of the complex while providing modern amenities (such as a swimming pool on grounds). Manager Dorcas Mussett is an artist who lives on premise, and it's worth taking a peek at her art, even though Comfort offers numerous stores for shopping. Because of the setting, The Meyer has the feel of a comfortable old river estate.

Idlewilde Lodge

Hosts: Hank and Connie Engle, 115 Texas Hwy. 473, Comfort 78013, (210) 995-3844, 2 cabins, full breakfast, $$, smoking in restricted areas, pets allowed, no cr

Idlewilde, a girls' camp for more than 60 years, retains much of the country flavor, from the Engle's pet pot-bellied pigs who roam about (Mr. Pig-Pig and Snow White) to the friendly burro (who loves to munch on a melon rind you can recycle from breakfast). The main house, where you're served breakfast and, if you choose, a five-course dinner, is like Grandmother's house—big, comfy couches and chairs mixed in with Connie's doll collection, her stuffed and carved rabbits, and the hand-stenciled designs around the ceiling. The Early Western house offers a huge fireplace and even larger porch to while away the evenings if you want to socialize. No TV or phones are in the cabins by design. If you arrive for July 4th, you're recruited into building a float for the town parade and you'll be treated to one of the best country fireworks shows you've ever seen. A large pool, one of the oldest in the county, has been modernized and is available for your enjoyment, as is a volleyball net, pavilion, child's fort, and sandbox. The Engles take pets, for which they provide an area to pen on their 13 acres. There are no check-in or check-out times, as there are no set times for breakfast. As they say, it's "customized."

DOSS

Quiet Hill Ranch

Hosts: Jim and Cindy Whatley, 110 Quiet Hill Road, Doss 78618, (210) 669-2253, (800) 544-2253, 3 cabins, full breakfast, $$$–$$$$ (depending upon the number of people), two night minimum on weekends, children encouraged, no smoking, no pets, all cr

Quiet Hill Ranch, a "mom-and-pop" operation, will prove to be one of the best B&Bs in Texas that caters to kids. Hidden in Doss (population 16 during the day, 8 at night) located about 30 minutes west of Fredericksburg, "the livin' here is easy"—a back-to-basics existence perfect for bonding. The hosts, Jim and Cindy Whatley, are proud of their spread, a 2,100 acre parcel of grazing land that has been in Cindy's family for generations. Theirs is a small operation with only three cabins, enough to house visiting families, but there's a brand new lodge, where guests are served a prompt 8 o'clock full country breakfast. The lodge also acts as the ranch's focus, unless one takes advantage of the "old stock tank," a new stone, above-the-ground pool that is a safe three-to-four-feet deep. The kids love it, but not as much as their visit to the chicken coop to gather green-hued eggs from a Chilean breed of cluckers called the Araucanas, translated "Easter Egg Chickens."

Parents join their offspring in a game of washer pitching, basketball, or volleyball, walk along the "strolling path," or gaze up at a star-studded horizon obscured only by the flight of an occasional hawk. Animals are also very friendly here. Pork and Beans, the Whatley's two pot-bellied pigs, will pay an uninvited visit to each cabin porch if guests are present. The hosts' children, Holden and Naomi, show visitors how to milk ranch goats that roam free among the cactus and central Texas live oaks.

The best part of Quiet Hill Ranch, though, is the resident wrangler, Kerry Hellums, who, as he leads trail rides, gives a running commentary about this "Old Yeller" country, also home of the long-gone Comanche and the indomitable cowboy, Kerry's heroic ideal. Dressed for the range in authentic wear of the nineteenth-century cowpoke, Kerry and his horse "Roho" are both so animated that one wonders how Hollywood has missed this colorful duo. Actually, TV watchers have seen them both in the movies, *Glory* and *The North and the South.* Kerry also has appeared in Smithsonian specials.

Here neat accommodations lack frills, but a country breakfast, good conversation, simple pleasures, and the natural beauty of the land and the sky make the Quiet Hill Ranch experience a truly memorable one. One word of advice—arrive before dark, and be sure you understand the directions. The ranch is close to Doss, but the little town is a far piece from Farm Road 783.

DRIPPING SPRINGS

Dabney House

Hosts: Jack and Patti Dabney, Autumn Lane, Dripping Springs. Wimberley Lodging Reservations, (800) 460-3909, room with king-sized bed and cottage suite with queen-sized bed, $$–$$$, smoking in restricted area, children accepted, no pets

Quiet and picturesque, the Dabney House requires extensive instructions to locate (cross a creek bed, turn on a road that looks more like a path, drive another 3.4 miles), but it's worth the visit. Friendly dogs greet you, llamas watch your arrival (and will give you llama kisses if you'd like), and a delightful hostess will make you at home in separate quarters from the house should you choose the suite, which has a beautiful Hill Country vista from its small porch. The Dabney House itself (in which the other room is located) is a Texas-style home with a beautiful wraparound porch on three sides so you can watch the deer come in to feed or enjoy your breakfast overlooking the 21 acres.

Short Mama's House B&B

Host: Keely Peel, Manager, 101 College, Dripping Springs, (512) 858-5668, 4 bedrooms with baths (1 bedroom has an extra room with a twin bed), continental breakfast, $$–$$$, no smoking, no children, no pets, cr

For 60 years, "Short Mama" Hayden spent many hours working in her yard or sitting on the front porch of her 1880 farm house, which had originally been constructed as the Lou Breed Boarding House. Three years ago, it was beautifully restored into a four-bedroom B&B

with English-style gardens and berm, which muffles passing cars because it's located just off U.S. 290 in Dripping Springs. No TV or phones in the rooms, a living room area with fireplace and television provide an entertainment area if the porch swing doesn't suffice. Dripping Springs is just down the road from Wimberley, Johnson City, Blanco, and the Pedernales Falls State Park.

ELGIN

Brinkley's Bed and Breakfast

Hosts: Gary and Rosalind Brinkley, 1212 Main, Elgin 78621, (800) 231-5426, (512) 321-7002, 2 upstairs bedrooms with parlor, downstairs master with private bath, across from park, full breakfast, $$–$$$, smoking restricted to outside areas, accommodates children, no pets, no cr

The 80-year-old house, a sentimental favorite of the people from Elgin, is actually a replica of George Washington's birthplace in Wakefield, Virginia, so Easterners will particularly feel at home here. On a one-acre, beautifully landscaped lot across from Elgin Memorial Park, Brinkley's is charming. It is located in a town primarily known for its railroads and its excellent Elgin sausage, which is included in their full breakfast. The Brinkleys take extra efforts to make their guests feel at home, from home-baked cookies when you arrive, to popcorn, soups, and bubble bath routinely made available during your stay.

But it's because of your hosts' interest in Texas history and genealogy that this B&B is spectacular. For someone wanting to know something about their Texas roots, you MUST go to Elgin. The Brinkleys have a library of books on genealogy, graveyards, family trees, DAR, Civil War, and over 2,000 genealogy lines in their computer database—all of which are available for guests interested in discovering their roots. Frankly, how anyone interested in genealogy gets any sleep around Brinkley's is amazing, because the hosts bubble with their recent discoveries and they love finding out something about their guests. Can you imagine a greater gift from a B&B than to find out, as some guests did recently, that their hosts were their distant cousins 20 times removed, originating from Jesse Billingsley ("Remember the Alamo, Remember Goliad")? For genealogists, this B&B is an aphrodisiac to which they will repeatedly return (perhaps for their hosts' Texas vignette in which descendants are invited to celebrate a famous Texan).

Ragtime Ranch Inn

Hosts: Roberta Butler, Debbie Jameson, County Road 98, Box 575, Elgin 78621, (512) 285-9599, or contact Bed & Breakfast Texas Style (800) 899-4538, 4 guest rooms, 4 baths, continental plus breakfast OYO, $$$, children and pets welcome, 2 smoking, 2 non-smoking rooms, all cr

Grab your saddle and head out to the Ragtime Ranch Inn where you can stable and pasture your horse, if you bring one. You'll truly enjoy this quiet getaway. Each 450-square-foot room has a fireplace, two queen-sized beds, a refrigerator with ice maker, microwave, coffee pot, and private screened porch or deck, where you can rock away your cares. You'll have a good view of the pastures or woods. The Ragtime Ranch Inn also has a stocked pond, shaded pool, and 24 acres of nature trails. Borrow a TV and VCR from the hosts if you wish, and use the video or reading library. A fax machine is available.

From this Central Texas retreat, you are just a short drive from two public golf courses and Manor Downs as well as downtown Elgin, which has specialty shops and restaurants in its Historic District.

FAYETTEVILLE

Fayette House Guest Cottage

Hosts: Hal & Dorothy Stall, 211 W. Fayette St., Fayetteville 78940, 1-800-256-7721, fax (409) 378-2240, 3 bedrooms, 2 baths, full breakfast OYO, $$$, no pets, no children under 15, smoking designated areas, no cr

Fayetteville, settled by three families of the Stephen F. Austin's Old Three Hundred, was once called Lick Skillet. The name derived from the inability of festival organizers to ever accurately predict the number and appetites of its visitors. In 1844, a town planner renamed it Fayetteville after his North Carolina hometown, and festival goers have been adequately fed since then.

Fayetteville is still called home by its friendly 283 residents. Time to these folks seems unimportant, but if you must keep track of the minutes, you can set your watch by the old courthouse's tower clock that chimes every half hour. You'll hear it from the porch of the romantic Fayette House Guest Cottage, which is a short walk from the small shop-filled town square. The unhosted historic B&B, which sleeps 8, has been authentically restored by Hal & Dorothy Stall even down to the period colors, gingerbread trim, and inside stenciling. The Stalls, who share a variety of interests from piloting to antique auctioneering to historic restoration, provide a country-sized breakfast of local bacon from the "down-the-street" Westside Market to fresh brown eggs. You cook the meal yourself on the 1336 white porcelain stove. Other notables include the Ben Franklin wood stove, a working player piano, and the clawfoot tub, original to Fayette House.

The Cottage

Hosts: Hal & Dorothy Stall, 111 E. Market St., Fayetteville 78940, 1-800-256-7721, fax (409) 378-2240, 1 bedroom, 1 bath, full breakfast OYO, $$, no pets, no children under 15, smoking designated areas, no cr

Also owned by the Stalls, The Cottage is one block off the town square on Market Street. Because Fayetteville is so small, nobody uses house numbers in this quaint little central Texas community that hosts a number of festivals each year. This B&B, a single-story painted gray with blue shutters, is over 100 years old. The tin roof, antique picket fence and the backyard brick patio invites its guests to rest a spell before expending energy to ride a bicycle-built-for-two down to the local museum or the courthouse. While in Fayetteville, be sure to bring your fishing poles because the Colorado River and Cummins Creek are nearby. You may also want to plan a trip during Labor Day when the Fayette County Country Fair is held in LaGrange or the third weekend in October when the town is bustling with Lickskillet Days, a heritage festival with parade, arts & crafts, barbecue, and Czech performers.

Fayetteville has recently given birth to a new art colony, the brainchild of Dorothy Stall. Located in the historic Sarrazin Building, artists work here in this gallery-like atmosphere and stop to sell their pieces to browsing tourists.

FREDERICKSBURG

In 1846 a handful of industrious Germans, who, to their advantage and safety, made quick friends with neighboring Comanches, founded Fredericksburg. Today this small town has become a B&B haven with over 100 vintage accommodations catering to a steady influx of visitors in need of a relaxing getaway. Tourists may view the quaint old town from a horse-drawn carriage or walk down Main Street, crowded with unusual shops, museums, and German restaurants. The majority of accommodations in Fredericksburg, however, are unhosted with "just adequate" continental morning fare, although the facilities are outstanding in decor and location. Among these, however, is a small number that classify as "traditional" bed and breakfasts. The following list is a mixture.

Admiral Nimitz Birthplace and Country Cottage Inn

Hosts: Michael and Jean Sudderth, 249 E. Main, Fredericksburg 78624, (210) 997-8549, 9 suites, gourmet breakfast, $$$–$$$$, no pets, no smoking, MC, V

World War II buffs know all about Admiral Chester W. Nimitz and the educational Nimitz Museum in Fredericksburg. Just across the street from the museum is the small rock house where the noted naval man was born. Beautifully restored to preserve its historic significance, the admiral's home is now one of the outstanding B&Bs in Fredericksburg. Rough walls, beamed ceilings, and bare floors complement these suites, enhanced with unique antiques, comfortable rockers and sofas, and country decor. Some are equipped with Jacuzzis and fireplaces that crackle in the winter. Best of all, from the front porch swing, guests can watch the world enjoying Main Street, Fredericksburg.

Country Cottage, built in 1850, is one of the oldest houses in Fredericksburg and is much on the order of the Admiral Nimitz Birthplace, with its rock walls, fireplaces, beautiful antiques, and early Texas ambience. The Cottage has two rooms and three suites, all with private baths and mini-kitchens. In the back is a huge, peaceful yard, where the noise of Main Street's busy traffic goes unheard. Both have been featured in national magazines and are the pride of the Sudderths who also offer the Courtyard Houses, circa 1995.

Country Cottage Inn

Austin Street Retreat

Unhosted: Contact Gastehaus Schmidt, (210) 997-5612, 5 separate quarters, OYO continental breakfast, $$$, no pets, children allowed, no smoking, all cr

Gastehaus Schmidt's hottest property and one of the most frequently photographed sites in Fredericksburg, the Austin Street Retreat is a collection of cabins dating back to 1867 and the John Walter clan. As this prosperous pioneer family grew, so did their home. The cottages are connected by stone walkways that join with each private ivy-laden courtyard, most with picturesque fountains. All accommodations sport elegant decor that emphasizes queen- or king-sized beds, most created by local craftsmen. Each cabin is uncluttered, the opposite of "country cute." Maria's cabin, circa 1867 and most suggestive of founding father days, features a whirlpool for two, as do the others. Although all five cabins are recommended, a personal favorite is Kristen's. The huge romantic fireplace complements the exquisite iron bed patterned after an intricate woven design of a French vegetable basket. The Italian tapestry sofa and chair add European elegance, and it is hard to believe that Kristen's once served as a stable, a dining room, and for a short period in 1885, a jail. An ancient pecan tree protects a private terrace with three-tiered fountain, reminiscent of a Tuscan plaza.

Baethge-Behrend Haus

Unhosted: Contact Gastehaus Schmidt, (210) 997-5612, guest house with 2 bedrooms sleeps 6, 2 baths, OYO continental breakfast, $$$, children welcome, no pets, smoking outside only, all cr

For elegance in country living, guests travel three-and-a-half miles northwest of Fredericksburg. An unhosted historic accommodation built in 1867, the house sits on land unspoiled by progress, but adorned with giant yellow chrysanthemums, petunias, crepe myrtle, and cannas. Restored to keep nineteenth-century flavor, yet provide guests with all the conveniences of home, the Baethge-Behrend Haus easily sleeps six. One bedroom features a king-sized bed with a headboard made from the property's old corral. White marbleized walls accent high-gloss wood floors and beaded board ceilings. The best part of the house, though, is the long inviting porch with swing and hummingbirds fluttering nearby.

Quilts, old trunks, fabrics, braided country blue rugs, and boxes of dried flowers add flair and warmth along with family pieces and a rock fireplace. A complimentary continental breakfast includes German-style pastries, coffee, teas, and juices, although hosts here are unseen. Jacuzzi, microwave, phone, and barbecue grill remind guests that we're approaching a new century.

Bed and Brew

Hosts: Richard Estenson and John Davies, The Fredericksburg Brewing Company, 245 E. Main, Fredericksburg 78624, (210) 997-1646, 12 rooms with private baths, brew in lieu of breakfast, $$–$$$, no pets, no children, smoking outside only, AE, V, MC

Are you not one for breakfast but love the taste of quality brew? "This one's for you!" Operated by the Fredericksburg Brewing Company, a dream realized by partners Richard Estenson, John Davies, and Laird Laurence, a local veterinarian, this boarding house-styled B&B is certainly a little different twist from the traditional ones. Twelve rooms, each done in a different theme, open to a common dimmed-for-effect hall just like in the old days. Artistically decorated by located artists and craftsmen, each reflects the sense of humor and a flair for adventure shared by these three businessmen. The Rustic Styles Room (the iron bed here is made from the wheel rims of an 1800s covered wagon), with its western theme, provides quite a contrast to the deep-hued Bordello Suite, adorned with mirrors and velvets of burgundy. There's no TV here to keep your mind off more important things like going downstairs to enjoy the frolic, food, and froth served daily. Male visitors particularly like "The Lodge," a masculine abode complete with sports motif.

As for the old fieldstone building itself, it once was the Silver King Saloon that enlivened Main Street in the 1890s. Recently transformed into a highly successful endeavor, this B&B with its popular dining room and biergarten shares a common wall with the birthplace of Admiral Chester Nimitz. The huge stone fireplace, high ceilings, and rustic metals and stonework of the brew pub hint of Fredericksburg's past and smells of homemade pretzels, Wiener Schnitzel with red cabbage and spaetzle (German egg dumplings), hard-boiled and deep-fried Scotch eggs (captured in sausage), and freshly brewed ales and lagers just drawn from four gleaming stainless steel tanks. Also in sight is the copper-clad mash tun and kettle flanked by four-cylindro-conical stainless steel fermenters.

In lieu of breakfast, B&B guests are served the ancient libation. They say the word and are served samplers of the pub's four specialty beers, including their Enchanted Rock Ale and Pedernales Pilsner. If you must have breakfast, however, walk across the street to the Dietz Bakery or a block down at the Fredericksburg Bakery for a taste of German pastry at its best.

The Delforge Place

Hosts: George and Betsy Delforge. Contact Gastehaus Schmidt, (210) 997-5612, 3 rooms, 3 baths, 1 suite, gourmet breakfast, $$-$$$, no pets, no children, no smoking, D, MC, V

George and Betsy Delforge offer one of the best traditional bed and breakfast homes in Texas. Built in 1898, the stained- and etched-glass doors and windows of the house are all original, as are the floors, 12-foot ceilings, and chandeliers. The home is exquisitely furnished with American, European, and Oriental pieces and antiques. Betsy's ancestors were seafaring men and played major roles in American history and the opening of the Orient. She has wonderful stories about them and her treasures. (Some are on loan to the Smithsonian.)

The Map Room reflects the sailing clippership era, and The American Room focuses on the Civil War. The Quebec Suite presents the American Revolution, and The Upper Deck (a favorite choice) is upstairs with an outside entrance, private deck complete with ship's mast, and flag pole. All rooms have small refrigerators, and The Deck has a mini-kitchen, phone, and TV. Yes, it's decorated in tones of ocean blue.

As for the breakfast, you'll never have better. That's because Betsy, who specializes in German sour cream twists and Belgian waffles, studied the culinary arts from the master—Julia Child. Betsy also creates tasty "Special Day" gift baskets upon request.

And, if you're in town but need to do business, the Delforges, who have their own E-mail address, allow access to the Web, as well as offer weekday business discounts.

Fredericksburg Bakery Bed & Breakfast

Hosts: Mike and Patsy Penick. Contact Gastehaus Schmidt, (210) 997-5612, 3 suites, continental plus breakfast, $$$, no pets, no children, no smoking, D, MC, V

Have you ever wanted to wake up to the heavenly aroma of fresh bread browning in the oven? Well, just stay at the Fredericksburg Bakery, and your wish will come true, and best of all, it's your breakfast. Just upstairs over the actual bakery you will find B&B accommodations with a living area of two large rooms, dining room, huge fully equipped kitchen, three spacious suites, a front porch overlooking the town's Main Street, and a secluded shady back porch with a treetop view of the patio.

The front suite is the largest with rock walls, antique quilts, and king-sized bed. The middle suite is charming with more colorful quilts and pine sleigh bed. In the back suite there are two bedrooms, each with a queen bed. All suites are elegantly furnished, and each suite has a private bath, TV and VCR, and seating area. A telephone is also available for guests. Not only do you stay in one of Fredericksburg's finest B&Bs, you can shop Main Street with easy walking.

Hill Country Guesthouse and Garden

Unhosted: Contact Gastehaus Schmidt, (210) 997-5612, 2 suites, full breakfast or continental plus, $$$, no pets, no children, smoking outside in designated areas

Owners of one of the few B&Bs in town to offer a hearty breakfast, Peter, a self-taught chef, and Corine Danysh serve Eggs Benedict or crepes, along with freshly home-canned goods, when they're in town. This B&B, five blocks from Main Street and built in 1921 by Felix Stehling, is a happy one—neat, spacious, and well-decorated—truly a labor of love passed from generation to generation. Musicians especially appreciate the parlor piano, a gift Felix gave his devoted wife many years ago.

Vivid colors mixed with white, testimony to good vibes, give the old, yet, nurtured, house new life. The Sun Room Suite, huge and open, features a king-size-adapted antique bed, pretty fabrics, and a wicker rocking chair among other interesting pieces. The Moonglow Suite, colored in hues of rose and pink, calms the frazzled nerves and promises restful Fredericksburg slumber. Both accommodations have private baths.

Outside, visitors spend quality time under the 60-year-old pecan tree in the sprawling stone-trimmed backyard that is full of coreopsis, antique Texas roses, mint and basil, just to name a few. There's a landscape horticulturist in the family, and it shows. The family vegetable garden also provides fresh produce for the breakfast table.

Hotopp House

Unhosted: Contact Gastehaus Schmidt, (210) 997-5612, 2 separate suites or entire house available, OYO continental plus, $$$$, children welcome, no pets, no smoking, all cr

Owned by German natives of Fredericksburg, this accommodation is indicative of German precision, quality, and neatness. A pristine red brick house built in the 1800s but recently restored, the Hotopp House with its fashionable decor is a showplace. The 1914 Suite includes a parlor, two bedrooms, a kitchen, and bath. The Victorian parlor, a perfect place to watch TV (it's hidden in an elegant secretary) is tinted by its stained-glass window and stylishly homey with its sofa and chair of floral and striped designs. In the bedroom, German laces and silk ivy adorn a canopy bed with its white spread of delicate embroidery. The rose bedroom has twin beds, a romantic pink crystal lamp, and double mirrored armoire. The red brick hallway points to a kitchen of limestone rock and modern appliances, and the bath with shower and whirlpool meets all needs.

Across the hall is the Fireplace Suite, which consists of a bedroom with a child's sleeping loft full of toys. The den here, though, is a dream-come-true. Graceful French doors overlook a patio and summer garden, and opposite, through another large window, is a view of church steeples. Fine sofa and chairs are accented by a large antique spinning wheel and antique bar. The bathroom features a claw-foot tub, dreamy in the light that drifts through the stained-glass window.

Magnolia House

Hostess: Joyce Kennard, 101 East Hackberry, Fredericksburg 78624, (210) 997-0306, fax (210) 997-0766, 4 rooms, 4 baths, 2 suites, full breakfast, $$–$$$, no pets, no children, smoking in common areas only, MC, V, AE

Magnolias conjure up visions of the coy Scarlett, sitting on her veranda sipping her minted iced tea. So, the huge gold-throated white blossoms seem somewhat out of place in this Hill Country town where mesquite and cedar dot the arid countryside. Edward Stein felt differently, though. When he built this home in 1925, he lined the street with five magnolia trees. How could he have known that 70 years later they would commemorate the southern-style hospitality Joyce Kennard would be serving at her Magnolia House?

Rather than the German and Texas primitive antiques that fill so many local B&Bs, this one has an English/American mix. Flowered prints, eyelet curtains, and overstuffed couches make rooms inviting. Here guests like the game room and enjoy a glass of wine on the patio and wicker-furnished porches. As for the country breakfast, it's served in the formal dining room on antique china and crystal. Of course, you can't get more southern than this. ·

Schmidt Barn

Hostess: Loretta Schmidt. Contact Gastehaus Schmidt, (210) 997-5612, 1-bedroom barn, continental plus breakfast, $$, no restrictions, D, MC, V

Just on the outskirts of one of Texas' favorite tourist towns is an old stone barn more than a hundred years old. The exterior is totally unchanged, but inside is a lovely little guest house. Rough rock walls and a brick floor polished to perfection add to the downstairs ambience. Even the sunken tub in the bath is brick. Rafters cross the high ceiling, and stairs take you to a cozy sleeping loft with its queen-sized bed. The sofa bed in the living area will sleep two more.

Your kitchen area is fully equipped, and Loretta supplies a German-style continental breakfast with a meat and cheese plate and homemade sweets. A small wood-burning iron stove works, but really it's just decorative and a reminder of how Grandfather Schmidt made his living

Schmidt Barn

selling these cranky appliances. It is no surprise that this little barn is one of the most popular B&Bs in Fredericksburg. Although small, the Schmidt Barn has been featured in several national magazines including *Country Living.*

The Yellow House and the Keepsake Kottage

Unhosted: Contact Gastehaus Schmidt, (210) 997-5612, both have queen-sized beds, OYO continental breakfast, $$–$$$, infants and children 12 and over, no pets, no smoking, all cr

Both adult-sized doll houses, these little B&Bs represent both the old and the new. The Yellow House, a true German Sunday House built by Emma "Oma" Stein (?) in 1896, sits high above the street under an old tree that surely saw Haley's Comet during Twain's time. Although tiny, the little house is decorated so well it appeared in *Country Living* magazine. The kitchen accommodates light cooking, so if you stay here, plan to eat out for noon and evening meals. A German-styled breakfast of cold summer sausages, cheeses, fruits, and juices is left in the compact refrigerator.

The Keepsake Cottage, also small but charming, is one of the town's newly built guest houses. Just one block off Main Street, this rock and stucco cottage is patterned after the historic Sunday Houses with its tin roof and front porch. Inside, visitors first notice the stencil work along ceilings accented by white-beaded walls. Colors range from blue to pink and white. Such touches as the country blue-and-white checked Queen Anne chair, homemade quilts, and little stuffed dolls add to a feeling of warmth. Also, vintage clothing and accessories hang from the pegs to add romance and charm.

Note: Also ask Donna Mittel about **Settlers Crossing,** a cluster of guest houses written up in five national magazines including *Country Living* and *Country Homes.* Situated outside town, there are four authentically restored cottages, each decorated by professionals in a way that preserves their history.

Watkins Hill Guest House

Host: Edgar Watkins, 608 East Creek Street, Fredericksburg 78624, (800) 899-1672, (210) 997-6739, 2 suites, 2 log guest rooms, all with private baths, gourmet breakfast, $$$$, no pets, infants, or children over 12, smoking outside in designated areas, MC, V

The Watkins Hill Guest House, governed by Edgar Watkins, whose family came to Texas in the 1830s, is a complex of guest houses, a livery stable, a Main Lodge containing a log frontier ballroom, entertainment facilities, two turn-of-the-century-style board and batten cottages, and at the center, an 1855 pioneer stone house that Edgar calls home. One of the "traditional" accommodations among Fredericksburg's one-hundred-plus B&Bs, this one features a gourmet breakfast delivered to your door. Fare usually includes a heart-shaped basket of fresh fruit compote, an egg casserole, biscuits, butter and jam. Each room has a butler's pantry equipped with coffee, tea, oatmeal, Perrier, fruit juice, apples, two kinds of snacks, and a bottle of chilled wine. Fine bed linens, canopied queen-sized beds, eighteenth- and nineteenth-century pieces add an air of elegance.

GEORGETOWN

The Harper-Chessher Historic Inn

Hosts: Leight Sumner Marcus; Manager: Kathy Frye, 1309 College Street, Georgetown 78628, (512) 863-4057, 4 rooms, 4 baths, buffet continental breakfast and noon high tea, $$$, no pets, no smoking, AE, MC, V

One of the oldest, if not the oldest (1847), house in Georgetown, this B&B is beautifully decorated with grand pine tables and sideboards in the dining room, exquisite antiques, and elaborate friezes and murals in every room painted by Jacque Muso. Flowers, fruit, dogs and rabbits, birds, baskets full of wine and food, angels, and just whimsical designs scroll out from light fixtures, ceilings, cabinets, fireplaces, and just about everywhere else there's wall space in the house. The enormous professional kitchen, enhanced with a stone fireplace and wine cellar, is worth seeing anyway, but Muso's art makes it a "must see." High noon tea with scones and clotted cream is served daily on the veranda overlooking a quaint English garden, designed for weddings and special parties. The murals, painted in the romantic impressionistic fashion, make the Harper Chessher well worth a visit, but the four bedrooms, all with their own fireplaces and bathrooms, create their own beckoning getaway in a town renown for its small-town character and charm.

Right At Home B&B

Host: Barbara Shepley, 1208 Main Street, Georgetown 78626-6727, (512) 930-3409 or (800) 651-0021, 4 rooms (2 with shared bath), full breakfast, dinners by request, $$, well-behaved children accepted, smoking outside, no TV in rooms (by design), MC, V

Right At Home is appropriately named, not only because the decor is family-friendly (no bric-a-brac here, even though there are antiques) but, primarily, because the hostess, Barbara Shepley, loves people and believes she truly adopts everyone who walks through the door. She'd rather sit and talk to you over coffee in the sun room than make a bed to have the room perfectly ready (which isn't everybody's idea of the perfect B&B), but her personality overcomes just about everyone's stressed-out personalities. She's combined 40 years of interior design and real estate to create Right At Home, which is a B&B in transition. It still needs a little paint here or something there, but that all makes it a little more like home. A new Southwestern University student can feel free to play his guitar, to entertain the guests, just as an adult can ask for seconds in the family-style setting for breakfast. Georgetown is known for Texas' first university and its large collection of commercial Victorian structures in its charming downtown. Both of these are just down the street from Right At Home, which is adjacent to a commercial district.

Claibourne House

Host: Clare Easley, 912 Forest Street, Georgetown 78626, (512) 930-3934 and (512) 913-2272, 4 bedrooms, each with private bath (although 1 is on a separate floor), expansive continental breakfast, $$$, smoking in restricted area, children with prior arrangement, accommodates pets

Beautifully decorated with a mixture of antiques and contemporary art, the Claibourne House offers one bedroom with twins (something unusual in B&Bs), along with the more traditional full-sized bedrooms. The 1896 house, with a grand hall and parlor and wraparound porch with rockers, overlooks an incredibly huge live oak tree. Former model and real estate agent Clare Easley has personalized the house with family pictures and striking selections of art, including an ancient Indian blanket with friendship signs in the sitting room upstairs. The Claibourne House is located on a quiet residential street just six blocks from the delightful Georgetown Square, punctuated by excellent restaurants and a coffee shop worth visiting.

GONZALES

Houston House Bed and Breakfast

Hosts: Diana and Gene Smith, 621 East Saint George St., Gonzales 78629, (210) 672-6940, 4 guest rooms, 3 baths, full breakfast, $$$–$$$$, no children, no pets, smoking in designated areas, all cr

Built in 1895 by a well-known Texas trail driver William Buckner Houston, this late Queen Anne Victorian home has it all—turrets, wraparound porches, arched windows, embossed ceilings, towering pillars, and glass pocket doors. Painted celestial murals adorning parlor ceilings and dining room walls, all executed by Sue Jones Houston, the cattle baron's wife, hint of gracious Texas times when the cattle industry reigned supreme.

Four guest rooms, formally decorated, compete with each other for the title of grandest. In the Emerald Room, for example, guests enjoy a finely crafted marble-top dresser and a Prudent Mallard gentleman's armoire along with a fireplace, original to the home.

Breakfast here is also elegant with hot apple and cherry Bavarian pancakes or cinnamon raisin French toast with real maple syrup, both served with crispy bacon or sausage links, a fresh fruit smoothie or juice, coffee, tea, and milk. Other choices include omelets or hotcakes.

St. James Inn

Hosts: Ann and Rew Covert, 723 St. James, Gonzales 78629, (210) 672-7066, 2 suites, 5 guest rooms, private baths, full breakfast, $$–$$$, no pets, no children, no smoking, MC, V, AE

Gonzales is often called the "Lexington of Texas" as the first shots for Texas Independence were fired in the Come & Take It Battle in October 1835. Now one of the most delightful and historic small towns in Texas, Gonzales boasts of its 1914 St. James Inn. Built by cattle baron Walter Kokernot and son of Texas Revolutionary hero D. L. Kokernot, this Greek Revival-styled mansion is grand, spacious, beautifully furnished, and yet has a warm inviting charm.

Many of the Covert's antiques and special collections add to the ambiance of each room and blend with modern pieces to make the atmosphere eclectic, yet tasteful. The home has especially large rooms, private baths, fireplaces, and porches.

As for breakfast, don't eat your dinner the night before so that you can finish a mile-high French pancake, delicate southern crepes, and many other specialties. Also be sure to have Ann and Rew arrange a romantic candlelight picnic with a basket of goodies and wine to enjoy in a nearby park on a balmy evening.

GRANITE SHOALS

La Casita

Hosts: Joanne and Roger Scarborough, 1908 Redwood Dr., Granite Shoals 78654, (210) 598-6443, 1 bedroom, 1 bath cottage, full breakfast, $–$$, no pets, no smoking, no cr

Two reasons make La Casita an enjoyable B&B: your hosts, who are charming retired-Navy, full of stories should you want to wile away the afternoon or evening enjoying their company, and the cuisine. Roger prides himself on his 12-item breakfast menu, which, truly, is the most unique selection seen in any B&B (one selection includes fish, not often found on most breakfast menus; another more typical example: La Casida Omelet, which is migas made with eggs, cheese, vegetables, and herbs *du jour,* served with a meat dish). La Casita, or "Little House," began its B&B career as an artist's studio (with a darkroom that has become the bathroom) behind the main house. The queen-sized bed, Persian rug, and Bahrain trunk are enticing discoveries. The place is a bit difficult to find because Granite Shoals (west of Marble Falls) isn't on most maps. The Scarboroughs have created a little garden and fountain area for you, if you enjoy sitting with your morning coffee out front. Your hosts join you for breakfast, and they're always happy to share recipes or cuttings from the garden.

GRUENE

Gruene Country Homestead Inn

Hosts: Ed and Billie Miles, 832 Gruene Road, New Braunfels 78130, (210) 606-0216, conference room/entertainment center, 15 rooms all with private baths, conducted tours of historic Fachwerk buildings (1850s German-style architecture) and molasses-making, furniture-making facilities on Thursdays 2–6, open for self-tours at the same times other days of the week, buffet continental plus, $$$, smoking in restricted areas, children above 12, no pets, no cr

When the frugal and ingenious Germans settled New Braunfels and Gruene, they constructed their homes and workplaces using a Medieval building technique called Fachwerk (pronounced fawk-work) because of the scarcity of trees. Fachwerk buildings are half timber (in this case, cedar and cypress) and sun-dried mud bricks. The workmen created an outline of wood beams horizontally and vertically, then filled in-between with sun-dried mud bricks, often covering it all with mud plaster, adobe style.

Gruene Country Homestead Inn has two beautifully restored Fachwerk buildings, as well as several later Texas homes, capturing an unparalleled slice of Texas architecture from the early 1840s to the early 1900s in six country acres. From a Fachwerk barn (now a bed and breakfast complex in which even the root cellar becomes a bed and breakfast suite) and a Fachwerk outbuilding (now a conference center with swimming pool) to several later Texas structures, including an outstanding Victorian house (all with the typical front porches with swings and rocking chairs for your enjoyment), the Gruene Country Homestead Inn offers eight acres of German architectural history and charm. The Miles, like the early Germans, also make their own molasses from sugar cane (grown on the property and harvested in the summer), actually using the cooker and sugar press obtained from Edwin Hanz, the prior owner of the Fachwerk barn and property. The rooms, all with private baths, are exquisitely and ingeniously decorated, offering not only a comfortable and charming B&B experience, but one which is uniquely Texan. Gruene Country Homestead Inn is a "must-stay" place if you want to experience historic Texas at its best. You can also partake of their hot tub, Jacuzzis, and massage, if you want to totally luxuriate modern-style.

The Old Hunter Road Stagecoach Inn Bed and Breakfast

Host: Bettina Messinger, 5441 FM 1102 (Old Hunter Road), New Braunfels 78132, (210) 620-9453, (800) 201-2912, http://www.virtual cities.com, 2 cabin suites with private baths and porch, 1 room with private bath and entrance and fireplace (accommodates up to 3 people), gourmet breakfast, $$, smoking restricted, all cr

Just five miles from Gruene, between New Braunfels and San Marcos, the Old Hunter Road Stagecoach Inn is a road-stopper. If the historic restoration of the 1840s cabin or German Fachwerk house doesn't grab you, the Texas cottage garden out front will. Your hostess is a landscape designer and it shows in a blaze of color. Lovingly restored, the houses are furnished with primitives befitting the era. Warmly decorated cedar-beamed rooms are fragrant with the scent of herbs (dried flowers hang in the main house from square-nailed beams). The Log-Pen Cabin features some unusual amenities, including a bed actually handmade for LBJ's grandfather from old cedar trees, a cannonball bed (real round posts about the size of a cannonball), phones, desks and TVs in every room (for the traveling business person), and claw-foot tubs (one actually tin!). Breakfast features homemade breads, potato pancakes, New Braunfels sausage and, their specialty, Swedish

Pancakes served with fresh fruit sauce and whipped cream, at any time you want it (literally!). No wonder folks flock to this country door— something which started back in the mid-1800s when this was one of the biggest houses on this side of the Guadalupe. When the river was up, you stayed. They don't have to capture guests anymore because everything is cozy at The Old Hunter Road Stagecoach Inn.

HUNT

River Bend

Hosts: Conrad and Terri Pyle, Owners; Linda Brown, manager, Rt. 1, Box 114, Hunt 78024, (800) 472-3933, 14 rooms, 13 baths, 2 suites, full breakfast, $$$–$$$$, no pets, no smoking, all cr

Just around the corner from Stonehenge (yes, there is a replica of Stonehenge in Texas), the River Bend B&B blends in perfectly with the Hill Country landscape on the Guadalupe River. Once a hunting lodge, this trio of rock buildings is rustic in decor, but still comfortable. River Bend offers a full breakfast and a massive fireplace in the Main Lodge that never stops crackling when cool days hit. A porch with rockers, tables, and swings makes a great spot to watch the sunset or the kids drifting around the river just down the road. You can tube, paddle a canoe, hike the hills, or swim a few laps because River Bend has it all for entertainment, including a River Bend Round-Up Mystery Weekend. This has become such a fun institution in Hunt, you have to make reservations way in advance. Families with children do not stay in the lodge, and children aren't welcome there, so take that into consideration if you intend a family outing.

JOHNSON CITY

Bed and Breakfast of Johnson City

Hosts: Seven locally owned, hostless cottages distinctly decorated are handled by B&B of Johnson City, (210) 868-4548, private baths in each, multiple sleeping accommodations in each, $$–$$$,

smoking restricted to outside, children accommodated with prior arrangements, cr

The Tin House, built in early 1900, is on the Johnson City square, having been moved there in the early 1930s, when it housed the Johnson City *Record Courier* newspaper offices, for which Lyndon B. Johnson worked for a time as a "Printers Devil" for his mother, who edited the paper. Incredibly quiet except at Christmas when the courthouse becomes a spectacular light display of over 800,000 Christmas lights, the quaintly decorated Tin House accommodates at least six. Like all the B&Bs of Johnson City, fresh baked goods, fruit in season, cereals, juices, teas, and coffee are provided for your enjoyment. Owned by writer Cynthia Robichaux Smith, the Tin House has many items in the decor for sale (honor system, which is true of everything in Johnson City), including the award-winning *Potluck on the Pedernales,* a cookbook of the Johnson City's cooks (which we'd definitely recommend).

The Gingerbread House, a 1940s-style house located four blocks off the square on a quiet residential street, still has its original outhouse (with gingerbread trim), although the private bath inside complements the two floral-decorated bedrooms. The house was owned by the same family since its construction. The new owners, Harry and Patty Carpenter, now provide items of interest with pictures of Charles Hobbs with President Johnson and other memorabilia.

Carolyne's Cottage is reminiscent of a German Sunday House, constructed of native stone. Its interior is equally as quaint, with a pleasing mixture of English country and Texas antiques, chintz and lace, and the fragrance of spices and potpourri. A sitting room, a large but cozy bedroom with queen-sized bed, and a double hide-a-bed sofa offer spacious accommodations, should you want to bring family or double-up, but it's definitely a romantic hideaway should the two of you want to book it.

Hill House Guest House, one of the oldest homes in Johnson City, has a fireplace in the living room or a wood stove in the master bedroom, adorned with an unusual antique Queen Anne (queen-sized) bed. A second bedroom features an antique full-sized metal bed, and the couch also can accommodate two, in case you want a family outing in Johnson City. In the 1920s, a pressed tin exterior was added to the house, which adds an unusual twist, as does the kitchen table, which was constructed by your host from the old floorboards and porch posts. You literally can eat "off the floor" in this B&B.

Boot Hill Guest House allows you to step back in time into comfortable bunkhouse-style accommodations, which include beds made from welded horseshoes, towel racks made from cedar posts and wagon wheels, a dining room table made from old whiskey barrels, a wall painted with local ranch brands, and a library of Louis L' Amour books (which you can curl up and read in the rocking chairs on the porch after having your very own barbecue in the pit provided). A wood stove in a guest house, which accommodates up to six, adds to the Old West ambiance.

Lawyer's Loft, located on the square appropriately over a lawyer's office, offers twin beds in a beautifully decorated suite overlooking the Johnson City courthouse. While on the square, you should take in the old hardware store run by Nelson Withers (whose daddy went on the last turkey drive), that also has items we know you won't find in the city!

Hoppe House is a charming home of two bedrooms with beautiful Texas primitives, quilts, and rolling pin collection that would make rolling pin collectors drool. It has a picturesque patio (with a rabbit to greet you on the entrance porch) and a full dining room, in case you want to pull out the stops for dinner while here (although we'd definitely recommend The Feed Mill for a gourmet meal at low cost). The quilts on the wall, old crocks, wood stove, and other Texas collectibles add to the charm and ambiance.

Room With A View

Host: Heather Anderson, Ranch Road 3232 (north off 290 from Dripping Springs to Johnson City, the picturesque route), (210) 868-7668, 2 rooms with private baths, $$–$$$, no pets, children with prior arrangement, smoking outside

A well-appointed handcrafted bed in a huge suite, decorated with antiques and fabrics and styles reminiscent of a country French cottage, would be enough to draw the weary city dweller to this B&B, but the suite has an unsurpassed view of the hills. You'll want to stay up at night to watch the sun settle over the mountainous horizons in which you can see dozens and dozens of miles of the spectacular star display. It's almost criminal to miss the first red hues of the sunrise over the equally gorgeous eastern horizon (you're literally on top of the mountain), so you should plan two days to "un-pace" yourself. Your hostess offers a blueberry blintz pancake breakfast which is impressive, to say the least. You can eat on the porch, in the picturesque gardens of native plants which surround the house, or in your suite. Very close by is Pedernales Falls State Park, a 5,000 acre offering of river, fishing, tubing, swimming, hiking, biking, horseback riding, and birding. You're minutes away from the charming Johnson City and Blanco (both "must-see" towns), and you're just down the road from Fredericksburg. If you want to get away and enjoy the view, this is the place!

KERRVILLE

Hays House B&B

Hosts: Sharon McLaughlin, Manager; Dash Peterson, Owner, 201 Hays St., Kerrville 78028, (210) 896-8801, $$–$$$, accepts children and pets, smoking in restricted area, cr

The Hays House, named after famous Texas Ranger John "Jack" Coffee Hays, who actually raised the first company of mounted gunmen to act as Texas Rangers, is a Spanish-style home located across from Kerrville's River Restaurant. A beautiful courtyard secludes the house, which has an eclectic decor of antiques (all for sale) and "recent comfortable." Quotations are found throughout the house on the walls (e.g., "Share your wisdom—not your prejudice" or "Opportunity knocks just once, but temptation is a frequent visitor"). The most outstanding characteristic of this B&B, besides the fact that you're staying in a house named after the man who captured Santa Anna, is Sharon McLaughlin, a gourmet cook who whips up an unparalleled breakfast and will do special dinners by reservations in advance.

Napolitos Hideaway

Hosts: Rodney and Michelle Traeger, 7117 Medina Highway, Kerrville 78028, (210) 257-7815, 1 cottage with 2 bedrooms and private bath and hot tub, OYO breakfast, $$$–$$$$, takes older children, no pets, smoking in designated areas, no cr

Ten miles south of Kerrville, a completely appointed two-bedroom 2,000-square-foot rock house is hidden among huge oaks and cedars and offers a complete hide away. After sinking into thick carpet in the large living room—complete with big screen TV, VCR, and stereo—the guests step down to a screened-in porch complete with a cedar wood hot tub large enough for a dozen visitors or small enough for two. There's even a washer and dryer for bathing suits. All this behind a locked iron gate and patrolled by the friendly dogs; although, you might see deer, turkey, and quail also. Breakfast is left for guests and includes plenty of bagels, sweetrolls, yogurt, orange juice, and coffee. Not a traditional B&B, but definitely secluded, if that's what you want.

KYLE

The Inn Above Onion Creek

Hosts: John and Janie Orr, 4444 Hwy 150 West, Kyle 78640, 1 (800) 579-7641 or (512) 268-1617, 4 rooms with whirlpool, 5 with large tubs and separate showers, full breakfast and dinner included, $$$$, children 12 and over welcome, no smoking, VCR/TV, fireplaces in rooms, AE, V, MC

Spectacular blankets of wildflowers cover the ground as far as you can see from The Inn Above Onion Creek in the spring—some bluebonnets, a lot of Indian paintbrush, mostly black-eyed Susans. In the summer, you can watch the hawks or Mexican eagles hover in the air above the 10,000-foot stone structure with oversized pine columns and porches everywhere, or you can wander down to the creek that flows through the middle of the 500 acres, perhaps spotting some wild turkey. The house sits high on a hill, and visitors say you can practically reach up and touch the clouds. At night, the only light is from the moon and the stars (darkness that most city folks never see) or the fireplace in your room. You can snuggle in your extra-feather mattress bed and read a book by Katherine Anne Porter, who grew up in Kyle (and you probably never heard of Kyle before!). If you prefer, you can have a massage after taking a bath in a tub at least big enough for two. Everything in the Inn Above Onion Creek is oversized, it seems. Your hosts consider the cuisine "inventive regional," but chances are you will say it's simply delicious. Oriental rugs, a wood-burning fireplace, and a huge grandfather clock in the Inn's living room just add other luxurious touches to the ambience of the Hill Country B&B that gets our vote for one of the best anywhere.

New Tracks Llama Ranch Bed and Breakfast

Hosts: David and Shyrie Allen. Contact Wimberley Lodging, (512) 847-3909 or 1 (800) 460-3909, 1 cottage, full breakfast, $$$, no pets, no children, no smoking, MC, V

Just petting the llamas, miniature donkeys, and emus at this B&B would be worth the trip to New Tracks, but there's more—much more. Your Santa Fe-style cottage is filled with original art, weavings, and carvings of the Southwest. Rock walls, hand-hewn beams, and Saltillo tile floors add to the ambience. In fact, your definitely unique and big comfy bed is made from 100-year-old hand-cut logs. Even the chickens add to the charm of New Tracks. A basket of freshly laid eggs and fixings for a ranch breakfast is in your fully equipped kitchen.

You may never leave New Tracks during your stay. There are critters to pet, the Blanco River for swimming and tubing, an ideal picnic spot, and even a canoe, and a bicycle built for two. Who needs the big city when you have all this and a soft llama nose insisting you give it a contented rub?

LAKE TRAVIS

Chanticleer Log Cabin (Spicewood)

Hosts: Ceaser and Mallonee Mellenger, P.O. Box 232, Spicewood 78669, (210) 693-4269 or ph/fax (512) 346-8814, 1 guest room, 1 bath, full breakfast OYO, $$$, no pets, no children, smoking only on porch, no cr

Restoring this log cabin on their 75-acre farm that fronts Lake Travis was a labor of love for the hosts. From the moment you step onto the front porch overlooking a clearing with chickens, cows, horses, deer, and bird feeders, you know you have found a special place. The handmade log door, hinged windows propped open for the breeze (don't worry, it has central air and heat), and the porch log furniture filled with pillows are all an invitation to relax in this Hill Country hideaway.

Cotton linens, a down duvet, and beautiful fabrics on the queen-sized bed, a claw-foot tub and thick towels, and a well-equipped kitchenette that includes a modern touch—a microwave—are all there for your comfort. There is a gas grill outside, and a detached screened porch about 30 feet away, which has a stone fireplace, a hammock, and adirondack chairs. This is where your hosts, who live nearby on a hill, will deliver your breakfast, which usually includes freshly baked muffins or streusels, farm-fresh egg dishes, and more!

If you tire of walks along the lake or in the herb garden, you are only about 20 minutes away from restaurants, shops, and a restored movie theater in Marble Falls and 40 miles west of Austin.

Chanticleer has become popular for small functions, especially weddings, which Ceaser and Mallonee certainly understand since their wedding was held there, too.

Trails End

Hosts: JoAnn and Tom Patty, 12223 Trails End Rd. #7, Leander 78641, (512) 267-2901, (800) 850-2901, 2 guest rooms, 2 baths, 1 guest house, full breakfast, $-$$$, no pets, no smoking, MC, V

Only four miles from boat docks on Lake Travis and about 10 minutes from North Austin, Trails End B&B is an eight-acre retreat. A big gray house trimmed in white, with two wraparound porches and a sunburst transom over the front door, sits on a hilltop that covers two of the acres. You can see the water from the third-floor observatory. The two guest rooms and private baths are on the second floor. Breakfast is served in the formal French country dining room, while with advance reservations you can have a candlelight dinner by the wood-burning fireplace in the parlor on a special occasion like an anniversary.

The land slopes down about 50 feet to the pool, then steps lead down even more to a grove of trees—and the secluded guest house, which has a huge deck. Neither house can see the other because of the woods, so there is total privacy. The rustic guest house has a fully equipped kitchen, cable TV, a fireplace, a bedroom and a loft, both with double beds. It also has a single built-in bed, so the guest house can sleep five comfortably.

Here you can explore the wooded surrounding or the lake area. Let your road to a relaxing adventure begin at the Trail's End B&B.

LAMPASAS

Historic Moses Hughes Bed and Breakfast

Hosts: Al and Beverly Solomon, Rt. 2, Box 31, Lampasas 76550, (512) 556-5923, 2 bedrooms, 2 baths, full breakfast, $$–$$$, no pets, no children, no smoking, no cr

Lampasas is a fascinating town, dating from the mid-1800s, when Moses Hughes founded it because he had heard about its healing waters from the Indians, so he moved there for his wife's health. It, subsequently, became one of the biggest resorts in the South due to its natural mineral springs. Moses Hughes built his own native stone Texas ranch house in 1856 on a meandering creek in the country, now one of the most charming B&Bs in the state. The house survived and has been beautifully restored by the Solomons, but the old opera house, the largest hotel west of the Mississippi from the 1880s, and the bath houses burned down years ago (the bath house ruins are still there by the newly refurbished Hostess House).

The Moses Hughes house is furnished in period antiques that fit in perfectly with this Texas Landmark building. Both B&B bedrooms open out onto a balcony that overlooks the incredibly beautiful country, which is not far from the Colorado Bend State Park, a park that protects over 400 caves and the tallest waterfall in this part of Texas. If you listen carefully, you may hear the screeching cry of the bald eagle soaring high above you, because it inhabits this part of the country. You may want to track the bird by taking the Vanishing Texas River Cruise, which actually conducts eagle counts in the wintertime. If you're an outdoor adventurer, you can walk down to the fresh water springs on the property, where you may still find arrowheads, although your host, Bill Solomon, is obviously a collector and has probably beaten you to them. The living and dining rooms in the B&B house contain priceless pots, points, and arrowheads that he has found over the years, some of them dating back centuries. The idyllic setting, your hosts, and the gourmet meals at the Moses Hughes are so captivating, you might not want to leave, but you need to know that Lampasas offers free concerts on the square (from blues to big band) and numerous charming shops worth a visit. The Solomons purchased the Moses Hughes practically the minute they saw it, even though it was in a shambles at the time. As

Beverly describes it, "the house gave us a big hug." When you stay with them, you understand that, just as you realize Lampasas still contains healing powers, even though they may not always be in the springs.

LLANO

Fraser House

Host: Belle Laning, 207 E. Main, Llano 78643, (915) 247-5183, 4 queen bedrooms with private baths, full breakfast, $$–$$, no pets, no children, smoking in restricted areas, MC, V

The Upper Hill Country is, perhaps, the most scenic and spectacular in terms of high hills with large water vistas you can see as you wind through the country on your way to Longhorn Caverns State Park or the Colorado Bend State Park (known for its virginal, pristine condition, ideal for hikers and swimming). Llano (pronounced Lan-o, not ya-no, as if it were Spanish because its derivation is actually Indian) is a quaint town, packed with antique and gift shops, and a very decent restaurant in The Badu House. The town is centrally located to some of the most amazing experiences in Texas, including the Vanishing Texas River Cruise from Upper Lake Buchanan—well-known among birders for its bald eagle counts in the winter, as well as its summer and spring cruises; the mammoth Enchanted Rock (you *must* climb to the top); and the wonderful tours and tastings at Fall Creek Vineyards (and the annual August grape stomp). Llano is also in the midst of some of the most fabulous restaurants in the Hill Country, such as Russo's (Italian) and Jamin' House Cafe (Caribbean) in Marble Falls, and the Hilltop, between Mason and Fredericksburg, known for its seafood and steaks.

Just off Llano's historic square is the 1900 Fraser House, which offers four bedrooms furnished with antiques and upholstered walls to add elegance. Although stern and imposing granite on the outside, Fraser House is all warmth and charm inside, which is not only a reflection of the decor but also its hostess, Belle Laning. Belle is an unabashed enthusiast for Llano, which is understandable if you once visit it and her. Back at the turn of the century, Texans were convinced there was gold in Llano's hills, so it became a big boom town for minerals and such. Now it's simply a delightful place, with riches far beyond the early explorer's vision.

LUCKENBACH

Luckenbach Inn B&B

Hosts: Capt. Matthew Carinhas and Eva Carinhas, HC 13, Box #9, Luckenbach 78624, (800) 997-1124, (210) 997-2205, http://www.ccsi/~ elyons/luckenbach.html, 6 rooms, 2 with Jacuzzis and fireplaces, 1 with shared bath downstairs, gourmet breakfast, $$$, no TV/phones in rooms, accepts children and pets (with pet carriers), smoking in designated areas, Saturday night dinners by reservation, wine cellar

When you think of Luckenbach, you think of the old post office/store that is renown for Willie Nelson's 4th of July Picnic, Waylon Jennings' and Willie's song, and Jimmie Lee Jones, the strumming, singing (and really good!) song writer/bartender in the smallest town with the most stolen road signs in the state. Capt. Matthew Carinhas is changing that. Once you visit the Luckenbach Inn B&B, you won't think of Luckenbach any more without thinking of his incredible restoration of a two-story 1860s log cabin (and construction of a complementary property built around 1900) and his culinary excellence, which may only be surpassed by some of the most beautiful acres containing a deep water creek and 200-year-old cypress trees you've seen in this part of Texas.

Matthew came up from the sea, where his family runs shrimp boats out of Brownsville (thus, he's a captain of a ship), bringing his love for hospitality, food and cooking to create one of the most delightful B&Bs in the state. He's not entirely landlocked, because he didn't entirely leave the sea behind; he uses seafood in much of his preparations and he runs a seafood business on the side (ask about it, in case you want to take home some fish, shrimp, or crabs; he'll also offer peaches from the orchard). He'll knock your socks off with dinner (should you make reservations) and, certainly, with breakfast (how about banana walnut or blackberry pancakes, with apple-smoked bacon, grapefruit brulée and fresh squeezed orange juice?) The fireplace in the kitchen, where hot mulled cider greets you during cold weather, is just one more compelling amenity that is changing the definition of Luckenbach, Texas.

One more thing, in case you don't know: Luckenbach is just north of Sisterdale, where the Sister Creek Vineyards are located (their wine tasting room is located in a century-old cotton gin, which is not only charming but also offers a Cabernet that deservedly took top honors in national competition). The Grape Creek Vineyards, which also have several meritorious wines, including the Fume blanc and their Cabernet Trois, are to the north. Generally speaking, the Texas wineries are no schmucks but these two are especially worthy of a visit.

MARTINDALE

Forget-Me-Not River Inn

Hosts: Mamie and Edvin Rohlack, P.O. Box 396, 310 Main, Martindale 78655, (512) 357-6385, 4 rooms with baths, full breakfast, $$, children welcome, no cr

Known as the Nancy Martindale House locally, built in 1899, this B&B home beckons you with its setting of flowers, huge trees, a gigantic magnolia among them, with the yard terracing down to the San Marcos River, which flows behind this picturesque Victorian house. It's in a romantic setting—little Martindale, a place you have to search for, but well worth finding. It's a place many movie companies discovered as the hidden gem of the Hill Country. The warm, chatty hostess, Mamie Rohlack, named each of the rooms after her children's travels abroad, and she's converted the turret into a child's room that any child would want to burrow into. It's a place of warm fuzzies and breakfast anytime you want it. And someone said you can't go home again. Wrong. You can in Martindale.

Countryside Inn B&B

Host: Mary Ann Jones, ¼ Mile Country Road 103 East, Martindale 78655, (512) 357-2550, 3 rooms with 2 baths, full breakfast, $$–$$$, accepts children, no smoking, TV/VCR and fireplace in bedroom, no cr

Located in Martindale, the Countryside Inn B&B was built in 1874 and is reputed to be one of the first brick houses south of Austin. Originally a dogtrot, the high-pitched, tin-roofed house features soft pine floors, cedar beams, and two bedrooms upstairs with a sitting room in between and one bedroom downstairs. Mary Ann's homemade angel yeast biscuits are legendary. You can walk to the San Marcos River through her fields that pasture beautiful horses or wile away the day on the outside porches that circle the back and side yards. The original well stands in the yard as does the ancient cistern, both reminders of early times.

MASON

The Hasse House

Host: Laverne Lee, P.O. Box 58, Mason 76856, (888) 414-2773 (41-Hasse), (915) 347-6463, 2-bedroom, 2-bath rock house, continental breakfast, $$, no pets, smoking allowed in restricted areas, TV/VCR in living room, phone down the road, no cr

Laverne Lee may well have the only private two-mile nature path in the northern Hill Country alongside a picturesque 1883 house. The house is country-comfortable, not at all one of the historic restorations in which you have to be so very careful that you feel a little uneasy. And that's fitting, because you're out under the millions of stars in the 100-year old sandstone rock house on 320 acres by yourself—a joy few can appreciate until they've experienced it. Laverne, a fourth-generation Texan, loves this house and country, and any guest who misses her enthusiasm reflected in the detail with which she works to make her guests feel at home has missed the whole point of Hasse House. A vine-covered patio under the windmill in the back of the house captures its romance, but the small pieces of rocks, arrowheads, and other historic finds that guests have lovingly left in the house after their stay, most clearly reflect the uniqueness of Hasse House and its hostess. It's a house from another time, with a wood-burning stove to add to the ambience and a modern kitchen stuffed with goodies to add to its convenience.

Mason Square Bed and Breakfast

Host: Brent Hinckley, P.O. Box 298, Mason 76856, (915) 347-6398 or (800) 369-0405, 3 bedrooms, 3 baths, continental plus breakfast, $–$$, no pets, no smoking, TV and phone in common area, MC, V

Brent Hinckley has created modern bedrooms on the second floor of two historic commercial buildings he owns in downtown Mason. Not to worry about the noise of traffic, because Mason is a charming, quiet Hill Country town that relatively few "tourists" have discovered. Although Mason is known for its Texas topaz and one of the best bat caves in the state, it should be declared one of the more picturesque areas in Texas, with a wealth of sandstone architecture that is virtually unmatched in Texas. In the summer months at dusk, 3 million bats explode out of a cave in the hills—a truly memorable sight and a feat to find because you have to cross at least one river bed to get there (and there are hundreds of them on the back county roads, which aren't paved, by the way)! Brent has retained the original pressed-tin ceilings, Victorian woodwork, stained-glass transoms, and oak floors and has decorated the rooms with antiques and original artwork. He serves bakery products from the bakery just downstairs. Imagine the smell when you awake! It's fascinating to study his ancient maps of Texas, when it was "the Great Space of Land Unknown," or the first 1730 Texas map or a saddle bag map (1852) that was carried in a small leather pouch he now owns. Make sure you enjoy the veranda overlooking the square, available for all guests.

NEW BRAUNFELS

Antik Haus

Owners: Larry and Patsy Herring, Host: Alice Herring, 118 S. Union, New Braunfels 78130, (210) 625-6666, 3 rooms with queen bed and 1 single, all with shared baths, full breakfast, $$, no children under 12, no TV in rooms, MC, V

Just around the corner from the Schlitterbahn, Landa Park (with its 18-hole golf course, miniature golf, and swimming pools), and the entrance to tubing on the Comal or Guadalupe rivers, a delightful Victorian home, built in 1909, offers an oasis to all that activity. The house is nestled in beautiful floral gardens with ivy-covered gazebo for guests' enjoyment. The interior is beautifully restored and contains family antiques, including great-grandfather's hutch. Victorian shades, canopied beds, beautiful music, and a gracious hostess translate into a serene experience—something needed after a day partaking in the myriad of activities available in New Braunfels. The "fresh-from-scratch" cinnamon rolls are legendary, as are the German pancakes and large breakfast offered at the Antik Haus.

Danville School and Kuebler-Waldrip Haus

Hosts: Margaret Waldrip and son, Darrell Waldrip, 1620 Hueco Springs Loop Road, New Braunfels 78132, (210) 625-8372 or 1 (800) 299-8372, 8 rooms, 8 baths (1 handicapped access, 2 rooms with whirlpool), full breakfast, $$$–$$$$, pets by approval, smoking outside, dogs and cats in residence; hablamos Español, cr

Overstuffed chairs, Mexican artifacts, hand-painted pottery, hammered silver and numerous cats and dogs serve as a backdrop for the gregarious hostess of Kuebler-Waldrip Haus, a house built from limestone and hand-hewn timber in 1847, and the Danville School, a building Margaret Waldrip saved from demolition to resurrect as a B&B haus. Margaret Waldrip, ex-schoolteacher, bubbles with excitement, describing the restoration and yet another remodeling (something is always going on at Waldrip Haus), the latest "goody" she's found in Mexico (she travels frequently there and sells many of her finds), her son's latest undertaking (he is co-host and oversees the various activities, including volleyball, horseshoes, croquet, books, astronomy, if you want), and yet another historic discovery they or their guests have made about the house or the 43 acres of land upon which Waldrip Haus is located. (Example: the original owner of the land, Francois Guilbeau, is credited with saving the diseased French vineyards with the mustang grape vine cutting from this property).

It's the juxtaposition of things that captures the imagination: the fireplace is made from stones that came from the city's old jail and the Roman Catholic Church; the old school, chalkboard intact, is a comfortable living room and bedroom with Jacuzzi; a bathroom literally opens into an office; a sick deer actually became a real house pet. If you enjoy a rich texture of people, food (the breakfast, "the whole nine yards," always brings raves), animals, and conversation, the Waldrip Haus is perfect.

Karbach Haus Bed and Breakfast Home

Hosts: Capt. Ben Jack and Kathy Karbach Kinney, 487 West San Antonio Street, New Braunfels 78130, (210) 625-2131 or (800) 972-5941, 4 bedrooms with private baths and sitting areas, full breakfast, $$$–$$$$, TV/VCR, no pets, no children, no smoking, off-street parking, swimming pool and large spa, monogrammed robes, turn-down service, cr

Ben Jack and Kathy Karbach Kinney obviously have a love affair with this wonderfully restored, turn-of-the-century family home they've returned to after years of service in other parts of the world. Their love translates into a warmth and gracious hospitality, rather than a stilted form of preservation sometimes found in old houses. Understandably, guests often tell them that the house reminds them of their grandparents' home and happy days from their childhood. The giant magnolia, cypress, and pecan trees surrounding the pool, hot tub, and old carriage house create a canopy haven on their acre of grounds in the middle of New Braunfels, only four blocks from the main Plaza. Although the interior space, such as the delightful sun room, is well done and the furnishings—particularly the antique: Texas hand-made furniture crafted by their family forefathers in the 1800s—are interesting, it's your hosts, who offer conversation and taste of German wine upon your arrival, should you prefer it, which makes the stay in Karbach Haus memorable. They are fifth-generation New Braunfelsers, so they know the history of the town (the sausage capital of Texas) and this historic house in every detail, but they've also traveled the world and have a wealth of experiences. The huge German breakfast, including a fresh fruit salad with a sauce to go along (e.g., Kahlua sauce, brandy sauce, or Devonshire cream) is just the beginning of a spectacular eating event that sends guests away totally satisfied. They advertise Karbach Haus as a "very special place with an upscale casual elegance," and there's truth in their advertising.

The Rose Garden

Hosts: Dawn Mann, 195 S. Academy, New Braunfels 78130, (210) 629-DAWN (3296), (800) 569-3296, 2 bedrooms with private baths, full breakfast, $$, smoking in restricted areas, children allowed, wir sprechen Deutsch, MC, V

The Rose Garden is the personification of the German eye to detail, where the rose garden outside becomes translated into floral carpets, chairs, beds, china, even silver, meticulously kept for guests. Although small on the exterior, guests have their own parlor area as well as a beautifully appointed private room with bath. The sour-cream waffles, German apple puff pancakes, fresh-ground coffee in the formal dining room (or, if you'd prefer, in the garden, or a specially prepared tray to your room) make guests "feel so special"—the operating philosophy and goal of the hostess. From fluffy towels to scented soaps to breakfast on your schedule, Dawn wants everything fine for her guests. The Rose Garden helps you appreciate the German heritage that makes up New Braunfels in a personally indulgent and delightful way.

PIPE CREEK

Windmill Hill Bed and Breakfast

Hosts: Shirley and Buford Minter, Windmill Hill Lane, P.O. Box 1975, Boerne 78006, (210) 510-6736, fax (210) 535-6831, 1 bedroom suite, $$, no smoking, no children, no pets

The windmill, after which this B&B is named, provides the backdrop to the herds of deer that gather around dusk to nibble the feed the Minters put out. Your hosts have contemplated just about everything you might find appealing in "external accommodations," including superlative fishing, the creation of a verdant meadow with a unique swing for a quiet afternoon, a plentiful garden of flowers and vegetables, hummingbird feeders for birdwatchers, a horseshoe pit and basketball goal, paths for hiking, and, even, the identification of "kissing rock" on a cliff, overlooking the falls below their home, located on 14 incredible acres between Boerne and Bandera. If you can overcome the external appearance of their B&B house (a metal building that reminds Mr. Minter of his aircraft hanger days when he was VP in charge of maintenance for Braniff and, subsequently, Muse, among other airlines), you'll find the interior appointments to the approximately 800 square feet are beautifully well done. These include an old Saddler's sales trunk in a handsome brown-and-British-racing-green decor, punctuated by a quotation written on the walls around the queen-sized bed stacked with pillows and a down comforter, "Grow Old Along With Me! The Best Is Yet To Be." They have managed to create first-class "best" accommodations in the country out of tin. Ingenious.

SALADO

Brambley Hedge

Hosts: Billy and Carol Anne Hanks, 1530 FM 2268 (Holland Road), Salado 76571, (817) 947-1914, 4 rooms, 4 baths, "very full" breakfast, $$$$, no children, no pets, no smoking, MC, V, AE

One mile north of Main Street on 50 wooded, deer-filled acres, the Brambley Hedge has a distinctive country look, a metal roof with cupolas, and a covered porch. Arriving guests are greeted by the tantalizing aroma of chocolate chip cookies, because the host pops them in the oven as soon as guests come up the walk! Carol Anne may be new to B&Bs, but it didn't take her long to catch on to what B&B hospitality is all about! A floral interior designer, Carol keeps fresh flowers in the rooms.

The bed and breakfast quarters are in a wing to the right, with two guest rooms upstairs and two down. A dramatic common area with a 23-foot-high ceiling, a fireplace, a game room with a brick floor, and fountains contribute to the ambience of this country inn. Snickerdoodle coffee is served at 6:30 a.m., and later, a bountiful seated breakfast that may include a variety of muffins, caramelized French toast, marinated bacon, and other tempting fare from Carol's vast recipe collection that reflects the couple's travels round the world. (The treasured china displayed in a hutch belonged to the Rev. and Mrs. Billy Graham, who sent it to the couple as a wedding gift. Billy Hanks is a minister who works with the noted evangelist.)

Ask Carol, one of the most interesting hosts in town, to tell you about the Brambley hedges, relics of the past, and other fascinating historical tidbits about their property.

Country Place

Hosts: Bob and Elinor Tope, Holland Road (2290 FM 2268), Salado 76571, (817) 947-9683, 5 bedrooms, 5 baths, country breakfast, $$–$$$, children over 12 welcome, no pets, no smoking MC, V

Two-and-a-half miles from the heart of Salado is a white, one-story farmhouse with blue trim, a wraparound porch, and a white picket fence. You'll see roses everywhere—on the fence, the trellis over the front gate, by the porch, and in back when they are in bloom. Bluebonnets and other wildflowers on the family's five-acre property are something to see as well.

One guest room, the Blue Room in the main house, has stenciled walls and a country French decor. The other four rooms and adjoining baths are in an L-shaped wing, added in 1980. Referred to as the Bunk House, the rooms have different decors because Elinor says three of their daughters each chose a room to decorate. She's pleased with the results, and you will be, too. Make yourself at home in the sitting room, where you'll find shelves filled with hundreds of books, a TV, phone, desk, two game tables, and antique wicker furniture. Country breakfast favorites include grits and gravy, almond French toast, and apple cinnamon or baked German pancakes.

Open to bed and breakfast guests since 1992, the Country Place is a nice alternative to the B&Bs in historic homes that long have been part of Salado's charm and popularity.

Green Gables

Hosts: Trisha and Ken Norman, 433 Royal, Salado, Texas 76571, (817) 947-0520, 2 rooms, 2 baths, gourmet breakfast, $$, no pets, no smoking, children welcome, no cr

"Anne of Green Gables" has always been a family favorite, and their new house was green (a pale Victorian green), so the Normans decided Green Gables was the perfect name for their little guest cottage next door, which they opened early in 1996. The cozy cottage has two small rooms—one with a queen-sized bed and the other, a full— with a Victorian decor and antiques. A gourmet breakfast is served in the dining room in their own home that looks like vintage Victorian, but was built about 12 years ago.

Transplanted Houstonians who once lived in Alaska, the Normans live in a rural area amid pastures and cows, though they are just minutes from the heart of Salado with all its shops, and they love it. If she is not at home with her family or guests, you can usually find Trisha in one of those shops, Another Day, because it's hers.

Halley House

Hosts: Cathy and Larry Sands, P.O. Box 125, Salado 76571, (817) 947-1000, fax (817) 947-5508, 5 rooms, 2 suites, 7 baths, gourmet buffet breakfast, $$–$$$$, no pets, no smoking, all cr

Next to the Old Red School House on Salado's Main Street is the Greek Revival 1860 Halley House, which is on the National Register of Historic Places. Beautifully decorated in fine antiques, three of its guest rooms have fireplaces, and all have private baths. The Captain's Room can sleep six, and the Star of Texas Suite, four (extra beds are available). Breakfast—a gourmet buffet that includes home-made pastries, fruit, and a variety of main dishes—is in the formal dining room. Relax on the patio under the massive oak trees while you enjoy those extra cups of coffee.

Three more inviting rooms, also with private baths and queen beds, are in the Carriage House behind the impressive Halley House. Two queen sofa sleepers are available downstairs for children or overflow, along with a half bath at a nominal charge—unless the downstairs, the Gathering Room, is being used for a meeting or function of some sort. Especially popular for receptions as well as seminars, it can easily accommodate 100 and has a kitchenette.

The Sands have been involved in B&B for many years, and know how to make their guests feel special indeed.

Inn at Salado

Host: Suzanne and Robert Petro, P.O. Box 320, Salado 76571, (800) 724-0027 or (817) 947-0027, fax (817) 947-1003, 9 rooms, 9 baths, gourmet breakfast, $–$$$, no pets, no smoking, all cr

Beautifully restored to its original 1872 splendor, The Inn at Salado on North Main by Pace Park was this growing hamlet's first B&B. Once the home of Col. James Norton, who donated the granite used in the present state capitol, it is listed on the National Register of Historic Places and boasts a Texas Historical Marker. A hand-dug well, two tree-shaded terraces, five covered porches, six swings, and two acres of landscaped grounds framed by a white picket fence add to the postcard pretty ambience.

Tastefully furnished with antiques and other fine pieces, the historic inn has four guest rooms; three more are in an adjoining Carriage House. Two guest rooms are in the Baylor House, a turn-of-the-century Victorian cottage. Most rooms have queen-sized beds, but one has a king, while twin beds are in a room named for General George Custer, who supposedly visited Salado. Sitting areas and working fireplaces are other features that guests seem to enjoy.

Adding another dimension to the property is a historic 1901 Methodist chapel that was moved to the site from another small town by the B&B's former owner, George Kolb. Converted into a meeting hall, Allen Hall can accommodate 75 people theater-style and 50 people seated at tables, and larger gatherings if the grounds are used. Audio/visual, and video resources are available, along with office services.

Inn on the Creek

Hosts: Lynn and Suzi Epps, Sue and Bob Whistler, Center Circle, P.O. Box 858, Salado 76571, (817) 947-5554, fax (817) 947-9198, 20 guest rooms, 20 baths in 6 houses, a fine breakfast, $–$$$$, children OK in two cottages, no pets, no smoking, MC, V

The original 1892 structure was brought into this idyllic location on Salado Creek from Cameron, Texas, and then doubled in size. Next, a restaurant was opened in another Victorian house that was relocated on the adjoining lot and linked to the first by a wooden walkway. B&B guests have breakfast in the restaurant, which also is open to the public on weekends for dinner with a fixed menu and by reservation. Because of the ambience and superb food, the Inn on the Creek is in demand for special events and business meetings.

In recent years, a restored, beautifully furnished, four-bedroom annex, The Reue House and the Osage Guest Cottage adjacent to it, which has a lighter, more casual Southwestern decor, and Sally's Cottage were added. Victorian pieces enhance the latter, a one-bedroom charmer that includes a living room and accommodations for all three, which are a block or two from the main house. Just across the street from the main inn is still another one of their properties that offers lodging to overnight guests. Built in the 1880s in Holland, Texas, and relocated to this site and restored by the Epps and Suzi's parents, the Whistlers, it has five bedrooms and baths, and like the rest, an elegant decor. The Giles-Kindred House, a two-bedroom, two-bath house with living room, dining room, and kitchen, is ideal for a group or family.

While most of the properties have queen-sized beds, a few have king or double beds, and one, twin beds. A favorite, though, is still the original B&B, because you can sit on the back porch in a swing or rocker and watch the Salado Creek trickle by.

Suzi, by the way, shares some of the wonderful recipes that have made the Inn on the Creek's restaurant so renowned for fine dining in a new cookbook.

Rose Mansion Inn

Hosts: Carole and Neil Hunter, P.O. Box 613, Salado 76571, (800) 948-1004 (weekdays, 8 a.m.–5 p.m.), (817) 947-8200, fax (817) 947-1003, 4 rooms, 4 baths, 2 log cabins, 2 cottages, gourmet breakfast, $$$–$$$$, "very well behaved" children welcome in cabins and cottages, no pets, no smoking, MC, V, AE, D

Built in 1870 by Major A. J. Rose, the Greek Revival Rose Mansion has four bedrooms, all furnished with antiques and Rose family memorabilia. Three of the bedrooms have working fireplaces. For something different, spend the night in one of the rustic log cabins. The terrace with its creaky windmill, storage tower, and rock smokehouse all add to the charm of this wonderful B&B. You'll enjoy the hammock on the grounds, too, along with shaded seating areas and swings. Picture postcard pretty with a white picket fence, the Rose Mansion Inn is one of the state's most scenic.

SAN ANTONIO

One of the most romantic yet progressive cities in Texas is San Antonio. Steeped in revolutionary history, "Old San Antone" holds within its environs the most sacred shrine of every Texan—the Alamo. Here the likes of such men as Davy Crockett, William Travis, and Jim Bowie shed their blood so that Texas could be free from Mexico.

Today, visionaries of city government have made San Antonio a mecca for tourism, which has brought millions to its multicultural population. Now visitors can stroll along downtown's Riverwalk that flanks the San Antonio River, walk through Hemisfair Plaza, and shop at the historic Mexican square, El Mercado. They can learn from the Guadalupe Cultural Arts Center or remember their childhood when they wile away time at the Hertzberg Circus Collection. As for overnight accommodations, many of the B&Bs are in the historic King William District, which within the past two decades has enjoyed a renaissance. A few, however, sit elsewhere in this city, but each offers its own unique experience. Remember, though, that there is a 15% hotel tax, so include it in your vacation budget.

Beckmann Inn and Carriage House

Hosts: Don and Betty Jo Schwartz, 222 E. Guenther (King William District), San Antonio 78204, (210) 229-1449 or (800) 945-1449, 4 bedrooms, 4 baths, gourmet continental, $$$–$$$$, no children, no pets, smoking in designated areas only

A listing on the National Register of Historic Places, the Beckmann Inn and Carriage House has a long history of respectability. It was built in 1886 by the prominent German, Alfred Beckmann, for Marie Dorothea Guenther, his bride and the daughter of Carl H. Guenther, founder of the Pioneer Flour Mills. Guenther's company, established in 1859, has staying power for it is still in operation today. As for Alfred, he may have been of the first German family to settle permanently in San Antonio in 1846, says one historian. Swiss-trained in architecture, he designed the Queen Anne residence, which in 1907 provided the distinguished setting for the funeral of Alfred's father, Johan.

Located in the King William District, this 3,200-square-foot one-story inn has tall classic beveled-glass and shuttered windows, and a graceful wraparound porch. Having gone though several renovations—the result of the numerous architects who either purchased the house, were Beckmanns, or married into the family, its simple hip roof with intersecting gables has now changed to one with 18 planes. The once Victorian style has been transformed into Greek Revival. Yet, in spite of drastic changes, this B&B has tasteful lines because the Schwartzes have spent a fortune in the restoration and furnishings, characterized by antique and white wicker furniture accented by vividly colored fabrics and window treatments.

If the inn is full or if you choose to be more "private," an adjoining two-story, shuttered Carriage House with flower-filled window boxes, is available. Guests are greeted with "welcome tea" and in the mornings look forward to freshly ground coffee, specialty teas, fruit juices, a main entrée, muffins, coffee cake or hot bread. Sometimes the hosts feature a theme-oriented breakfast, for example cranberry, that begins with the juice of that fruit and ends with a dessert that also uses the fruit of the day.

Bonner Garden Bed and Breakfast

Hosts: Noel and Jan Stenoien, 145 E. Agarita, San Antonio 78212, (210) 733-4222 or (800) 396-4222, fax (210) 733-6127, 5 bedrooms, 5 baths, 2 suites and 1 studio, hosted full breakfast, $$$–$$$$, call about children, no pets, smoking outside only, V, MC, CB, D, AE

Artist and printmaker Mary Bonner was a free thinker who chose world travel to home and husband. Yet, she did stop long enough to build a stunning Italian villa, completion date 1910, in the heart of San Antonio's Monte Vista Historical District.

The intriguing feature about this fireproof accommodation is that it was designed and constructed by the noted architect, Atlee B. Ayers, one of the few in his field in the southwest to use concrete to build a steel-reinforced residence. Bonner commissioned him because she watched as her Louisiana home burned to the ground incredibly on six separate occasions. But safety was not the only priority of this internationally known artist. She chose stucco for the exterior and Italian-made fireplaces, tiles, and fixtures for the inside.

Art lovers will find hand-painted wall designs of particular interest. In the Garden Suite, for instance, delicately painted flowers are
carried from bedroom to bath. Furnishings are costly. The Ivy Room
features a sleigh bed that is contrasted by an impressive armoire that
hides the TV and VCR. For newlyweds, the Bridal Suite has a canopy
bed draped with Italian lace and linens. A two-person Jacuzzi tub awaits
lovers or singles who like plenty of soaking space.

There's also a raised-garden rooftop here where wine is served. At
night, guests admire the sparkles of San Antone's downtown district
as well as the resident swimming pool surrounded by lush foliage that
reminds the overseas traveler of European affluence.

Even though Monte Vista is a drive from the Riverwalk and downtown, guests are in walking distance to Trinity University and convenient to the zoo, the Botanical Gardens, the Witte and McNay
Museums, and Incarnate Word College. This one's perfect for not only
parents visiting their college offspring, but it is a luxury for visiting
professors, lecturers, and other professionals. Noel and Jan are very
gracious hosts who serve a varied full breakfast from stuffed French
toast to traditional fare such as pancakes, bacon, fruit, and muffins. If
you wish to be absolutely alone, Bonner's artist Santa Fe-styled studio is separate from the house and is also available.

Brackenridge House

**Hosts: Bennie and Sue Blansett, 230 Madison, San Antonio 78204,
(800) 221-1412 or (210) 271-3442, fax (210) 271-3442, 5 guest
rooms each with private bath, gourmet breakfast, $$$–$$$$,
no smoking, all age children and pets in carriage house, children 12
and over in main house, V, MC, AE, DC**

Recently purchased by retired Air Force colonel Bennie Blansett and
wife Sue, the 1906 Brackenridge House received the prestigious restora-
tion award from the San Antonio Conservation Society in 1987. Every
room is a showplace with period antiques softened by emerald fabrics
and rich deep tones offset by quality laces, homemade quilts, and silk
flower arrangements. The unusually placed upstairs dining room is for-
mal with fine crystal and china enough to serve ten people.

Formally known as the Norton-Brackenridge House, this B&B not
only has style but a warm host couple skilled in the art of entertain-
ment. The service took the Blansetts all over the world—testimony to

their vast experiences can be seen on the walls of Bennie's office. In one photograph, the distinguished colonel, accustomed to skies clouded with battle, is greeting former president Ronald Reagan.

Two rooms can be made into a suite as they share a common, easily closed-off kitchen. The bridal room, with decor of white lace and quilted fabrics and old claw-foot tub with shower, is romantic for honeymooners. Creme sherry and candy are provided to guests as well as fresh peach cobbler before or after a full breakfast of watermelon and other fruits in season, eggs and artichokes in sherry sauce, ham, croissants, and hash brown potatoes. Non-egg eaters still have plenty of other choices. Hairdryers and robes are furnished, and there's a hot tub in the garden. Kids and pets welcome in the carriage house, called the Blansett Barn, a two-bedroom guest house up the street at 206 Madison.

The Ogé House

Hosts: Patrick and Sharrie Magatagan, 209 Washington St., San Antonio 78204, (210) 223-2353, fax (210) 226-5812, 5 bedrooms, 5 baths, 5 suites, continental plus breakfast, $$$$, no pets, no children, no smoking, AE, MC, V

The Ogé House (Oh-jhay), built in 1857, and magnificently restored, is historically one of the crown jewels of the King William District. Originally owned by a Texas Ranger, cattle rancher and businessman, Louis Ogé, it is also one of the crown jewels of the B&Bs in Texas. The large foyer and library with its glowing hearth and view of the river make these public rooms ideal for meeting friends or small conversations. Breakfast is served in the beautiful formal dining room or on the sunny front veranda.

Throughout the entire mansion are exceptionally fine antiques, and each room is exquisitely decorated, yet each is comfortable and inviting. Most bedrooms have a fireplace, and all have cable TV, a telephone, and a refrigerator. Each suite opens onto a porch with a scenic view of old San Antonio, and massive oaks and pecans shade the wide lawns of Ogé House. Draw up a big wicker chair, contemplate the perfection of the setting, and then plan your brief walk into the heart of San Antonio. Waiting for you on your return will be the wonderful Ogé House where you step back in time to a romantic bygone era in Texas history.

Pancoast Carriage House

Host: Don Noble. Contact Bed and Breakfast Hosts of San Antonio (512) 824-8036 or 800-356-1605, 1-bedroom, 1-bath carriage house, continental plus breakfast, $$$$, no pets, no smoking, AE, D, MC, V

This beautifully restored carriage house in the King William District is furnished in Victorian antiques and accentuated with brick walls, decorator fabrics, and draperies. The spacious living area is lighted by French doors opening onto the patio. Just outside your B&B is a garden, swimming pool, and spa for your use, a most welcome relaxation after touring San Antonio. But, Don has not overlooked other amenities such as a full kitchen with a refrigerator stocked with tasty tidbits, telephone, and cable TV.

Your handsome bedroom is furnished with a queen-sized brass bed, and the white marble bath includes a claw-foot tub with shower. For that absolutely perfect little hideaway, don't miss Pancoast Carriage House.

Riverwalk Inn

Host: Johnny Halpenny, 329 Old Guilbeau, San Antonio 78204. Contact Bed and Breakfast Hosts of San Antonio (800) 356-1605, (210) 212-8300, (800) 254-4440, fax (210) 229-9422, 11 guest rooms with private baths, unhosted, "expanded" continental, $$$–$$$$, children welcome but only two people per room, no pets, smoking in designated areas only, V, M, AE, D

Located on the banks of the San Antonio River, the Riverwalk Inn is one of San Antonio's newest and most picturesque B&Bs. The history of this comfortably country accommodation dates back to 1842 when five two-story cottonwood log homes were built in Tennessee. Builders dismantled the homes and brought them log by log to San Antonio where they are now combined to make the Riverwalk Inn. Although the authenticity of the historic structures was preserved, you'll not find any "rustic conveniences" here. Working fireplaces, refrigerators, private baths, phones, balconies with a view, TV, and a conference room meet the needs of every tourist and business person. Located within downtown makes travel to attractions and meetings easy and quick.

Modern comforts here differ from hotel stays in that the decor emphasizes quality four-poster beds laden with antique spreads, inviting rockers lined along a long pioneer porch, and rough board halls accented by polished wood and flagstone floors with woven rugs. If you stay here, remember that there is a two-and-three-day minimum visit during special city events.

Royal Swan Guest House

Hosts: Curt and Helen Skredergard, 236 Madison, San Antonio 78204, (210) 223-3776, 5 guest rooms with private baths, gourmet breakfast, $$$–$$$$, children over 12, no pets, smoking in designated areas only, MC, V, D, AE

In 1890 a successful dentist, Dr. Jabez Cain, built the Royal Swan Guest House in King William District. Only a block away from the River Walk, this gracious lady stands for the elegance of living shared by the socially elite of the Victorian era.

Rich, shining loblolly pine woodwork and plush floral carpets greet guests as they come in from a day's sightseeing. Stained glass, transoms, and original, refurbished pocket doors that still work join with tiled fireplaces to add interest to the entire house. While the parlor and dining room are dramatically elegant, the morning room acts as an appropriate contrast with its light, airy colors and wicker furniture.

This B&B has five guest rooms, each decorated to fit a mood. The Texas Room, cozy with western decor, a rocking chair and braided rugs, reminds one that Texas is best. The Crystal Room, with its gleaming bed and bath chandeliers, shades of rose and creme, and a cherub motif mixed with lace, whispers of romance. The Emerald Room features a great mahogany "rice" carving bed, fireplace, and claw-foot tub as well as a private veranda. If sky blue is your favorite color, the Veranda Suite, which also joins a private porch, is made up of two rooms, a bedroom and a sitting room, all in blue and white. For those with a dramatic flair, the downstairs Garnet Room, with its pewter bed, original fireplace, and large claw-foot tub, has its own private entrance.

This B&B abounds with extras. Afternoon guests enjoy chocolate-filled dishes, snacks, and sodas while coffee makers in each room give slow risers a chance to sip a cup in private. Hosts here are on-line with computer hookup capabilities. Each room also has its own phone and telephone number. As for the fare, the hosts here are creative and specialize in egg soufflés and quiches as well as cobblers and muffin cakes.

Of special note here is the original carriage curbstone that past visitors used to secure their horsedrawn carriages and the exquisite "bridal bow," a halfmoon-shaped balcony perfect for a blushing bride to gaze down at her admiring guests.

The Tara Inn

Hosts: Douglas and Donna West, 307 Beauregard, San Antonio 78204, (210) 223-5875 or (800) 356-1605, fax (210)226-7136, 4 guest rooms, 4 baths, full breakfast, $$$–$$$$, children over 10, no pets, smoking only in designated areas, all cr

Have you ever felt like pretending to be Scarlett O'Hara or Rhett Butler, if only for a weekend? Well, although your chances are slim of ever digging sweet potatoes out of the soil with your bare hands or gun-running for the Old South, you do have the unique opportunity of experiencing the atmosphere of Scarlett's era. All you have to do is call the Tara House in Old San Antone. This antebellum home on Beauregard Street in the city's most historic sector, King William District, is a fitting tribute to Margaret Mitchell's book, *Gone with the Wind,* even down to the pictures on the walls. All that's missing is the threat of Sherman and his army of Yankees marching through Georgia.

Built in 1905, the grand old home, recently restored by owners Douglas and Donna West, has four guest rooms, each christened for Scarlett, Rhett, Melanie, and the heroine's family name, O'Hara. The indecisive Ashley must still be paying for his weaknesses as he has no namesake here. Rhett's Room features flickering lights, a richly adorned queen-sized bed, complemented by man-sized windows, and a portrait of Robert E. Lee to stand watch. Mrs. Butler's room projects an ambience of delicacy balanced by strength. The Wests (Donna is the director of Bed and Breakfast Hosts of San Antonio and South Texas) have spared no expense in bringing their B&B back to its original luster. Walk through windows, expansive first- and second-story verandas, and fabrics of green (to commemorate Scarlett's eye color and the O'Hara name) all mark this hosted accommodation as one of the best in the King William District.

The full breakfast is enough to satisfy even the most genteel of palates with three courses including an egg dish, on occasion, Eggs Benedict. Other amenities include chocolates and fresh flowers in every guest room. Afternoon tea is also served.

Terrell Castle Bed and Breakfast

Hosts: Katherine Poulis and Nancy Haley. Contact Bed and Breakfast Hosts of San Antonio, 800-356-1605, 4 suites, 5 rooms, 5 baths, gourmet breakfast, $$–$$$$, no pets, no smoking, AE, MC, V

All the castles aren't in Spain; there is one on Grayson Street in San Antonio with rooms and meals fit for royalty. And, you are definitely given a red carpet welcome by owners Katherine Poulis and her daughter, Nancy Haley. Edwin Holland Terrell built this 26-room mansion in 1894 for his bride and named it Lambermont. Complete with tower, turrets, and just about every castle feature except a moat, Terrell Castle offers spacious rooms, charming suites, delightful antiques, fireplaces, and in spite of its four stories, full heating and air conditioning.

When you think of the "groaning board," think of breakfast at Terrell Castle. It is served at your convenience in the huge impressive dining room (no, you don't get a throne, just a chair), and you have your choice of everything you ever dreamed about eating for breakfast, and it is all prepared daily. Guests rave about the breakfast at Terrell Castle, and they probably do not eat the rest of the day.

SAN MARCOS

The Crystal River Inn

Hosts: Mike and Cathy Dillon, 326 West Hopkins, San Marcos 78666, (512) 396-3739, 12 rooms and suites, all with private baths, full breakfast, $$–$$$, TV in room, AE, D, MC, V

The Crystal River Inn is a romantic 1883 Victorian inn and garden complex, featuring roses, topiaries, fountains, and beautiful old pecan trees. The gourmet breakfast is a headliner event—Eggs Benedict,

Crystal River Inn

Bananas Foster crepes, and raspberry French toast. Known for theme weekends, the Crystal River Inn also offers other unique amenities, including fireplaces, carriage rides, and rooms with canopied beds and claw-foot tubs. Vivacious owner Cathy Dillon can tell you just about anything you want to know about the area she loves, including its antiquing, the wineries, whitewater sports, its history, and shopping at the biggest outlet mall in Texas (150 stores). In their brochure, they say that "some of the peace, the beauty, the history, and the happiness of this unique chunk of Texas has been bottled up right here, waiting to be sampled." The description is apt; the bottle is full.

SEGUIN

Weinert House Bed and Breakfast

Hosts: Tom and Lynna Thomas, 1207 North Austin St., Seguin 78155, (210) 372-0422, 4 bedrooms with private baths, full breakfast, no pets, no young children, smoking in restricted areas, MC, V

The history of the immaculately restored Weinert House is compelling. It was built in the early 1840s by the "Warhorse of Guadalupe County," Senator Weinert, who was responsible for reforms in the Texas Penal Code (for which prisoners were so grateful they built in a ten-foot armoire which sits on the upstairs landing, next to one of his daughter's hand-carved hope chests, also from the same source). The Senator is also credited with the creation of the first electric coop (the lights over the vineyard on the grounds under the Senator's "sleeping porch" twinkle through the night), and the introduction of the first Pasteur Institute in Texas (because of the loss of a valued friend to polio) among other significant contributions. Aggies should make the Weinert Home their mecca for no other reason than Weinert's son, Arthur, played on the first football team and took his dog to the games. His picture is in the music room, with the original furniture, *fleur de lis* pattern around the ceiling, and fireplace screen from the house. Oh, do we need to tell you the dog's name? No matter what your alma mater, anybody in Texas who doesn't know the name of the A&M mascot can't claim this state as their own. That's the rule. Okay, just in case you forgot, it's Reveille. The magnificence of the house is captured by its enthusiastic hostess who, literally, brings the home alive with stories and articles (including the Senator's glass eye and eyeglasses, believe it or not), should you take the time to visit with her during your stay. The beds are large, the detail with which you are luxuriated is exact, and the food is unparalleled (no one can beat a fat-free banana split for breakfast—no one!). What more can be said except you're missing a true Texas treat if you don't stay the night at the Weinert House.

SHINER

Old Kasper House Bed and Breakfast Inn

Hosts: Hubert & Mary Ann Novak, 219 Avenue C, Shiner 77984, (512) 594-4336, 8 bedrooms, 8 baths, full breakfast, $–$$, no pets, children in cottage only, smoking in designated areas only, DC, MC, V

Shiner, a Czech and German community founded in 1887 and located 85 miles east of San Antonio, now has something more to shine about other than its beer. The Old Kasper House was built in 1905 by cotton gin operator, John F. Kasper, whose claim to fame was descendant Gregor John Mendel, who uncovered the secret of genetic inheritance. A master craftsman, Kasper used his Old World skill to build Shiner's quaint yet sturdy B&B.

Now owned by Hubert and Mary Novak, the home, painted blue and ivory with gingerbread trim, is filled with comfortable antiques accented by fabric-lined walls. When outside, note the front yard planter, anchored by a petrified lighthouse that symbolizes a welcome to the New World. You'll also see the outback cottage, open to families, not concerned about frills. Recently, the Novaks have added a spacious Honeymoon Cottage, a two-room, "very private" accommodation complete with Jacuzzi and canopied king-sized bed. Furnished in the French country motif, the suite also has its own sitting room. The cottage is separated from the B&B's one-and-a-half acres by a picket fence, which also keeps out the rest of the world.

Whatever you do, though, be sure to catch Sunday brunch with the Novaks. Hubert plays the accordian for their guests.

While in Shiner, visit Spoetzl Brewery, the home of Shiner Beer, a product made, bought, and consumed in Texas.

SMITHVILLE

The Katy House

Hosts: Sallie and Bruce Blalock, P.O. Box 803, 201 Ramona, Smithville 78957, (512) 237-4262, (800) THEKATY (843-5289), 2 rooms in the house with private baths, 2 rooms with private baths (conductor's quarters over the garage and the carriage house), full country breakfast, $$–$$$, children with prior arrangements and in certain areas, pets with prior arrangements and in certain areas, smoking outside, AE, MC, V

The Katy House is appropriately named because it was for years the residence and offices of the Katy Railroad's physician, who was based in the town that served as the division point for the Katy Railroad. The real reason for its name, however, is that the 1909 home is packed full of American antiques and authentic railroad memorabilia, collected by your host, who is an unabashed railroad aficionado. Maybe that term is too loose, because, to stay at the Katy House and not tour the treasures Bruce has collected over 30 years is to miss the treat of a lifetime, particularly if you love the romance of trains. They have items that would make a museum curator salivate, from the silver and dishes you use for your meals to signs, ticket holders, clocks, conductors' watches—well, you have to see it to believe it.

The breakfast is noteworthy for its huge slabs of peppered bacon as well as the Sally S rolls (little cinnamon rolls). Their homemade bread toast, along with the fruit plate and egg dish round out a memorable meal.

Smithville is a lovely, small, central Texas town with huge trees (several are well over 500 years old), a wide main street with the Colorado River on one end and a railroad park on the other, and a wonderful restaurant called the Back Door, antique shops (where you can find some real bargains if you call for an appointment ahead of time), and one of the most unusual bars you'll ever experience. Huebel's, located just behind your garden gate at the Katy, doles out gigantic chunks of cheese and sausage, priced by the dollar (like, "this looks like a dollar's worth"), served on a piece of paper with your favorite brew under a ceiling with its paint falling off. You'll think you've sat down for a Renaissance feast in a place that looks about that old. If you want a true small town experience, ride your bikes (provided by your hosts) around town until you find a quiet nook for a picnic. On the first Saturday of the month, the stores in town stay open late and jazz musicians and other major small-town draws entertain (the Chamber often gives away $50). Smithville truly is a treat, the kind of place you probably thought didn't exist anymore except in old movies.

STONEWALL

Home on the Range B&B

Hosts: Don and Velna Jackson (known locally as The Stonewall Jackson), Route 2721, Stonewall, (888) 458 BEVO, (800) 460-2380, (210) 644-2380, or contact Hill Country Accommodations (512) 847-5388, 1 cottage (sleeps 6), full breakfast in refrigerator, $$, 11 stocked ponds, Longhorn lean beef, 2 barbecue pits, no pets, restricted smoking, cr

Your B&B quarters are the original ranch homestead built in 1927 in the middle of a registered Longhorn operation of 455 or so acres, with buffalo, antelope, Spanish goats (fun for the kids to chase), Mouflon sheep (those are the ones with the curly horns), kittens, huge bass and catfish (for catching), and one dog, Snoodles. The Range is known for the internationally famous Captain Twiggs, a gigantic red and white Longhorn steer that you can climb aboard for a photograph, if he is available. Twiggs will stand stock still, chew on his cud, and pose like the ham (or should we say steak) that he is. He is also the talk of Texas because he is the candidate for Bevo (need we tell you who that is, if you're in Texas?).

You have full breakfast fixings in the fridge, including grits, homemade breads, and fresh fruits, but, if you request ahead of time, your hosts will fix you a breakfast quiche with venison sausage. Although the two bedroom cottage has all the modern comforts, it also has a working wood-burning cook stove (called "Home Comfort"), an old electric stove, a claw-foot tub (from the home Velna grew up in), and a delightful country decor that makes you feel right at home on the range. No decent ranch house exists in Texas without puzzles, games, and a porch to rock on, to overlook your spread. If it's feeding time on the ranch, take a ride with your charming hosts because you'll end up nose to nose with the buffalo and longhorns (some will actually eat from your hand, as do the catfish) and you, also, won't want to miss Flagpoint Knoll, which looks like something out of the old West movies, where you stand under trees on a high knoll, overlooking the expansive Stonewall Valley and thousands of acres, including the LBJ Ranch below.

UTOPIA

Bluebird Hill

Hosts: Roger and B Garrison, Box 206, Hwy 1050, Utopia 78884, (210) 966-3525, 1 bedroom with bath, 1 suite, 1 hideaway cabin, full breakfast, $$, fireplace in dining room, no pets, children in the cabin only, smoking in restricted area, no guns, no hunting, no cr

The most beautiful, mountainous drive in the Hill Country is west of Bandera, headed over to Utopia, Vanderpool, and Leakey, so the vista from Roger and B Garrison's hill is spectacular. The suite is up in the trees with a great deck surrounded by live oak branches and you can enjoy the million stars at night that settle over their 250-acre mountainous ranch and creek. You can soak your bones in the hot tub in their sun room (if you've been out hiking or riding in one of various stables in the area) or you can enjoy B's stories (not only is she a professional story teller, she's amassed a huge variety of tales from the Hill Country and her people, who homesteaded the place at the turn of the century). Roger is ex-military-turned artist, whose works and charm would melt anyone's heart. If you want totally private, take the hideaway cabin that sleeps six, with its Texas decor featuring momentoes of pioneer ancestors and Native Americans. Adding to the cabin's charm is your very own hot tub and funky Victorian bathroom. At the cabin, a fireplace will cut the chill in the winter, but you'll have to appreciate the Hill Country breezes for air conditioning (the guests actually tell the Garrisons that adding air conditioning will spoil the cabin, so it stays as is). A truly comfortable B&B worth the drive, but make sure you travel the roads the first time during daylight for safety as well as appreciation.

Rio Frio Bed n Breakfast and Lodging

Hosts: LeAnn and Anthony Sharp, P.O. Box 155, Rio Frio 78879, (210) 966-2320 or (210) 232-6633, 15 vacation homes and cabins, 6 B&Bs

In the front yard of LeAnn's B&B Service is the largest live oak tree in the nation, estimated to be 500–1,000 years old. The limbs are so large, their weight pulls them to the ground. That, alone, is worthy of a visit to Rio Frio (the area between Kerrville and Uvalde), but the drive into the area is nothing short of incredible. The parks are legendary (with tubing, swimming, hiking, horseback riding, and fishing) and the fall foliage is, well, not exactly like the rest of Texas: it's actually fall foliage (Lost Maples has reason for its name!). The "Land of 1100 Springs" offers a wide variety of accommodations, from cabins (with cooking facilities, in which you cook and wash up) to rustic inns (such as Whiskey Mountain Inn that offers a continental breakfast in a 1869 German farmhouse surrounded by cabins, where you cook your own) to a 4,000-acre ranch with 16 miles of mountain bike and hiking trails (and two stocked fishing ponds).

LeAnn runs a service to find what type of accommodations you might need. Most aren't typical B&Bs, falling into the Dude Ranch, independent cabin or cottage, or continental breakfast motif, so to get the kind of accommodations you really want, be sure to tell her whether you want a private bath (if you're leasing a room), a full or partial breakfast (or none at all, in some cases), whether you want hosted or unhosted accommodations, and the kind of ambience (e.g., mountain isolated, country rustic, town, luxurious hosted) you'd like (and anything else you can think of, such as dinner arrangements). She can match your requirements because she can really isolate you in the hills or find you a place in a stone-structured house in town, depending on your desires.

VANDERPOOL

Texas Stagecoach Inn

Hosts: David and Karen Camp, Hwy 187, Vanderpool 78885, (210) 966-6272, 1 room with private bath, 4 rooms sharing 2 baths, full breakfast, $$, no smoking, no pets, children over 10 welcome, dog and cat on premise, catch-and-release fishing and canoeing on property, no cr

The two-story 1885 historic frame home, remodeled in the style of an early stagecoach inn, is located on the banks of the Sabinal River just down the road from Lost Maples State Natural Area (great Fall colors!), Garner State Park (fantastic swimming and tubing), and smack in the middle of just about the most scenic drive in Texas Hill Country. The 6,000-square-foot home reflects its ranch and western heritage, not only with a display case full of hundreds of arrowheads and other objects discovered by the Camps in their previous life as ranchers, but by the outstanding selection of art, most of which are landscape paintings by David, a professional artist worth collecting. From the furniture to the tableware, the western motif has been carefully constructed by the Camps to reflect the heritage of the community they obviously love. If you want to know anything about the area, ask your hostess. She is a font of information. Karen's breakfast, particularly her breakfast bread pudding (the recipe is in a book she sells in her gift shop), is simply to die for.

WACO

Judge Baylor House

Hosts: Bruce and Dorothy Dyer, 908 Speight, Waco 76706, (888) jbaylor and (817) 756-0273, fax (817) 756-0711, e-mail: jbaylor@iamerica.net, 5 rooms with private baths, full breakfast, $$–$$$, no smoking, no pets, children accommodated, MC, V

New owners Bruce and Dorothy Dyer were B&Bers the last ten years, so upon retirement from the health care industry, they purchased the Judge Baylor House in 1996 to fulfill their dream of running a B&B. The house was built in the 1940s by a Baylor chemistry professor. Their personal joy of operating the house shows in the immaculate rooms, the homemade goodies they put out for arriving guests, and small details, such as providing a large table and several small ones for people who like to breakfast alone or those who want to converse with other guests. The two-story red-brick house features a formal garden in the back, as well as a large porch swing that hangs from the big ash tree in the front (a favorite for guests who enjoy the morning streetscape before breakfast). Practically located smack in the middle of Baylor and a block and a half from the Armstrong-Browning Library, which houses the largest collection of Robert and Elizabeth Barrett Browning works and 16 stained-glass windows celebrating their contributions, the Judge Baylor B&B is convenient to most anything in Waco, including the Dr. Pepper Museum.

WIMBERLEY

Blair House

Host and Owner: Jonnie Stansbury; Shawn Leighton, Assistant Innkeeper, One Spoke Hill, Route One, Box 122, Wimberley 78676, (512) 847-8828, or Wimberley Lodging (512) 847-3909, 6 bedrooms with private baths, 3 with Jacuzzi, 1 cottage, full breakfast, $$$$, no pets, children in cottage only, no smoking, cr

Secluded on a hill overlooking Wimberley, the Blair House provides guests the ultimate B&B experience, from Jacuzzis to a sauna after a massage (by appointment) to the finest cuisine, served in the loggia dining room. The fine art plays center stage at Blair House, with all rooms featuring superlative artists, many from the Wimberley area, but also from all over North America, as well as Mexico and Europe. A retreat from the fast lane, Blair House is situated on 85 acres of beautiful Texas Hill country, available for your hiking, fishing, or napping in hammocks on the property. Guest rooms are meticulously decorated (such as the Austin Cottage, which offers a large room that opens to a huge private deck, a tapestry bed covering over Chinese cutout dust ruffle, and a cherrywood sleigh daybed with trundle). Blair House offers special packages, including catered weddings and dinners, although dinner is available with advance reservations every Saturday. Even if you haven't booked a room with Blair House, book dinner. The menus take advantage of the seasonal harvests from the Craftsman Organic Farm, as well as other local gardens, but whatever is on the menu, the cuisine is unparalleled. Homemade sausages, omelets, fresh baked breads, and fresh-ground French roast coffee are typical breakfast fare, if you can call anything "typical" at Blair House except its excellence.

Dancing Water Inn

Hosts: Artist David Bear and partner Kimberly Kruger, 1405 Mt. Sharp Rd., Wimberley 78676, (512) 847-9391 or Wimberley Lodging (800) 460-3909, 2 houses with 4 bedrooms, 4 fireplaces, 4 baths, screened porches, full kitchens, hot tub, expanded continental breakfast, $$–$$$, children accommodated, smoking restricted to porches, special arrangements for catering and massage (by advance reservation)

Two things distinctly separate this B&B from anything you've ever seen: it is literally a piece of art in which you live ("a living gallery"), and it is THE source of water for Cypress Creek—literally, a huge rock hole called Jacob's Well that is at least 240 feet deep and springs forth crystal blue waters from monolith boulders that create a natural amphitheater around the spring. In short, Dancing Water Inn is unique. Artist David Bear and Kimberly have transformed two native stone homes into a primitive folk art environment, in which the floors, walls, ceilings, and woodwork have become a gigantic canvas, painted turquoise, emerald, gold, any mix of colors, on and in which paintings, textiles and sculpture (often by Hayden Larson) coexist/exist beautifully. Even the furniture is hand-crafted (Carl Wilkins). As a result, the entire place is a work in progress, like a gigantic artist's studio, where patterns and colors, artwork and furniture are in transition—some, because people purchase the works and take them away, and some because the artist/owners are always visualizing more to do. It's not chaotic if you're delighted by surprise and ingenuity, but this is not a B&B for the compulsive personality. To the owners, everything about the place is peaceful, although they view Jacob's Well as perfect for an invigorating swim or reflective meditation. In any case, it's a place to respect, an amazing sight, alone worth a visit. The meadow leading down to the waters is one of the most beautiful imaginable, with a hammock strung for someone to lie in the blanket of spring wild-flowers or tall summer grass. Another "tree" is in actuality an oak and elm which have been wrapped together in the Indian marriage tradition that says a marriage is considered strong and would survive if two unlike trees were wrapped together at the time of the marriage and they survived. The grass is not manicured and the path not straight, but there's soul in the stones and wood at Dancing Water Inn (if you open your heart).

Old Oaks Ranch

Host: Bill Holt, County Road 221, Wimberley, (512) 847-9334 or contact Wimberley Lodging (512) 847-3090, 3 cottages, full breakfast with arrangements, $$–$$$, TV, no pets, no children, smoking outside, MC, V

The Holts' house, the original John Dobie house built over 100 years ago, is the centerpiece of the Old Oaks Ranch, with two historic buildings and a barn outback that have been converted into B&B accommodations. The one-bedroom Chicken House is decorated with Victorian antiques and has its original foot-thick walls. The Ol' Store-house Cottage has two bedrooms, (one a king and one with two doubles), complete with fireplace and living room. The Barn is a one-bedroom with sitting room getaway and an iron stove for winter fun. Old Oaks is known for the miniature donkeys they raise and their gigantic oak tree, which is estimated to be over 600 years old, obviously a tree under which Indians sat many years ago (and the arrowheads around the area substantiate that). Breakfast arrangements are unusual; you're given a chit to have a full breakfast at the Cypress Creek Cafe in downtown Wimberley, which allows you the flexibility to eat any time between 7:30 and 11:00. If you don't want to eat, you can use your coupon as cash in the Old Mill Store for supplies or other goodies.

Rancho El Valle Chiquito

Hosts: Jim and Karen Zombola, Rt. 3, 897M, (on County Road 218), Wimberley, 78676, (512) 847-3665 or Contact Wimberley Lodging (800) 460-3909, 4 suites with private baths and kitchens, 1 suite with 2 bedrooms, full breakfast, $$$, children accommodated, check on pets, smoking in restricted areas

If you want family activity on a Texas ranch, Rancho El Valle Chiquito offers everything but the cattle drive. Two rules exist: there's no smoking inside and no peeing in the pool (that's because the pool is a "Cowboy swimming pool," a metal trough filled with fresh water daily). You haven't lived until you've taken a dip in a cowboy swimming pool! A pond stocked with hybrid perch and bass, a golf green (par 3 hole), putting range, a skeet shooting area, gigantic barbecue pits with a wet bar, swings, and music piped into the terrace (with pool table), 22-acre hiking/biking paths, and a real barnyard, filled with peafowl, guineas, fainting goats, and chickens literally surrounds your barn B&B. That's right, you sleep in the stable (with the animals all around you), which has been transformed in the interior into two large well-appointed bedrooms, living room with balcony and library, cable TV, full kitchen and bath, all decorated with antiques and western bric-a-brac. A gigantic spread of longhorns and horses add to the ambience, as do your hosts, who serve complimentary wine and cheese upon your arrival and a cowboy-sized breakfast to your door in the morning. The kids can spend the night in the tack room, which is an old store front behind the barnyard, if they'd like (and most "like") and the staff offers "Barnyard Trivial Pursuit" banter that delights kids (e.g., How many feathers have eyes in a Peacock? Answer, 150. How many days does a chicken egg incubate for a chick? Answer, 21. What shape is a duck/peacock/chicken egg when it comes out? Answer, round, but it immediately changes to oval). You are guaranteed to catch fish, and you'd have to be blind not to spot quail, dove, and deer around the place. Wild turkey are also frequent visitors, which you will be too once you've enjoyed the Zombolas' hospitality.

Southwind Bed and Breakfast

Host: Carrie Watson, 2701 FM 3237, Wimberley 78676, (512) 847-5277, (800) 508-5277, or Wimberley Lodging (800) 460-3909, 3 guest rooms with private baths and two cabins, full breakfast (no meats), $$–$$$, children and pets accommodated in cabins, no smoking, hot tub

On the outskirts of Wimberley, there's a sign which states "A Little Bit of Heaven—Welcome to Wimberley." Southwind most aptly captures that concept because it is a house built on to the side of a mountain with HUGE vistas of sky and earth. The decor is simple— no posh Orientals here—and, on the outside of the cabins, vertical cedar rustic, but both capture the philosophy of the owner, who appreciates Southwind as a quiet place, where someone can be one with nature (she offers books on wildlife and fossils, binoculars for viewing and a library of books, puzzles, and games for quiet days in front of the fire or on the porches overlooking it all). Each room opens onto a porch, and each room is named after a wind, from Zephyr, with the pencil poster bed; Cat's Paw, "which makes the ripple in the water"; Spirit Wind (king bed and fireplace); Earth Wind (Country Victorian decor); to Mariah (Western decor). Locals say Wimberley is the place "where heaven and the hills hold hands." You can see it most clearly here, without extraneous interruption. If you want simple natural glory, Southwind is the B&B because its goal is "to soothe your mind and feed your spirit."

DALLAS, FORT WORTH, AND NORTHEAST TEXAS

ALLEN

Blee House

Hosts: Tim and Amy Sherman, 103 W. Belmont Dr., Allen 75013, (800) 699-4754, phone/fax (972) 390-1884, 4 guest rooms, 4 baths, continental or full breakfast, $, no children under 12, no pets, no smoking, all cr

Tim and Amy, who met at the New England Culinary Institute, are both chefs, so you know you're going to get a good breakfast at the Blee House! In fact, they will even prepare special dinners for you (and groups) if asked in advance. Committed to making guests feel pampered and at home, the nice young couple enjoy hosting murder mystery weekends, meetings, and other events, too. Since moving to Texas from Oregon in 1996 to acquire the Blee House, the hosts have been involved in an ongoing renovation project.

Built in 1904 and owned by the same family (the Cundiffs) for 79 years, the cottage has a wraparound porch, the original wood floors and trim, and antique and family furnishings. The Attic Room, a quaint, dormered room, has twin beds, but the other guest rooms have queen beds. All have phones. An upstairs sitting room has a fax/copier and desk space for those in town on business. Games are available for rainy days.

Close to the antique and craft shops in the historic areas of both Plano and McKinney, this Collin County B&B is also near Lake Lavon, Southfork, and an 18-hole championship golf course. The Blee House is just east of the freeway, so the Telecom Corridor in Richardson and downtown Dallas also are easily accessible.

ARGYLE

The Roadrunner Farm

Host: Jan Michie, 10501 Fincher Road, Argyle 76226, phone and fax (940) 241-3089, 2 bedrooms, 2 baths, full breakfast, $$, no pets, no children under 5, smoking only on porches, no cr

On rolling terrain four miles south of Denton is a one-story sprawling limestone ranch house with limestone columns and a large veranda in front and back (the latter is screened in). These are great places to drink your morning coffee or margaritas or even have breakfast. Featured in *Southern Living* magazine in 1990 for its country elegance, The Roadrunner Farm B&B has Mexican tile floors, a fireplace, and total privacy for the two guest rooms. At one end of the house with full baths, both have queen beds; one has a twin as well. Relax by the fire in the winter, watch a video, or read.

Look out the windows and see the horses grazing in the pasture. A "cowgirl" who grew up on a northeast Texas ranch, Jan boards and trains horses for others. She also brings in Olympic-calibre riders and equestrian trainers from all over the U.S. to provide special instruction to area riders on her 32-acre spread.

Off the beaten path, The Roadrunner Farm B&B has wonderful walking trails. Encircled by a rail post fence, a swimming pool in back looks like a pond instead of a pool. Far from city sounds, only an occasional coyote howls at night.

Ranchman's Cafe, a steak diner in Ponder that is also famous for homemade pies and cobblers, and Texas Lil's Diamond A Ranch at Justin are two area places you might want to visit.

ATHENS

Avonlea

Hostess: Margaret Geng, 410 East Corsicana, (903) 675-5770, 5 bedrooms, full breakfast, $$–$$$, no smoking except in designated areas, no pets, children accepted, cr

Built in 1890, this beautifully restored Victorian boasts Victorian decor, including plates lovingly collected by your hostess's mother over many years. Renown for their fresh blueberry French toast, with fresh blueberries in season (Athens is the heart of the blueberry/raspberry/blackberry pick-your-own and wholesale operations), the breakfast is substantial, including their egg casserole, which is always a hit. One of the bedrooms is a king with a private bath, while the others, with queens, have semi-private baths. Your charming hostess resides on the premise and offers abundant advice on all there is to do and see in Athens, including shopping just down the street at Athens Alley (antiques, gifts, cosmetics, and dining) and Waldenwood, a charming gift shop just doors away. While in Athens, you can exercise or swim at the Cain Center, an unparalleled community center, which also offers meeting rooms and dining facilities for family reunions or large gatherings. The Avonlea is conveniently located in Downtown, so you're only a hop and skip away from several outstanding restaurants.

Carriage House B&B

Hosts: Carol and Larry Kelly, Rt. 2, Box 2153, Athens 75751, (903) 677-3939, (800) 808-BEDS, 2 rooms with private bath, full breakfast, $$$–$$$$, 1 suite with private bath, no pets, no children, no smoking

Immaculate white iron fences surrounding rolling hills of bermudagrass welcome you to the Carriage House B & B, a picturesque country estate south of Athens. In what used to be a horse barn, this B&B's downstairs has been transformed into two huge bedrooms (15x15), each with private bath and decorated with Oriental rugs, lovely antiques, queen beds, fluffy down comforters and down pillows. A large porch surrounded by lovely gardens under the trees is available for guests' use. Upstairs, in what once was a hayloft, an even larger suite called the Gable Suite contains a sitting room, large bathroom, and an even more substantial bedroom with an impressive country vista. The porch seems to be a favorite place to light, particularly because your hosts greet you with their legendary hors d'oeuvre (e.g., shrimp mousse) and cool drinks (almond or peach tea or cappuccino) to help you unwind. Carol and Larry have thought of almost everything, from walking trails (paths cut through the hay) to marked jogging trails (so you know how far you've jogged since you don't have the city landmarks), to providing tennis balls and racquets for their tennis court (should you decide to be more energetic). After dinner out, they have some dessert awaiting your return, with decaf coffee to top off the evening. It almost goes without saying that breakfast, at your convenience, is an event worthy of the visit to the Carriage House alone. Carol is well-known for her gourmet cooking. In case you plan a special event (e.g., a wedding celebration or a large dinner party) they have a pavilion that can accommodate up to 144 people, with musicians, dinner—well, the whole schmear, including horse-drawn carriage. Keep it in mind, because a more luxurious setting you couldn't have.

Dunsavage Farms Bed and Breakfast

**Host: Lyn Dunsavage, 2044 FM 804, La Rue 75770,
(903) 675-4193 or contact Bed & Breakfast Texas Style
(214) 298-8586, 3 bedrooms with private baths, full breakfast,
$$–$$$, smoking in restricted areas, dogs on premise, no cr**

From the two-story farmhouse porch, you'll marvel at the panoramic view of the constellations and hear the wild geese call as they spear their way though the East Texas sky. In the distance, roosting barn owls join the chorus. The soothing quiet at Dunsavage Farms is the envy of poets, but the best part about this B&B is journalist Lyn Dunsavage. An "urban pioneer" who wrote reams to save Dallas' inner city (some call her the "Mother of Deep Ellum"), Lyn will entertain you with stories told in gifted narrative, should you choose to catch her in a talkative mood. She founded the New York, Texas, Cheesecake, (a cheesecake to die for!), which you can buy from its new owners in Athens on the square, just seven miles down the road.

As for the accommodations, you'll wake up to the sun rising over wildflowers and the smell of Lyn's homemade biscuits and twice-buttered potatoes. She also prepares eggs topped with Cajun mushroom sauce that throws dietary caution to the wind. Her full ham with a raspberry-raisin sauce is legendary. Everything is laid back and casual at Dunsavage Farms, so expect to take off your shoes, read a book from her extensive library in front of a fire in cold weather, or enjoy a little refreshment on the porch, which always has a breeze in the warm weather. One other thing: the farm is located in the middle of the only hardwood country in Texas, so fall color enthusiasts and nature lovers should definitely make Athens a place to visit.

AUBREY

The Guest House

Hosts: Lynne Weil and her sister, Jeanne Shelton, 5408 Highway 377, Aubrey 76227, (817) 440-2076, 3 guest rooms, 3 baths, 1 cottage, continental plus OYO, $$, children and pets ok in cottage, smoking outside only, AE

Even horses are welcome here! About 14 miles northeast of Denton is a farm where horses are bred and boarded, but it is also a B&B. Since Aubrey is horse country, lots of people who are interested in horses or in the business bring their horses when they come to the area, so the Guest House keeps quite busy. Lynne lives in the east wing of the ranch-style home, while the three rooms with private entrances for guests are in the west wing. The Windsor Room has twin beds, period furniture, and a marble bath; Martha's Room, which has two queen beds, is named for Martha Stewart, because the eggshell colors that she favors are featured in the decor. It has a patio. Available as a suite or single bedroom with a queen-sized bed, the Great American West's lodgepole pine and scrub oak furniture creates a more rustic look. A fireplace and queen-sized sofa bed are in the living room. (Some of the unique furniture and art are for sale, says Lynne, who is into interior decorating as well as catering.)

Guests also have the option of a one-story, 50-year-old wood-framed farmhouse that looks more like a 1920s era summer cottage. It includes two-bedrooms, one bath, and a dining/living/kitchen area. A smaller bedroom with a single twin bed also is available, if needed.

Though both homes are right on the highway, across from a Texaco and a saddle and tack shop, the hosts have 70 acres. Guests enjoy walking around their lake or to the barn and back, a nice jaunt. Horses aren't the only ones who can exercise here!

BEN WHEELER

Arc Ridge Guest Ranch

**Hosts: Charlie and Reva Ogilvie, Box 7, Ben Wheeler 75754,
(903) 833-5337, or Bed & Breakfast Texas Style (972) 298-8586,
3 fully furnished guest houses, light continental breakfast OYO,
$$, well-behaved pets by special permission, no smoking, MC, V**

For an outdoor retreat with plenty to do, the Arc Ridge Guest Ranch can't be beat. Located about an hour and a half from Dallas, not far from Canton or Edom, the 600-acre working ranch is a wildlife sanctuary that includes a 25-acre pristine lake (stocked with bluegill and bass), picnic grounds, and marked hiking and nature trails abounding with wildflowers. For the bicycling enthusiast, maps of the county's scenic back roads are available. Since there are alligators in the lake, swimming is not encouraged.

Each of the three guest houses has two bedrooms, one bath, a living room, a fully equipped kitchen, TV with VCR (videos are available), and an outside grill. Each also has its own paddleboat and dock. Nestled on the side of a forested hill, the Dogwood Cottage sleeps four adults, and has an overflow couch in the living room. A large covered porch borders two sides of the house. The more spacious Lakota Lodge has a double hide-a-bed in the living room, and can accommodate six. Amenities include a dishwasher, stereo, and full bath. Decorated in a Native American motif, it has a "medicine wheel" at its entrance. The newer Trailhead, an "adults preferred" facility also sleeping six, has a Southwestern decor.

BIG SANDY

Annie's Bed and Breakfast

**Contact Bed & Breakfast Texas Style (972) 298-8586,
106 N. Tyler, Big Sandy 75755, (903) 636-4355, 12 guest rooms,
11 baths, gourmet breakfast, $–$$$, no children, no pets,
no smoking inside, all cr**

Located off the beaten path midway between Dallas and Shreveport and close to Tyler, Jefferson, and other places with a variety of attractions, Annie's attracts a steady stream of visitors year-round. And no wonder! Besides charming turn-of-the-century accommodations, Annie's has a needlecraft gallery, a gift shop with Victorian items, and a tearoom noted for superb food and high teas. Fashion shows, crochet seminars, arts and crafts fairs, and other events are often held on the park-like grounds.

Annie's is actually a traffic-stopping cluster of three Victorian homes, set off by white picket fences. The guest rooms are in the large gray and white seven-gabled house, which was only one story when built in 1901. Guest rooms have antique and reproduction furnishings, handmade quilts, small, old-fashioned refrigerators, and TV. Many have fireplaces and balconies. One suite has a spiral staircase leading to its own balcony, and two rooms have lofts.

An extraordinary breakfast that may include cold strawberry soup, Swiss eggs, or stuffed French toast is served in the tearoom seven days a week. The special herbed teas are wonderful, too. Open to the public as well as B&B guests, the restaurant serves dinner Wednesday through Saturday and lunch daily. Flowered wallpaper and lace tablecloths create a Victorian atmosphere.

BONHAM

The Carleton House

Hosts: Karen and Stephen Halbrook, 803 N. Main, Bonham 75418, (903) 583-2779, 3 guest rooms, 3 baths, full breakfast, $–$$, no children under 15, no pets, no smoking indoors, no cr

Each of the guest rooms in this two-story Victorian home was named for one of the Carleton daughters (Lillian, Bernice, and Mary). One room has a king, another a queen, and the third, a full-sized bed, while all three have antiques, TV, reading material, and cards. Baths have claw-foot tubs as well as showers. Cold drinks and homemade treats are readily available. On the National Register of Historic Places and built in 1888, the restored Carleton House is available for receptions and parties in addition to B&B guests.

The Sam Rayburn Library, which includes a replica of the late speaker's Capitol Hill office, antique shops, and an outlet mall are among area attractions. The Fannin County Fair is a fun event that has been held each October for more than 100 years.

BOWIE

Old Tucker Homeplace

Hosts: Robert and Martha Fuller, Rt. 2, Box 355, Bowie 76230, (817) 872-2484, 2 suites, 3 guest rooms, 2½ baths, country breakfast, $$, extra charge for pets, smoking on grounds, no cr

Horse-drawn wagon and hay rides, cookouts, and trail rides (available at an extra charge), along with crawdadding and fishing are among activities attracting B&B buffs to this 400-acre ranch, but being pampered with treats like breakfast in bed is also part of its appeal. Bargain hunters who come from miles around for Bowie's Second Monday Trade Day, held prior to the second Monday of each month like First Monday in Canton, often stay at The Old Tucker Homeplace, too.

About one-and-a-half hours northwest of the Dallas/Fort Worth Metroplex, The Old Tucker Homeplace is 10 miles south of Bowie on Texas 59, just off U.S. 287, a major thoroughfare to Amarillo. Picturesque with bay windows and wide porches, the two-story home was built in 1983 in a grove of trees—a spot Martha, as a young girl, loved when riding her horse around her family's property. Someday, she vowed, her home would be here, and so it is!

One spacious suite has a whirlpool bath, and the other, a claw-foot tub. The latter's adjoining sitting room has twin beds. The Fullers also have two queen hide-a-beds in a den, so can sleep 14 comfortably. Other meals and special activities, like a romantic candlelight dinner or afternoon tea, are available at an additional charge.

Martha hopes to do mystery weekends for groups at the Old Tucker Homeplace or in conjunction with the restored **Henrietta Township Bed and Breakfast.** About 20 miles away in **Henrietta,** the latter is in a building more than a century old on the square that has been everything from a bank to a florist shop. Jeannie and James Williams already offer the mystery weekends on a regular basis. Call (817) 538-6968 or (800) 450-4070 for more about their five guest rooms ($–$$$$) and restored historic property.

CADDO LAKE

Caddo Cottage

Hosts: Dorothy and Pete Grant, Mossy Brake Drive, Taylor Island, Caddo Lake, Uncertain 75661, (903) 789-3988 or (903) 789-3297, fax (903) 789-3297, a 2-bedroom cottage, 2 baths, continental breakfast OYO, $$$, no children or pets, no cr

The living and dining rooms of Caddo Cottage have a wall of glass on the second floor deck, which overlooks the water. The hosts, who live next door, have everything for your comfort—even wine glasses and a fly swatter. You'll find a fully equipped kitchen with a microwave, a gas grill on the downstairs covered patio, and a color TV. Two of the four sofas make into beds; there is also a king-sized bed upstairs. The first floor den bedroom has a full bed. Make reservations for one or eight, the cabin is yours. (A nominal fee is charged for more than two.) Special requests like wine or fresh flowers can be filled, for an added fee, too. Amenities include a canoe, a boathouse with a deck where you can sit and sun or fish from the Grant's private pier.

Twenty miles from Marshall as well as Jefferson, Caddo Cottage is an hour from Shreveport and the Louisiana Downs Racetrack. But you can find plenty to do on Taylor Island because the highly regarded Mossy Brake Art Gallery and Studio, where you can watch artists work; restaurants, marinas, and even beauty shops are within walking distance. Boat tours of Caddo Lake, the only natural lake in Texas, are memorable.

Having a guide, whether it is to fish or just to explore the maze of channels and bayous, is highly recommended! Norm Presson, recognized as one of the best guides in the area, and his wife, Pat, have an unpretentious one-room bed and breakfast, **Mossy Brake Lodge.** It has twin beds that can be used as a king-sized bed, a microwave, toaster, and TV, a full bath, and private entrance. (The Pressons live upstairs.) Children 10 and older are welcome. A continental breakfast is left in the fridge. A double hammock and glider, a boat house with two stalls, a fish cooker, and a BBQ grill are available. So is Norm, who has even fished on the National Championship Bass Circuit. (800) 607-6002.

Spatterdock

Hosts: Robert and Dottie Russell, Rt. 2, Box 66B, Uncertain 75661, phone and fax (903) 789-3288, 3 guest rooms, 2 baths, continental breakfast OYO, $$$, no pets, no smoking, no cr

The Spatterdock Guest House is located on Taylor Island where Caddo Lake merges with Alligator Bayou, one of the many entangled waterways on Caddo Lake. Spatterdock, by the way, is a type of water lily found on the lake. This spacious lakehouse is decorated with a unique collection of Caddo memorabilia and furnished with "semi" antiques, like a primitive plank lakehouse table and benches, rattan furniture from the '50s, and iron beds with quilts. Quality paintings furnished by Mossy Brake Art Gallery are on the walls. (Dottie helps organize workshops for the Gallery.) It includes a large living area, a fireplace, a modern kitchen, and a screened porch. A big bath with stained glass, a raised footed bathtub, and a picture window that overlooks the lake also add to the charm of the Spatterdock. A walkway leads to an over-the-water patio that is surrounded by huge, ancient cypress trees. The hosts have a canoe and a fishing boat you can rent. The Russells welcome and enjoy children. Board games, croquet, and horseshoes are available.

The Russells have another appealing unhosted B&B, **Duckweed Cottage,** which is next door to the Spatterdock. It has a screened porch with a panoramic view of haunting Caddo Lake and an over-the-water patio.

Other Caddo Lake B&Bs include the **Blue Bayou Inn,** (903) 780-3240, which has three suites with private entrances, a pier, and boat dock; and **Bell's View on Mound Pond,** (903) 679-3234. Amenities at the latter include a gazebo-enclosed hot tub. The **Cypress Moon Cottage,** (903) 579-3154 is another secluded B&B that is hosted.

The most luxurious B&B is **Whispering Pines Lodge,** an "old Southern" style brick home that was built in 1995. Three beautifully decorated rooms with private baths are available (one has a wood-burning fireplace) in the house, but you can also stay in the Williams' cozy guest house. Perfect for a romantic getaway, it also has a fireplace. Cindy and Victor are about the only B&B hosts in the area who serve a full breakfast. Call (903) 789-3913.

CANTON

Heavenly Acres

Hosts: Vickie and Marshall Ragle, Rt. 3, Box 470, Mabank 75147, 1 (800) 283-0341, or contact Bed & Breakfast Texas Style (972) 298-8586, 6 cabins, all private baths, 1 apartment, 1 bath, full breakfast OYO, $$$, children and pets welcome in specified cabins with prior approval, no smoking indoors, MC, V, D, AE

A number of bed and breakfasts claim Canton as their address to attract First Monday Trade business, but actually are in outlying towns, possibly as much as 22 miles away. Some, in fact, only open as a B&B for First Monday, but others, like Heavenly Acres, which is 12 miles from Canton in Mabank, are full-time bed and breakfasts.

Appropriately named, this 100-acre East Texas ranch has a variety of accommodations overlooking two well-stocked private fishing lakes. The Ragles provide paddleboats and small fishing boats with trolling motors. Fish away! All six fully equipped cabins have porches, private baths with showers, microwaves, TVs, and VCRs (an extensive video library is available in the main house).

Picking a favorite is difficult. Converted from an 1880's cowboy fenceline shack, The Ole' Lineshack has a rustic decor and a large room with a full-sized bed and a queen sleeping sofa. Like the Victorian Room, which has two private entrances, the romantic Rose Cottage is filled with antique dolls, angels, and lace. The latter has a double bed and a trundle (twins). Also sleeping four is The Ole' Homeplace, furnished in antiques and collectibles. Overlooking the lower 15-acre lake, The Caddo Lodge sleeps eight. Its decor pays tribute to the Caddo Indians native to East Texas. The Udder Place, once an old dairy barn that sleeps up to 20 in rooms with barnyard animal themes, is ideal for retreats and reunions. The Country Club is the meeting and dining hall for groups.

One of the nicest country getaways in the area, Heavenly Acres includes a petting zoo. Bonnie and Clyde (pygmy goats) and Peaches, the potbellied pig, are favorites. About an hour and a half from the Dallas/Ft.Worth Metroplex as well as Tyler, Heavenly Acres is a fun place to stay while exploring nearby Cedar Creek Lake, Purtis Creek

State Park, or Canton. Better book a reservation early for First Monday Trade Days!

Mamaw's House

Host: Lucia Deen, 681 W. Dallas, Canton 75103, (800) 38-MAMAW or (903) 567-4387, main house, 3 guest rooms, 3 baths, choice of continental breakfast OYO or coupon voucher at a local tearoom, $$, no pets, no smoking, no cr

Wear comfortable shoes when you go to Canton's First Monday (Friday through Sunday before the first Monday of each month) because the nation's largest flea market has 6,000 vendors spread over 100 acres! You can shop 'til you drop—then return to this quaint country inn to unload your "finds." Because it is within walking distance of the grounds, you can even rest your weary feet before resuming your bargain-hunting spree.

The front porch of Mamaw's House, which can accommodate six, faces SH 64. Filled with family heirlooms, it has two bedrooms and a large bath with claw-foot tub, a fully equipped country kitchen, and a living room with a full sleeper sofa. It rents to one family or group at a time. The unhosted B&B also has an attached wing in back with three inviting themed suites. Each has a private entrance, two double beds, a coffee maker, TV, and a bath with a dressing area. An extra rollaway bed can be put in two of the suites.

Mamaw's and **Buffalo Beal's Boardin' House,** which is in a building on the courthouse square at 133 Buffalo Street, and the tearoom next door offer Trades Day packages for groups. Within walking distance of the main gate of First Monday, Buffalo Beal's can accommodate 18 in five rooms with a turn-of-the-century decor, queen-sized beds, and quilts. Breakfast is served at the tearoom. The Boardin' House B&B is in the back portion of the Buffalo Street Gallery, which features original art and limited edition prints. Call Rollin and Carol Beal (800) 704-8769 for information.

Both Mamaw's and Buffalo Beal's are also within easy walking distance of Wild Willie's II Mountain, which has over 600 shops, working artists and craft demonstrations, an amphitheater featuring C&W singers, a children's fishing pond and more. Wild Willie's opens a week or so before First Monday.

The Willow House

Hosts: Skip and Flossie Owens, Rt. 1, Box 245 (FM 243), (903) 848-9008, Canton 75103, or Gayle Irby, East Texas Reservation Service (888) 327-8839, 3 guest rooms, 3 baths, country breakfast, $$–$$$, no children, no pets, no smoking, MC, V, D

On 11 acres seven miles from Canton, The Willow House is a nice retreat in winter as well as summer, because there are fireplaces in the den and the Garden Room. The two-story brick home has spacious living, dining, and kitchen areas and an oversized Jacuzzi and shower in one of the guest baths. Quiche, grits with potato casserole, muffins, and meat are often included in the hearty breakfasts here, along with a heaping helping of hospitality. You'll have The Willow House to yourself, but Skip and Flossie aren't far. Available for special events, The Willow House is only minutes from the Tanger Outlet Mall in Terrell, lakes, and golf courses.

Among other area options is **The Texas Star Bed & Breakfast,** (903) 896-4277, which has two guest rooms that share a bath and a living room with TV in the main house, and accommodations for eight in a cabin and guest house. Each room in the latter has a private bath and patio and a different decor reflecting Texas history or culture. David and Marie Stoltzfus feature homemade bread, pastries, and jam in their family-style country breakfast. Games, like horseshoes and croquet, are available, along with a VCR and videos.

A fishing lake, a deck, and gazebo are among amenities at **Saline Creek Farm,** a B&B eight miles northeast of Canton that can accommodate ten adults. Served in the dining room overlooking the lake, the full breakfast is a treat. The host, Karen Stanberry, is a talented artist who can be contacted at (903) 829-2709.

The Thornton's 100-acre **Crooked Creek Farm,** (800) 766-0790, offers three guest rooms in the hosts' home and three more in a furnished guest house (formerly a manufactured home). The friendly hosts serve a big country breakfast with homemade jams and jellies from their fruit trees. Dorothy has some interesting stories about celebrities she's met like Elvis and Conway Twitty.

Gayle Irby of the **East Texas Reservation Service** can tell you about other full-time area B&Bs that have appeal. Gayle and her husband, Brance, have a B&B of their own in a beautiful East Texas setting:

Sweet Creek Farm. A hot tub and pool are among amenities. One guest house sleeps six, the other, four, and both include a refrigerator, microwave, TV, and VCR. For reservations through the service or at Sweet Creek Farm, call (888) 327-8839 or (903) 479-4052, fax (903) 479-3158.

The Wind Sock Inn

Hosts: Ann and Hugh Thornton, Rt. 3, Box 60 B, Canton 75103, (800) 476-2038, (903) 848-0618, fax (903) 848-7013, or Bed & Breakfast Texas Style (972) 298-8586, 1 suite, 5 guest rooms, 5 baths, 3 cottages, full breakfast, $–$$$$, no pets, no smoking, MC, V, D

This 5,000-square-foot ranch-style brick home was actually built to be a bed and breakfast, fulfilling a long-time dream of the hosts. An airline captain and flight instructor, Hugh hopes to offer flying lesson packages to B&B guests, a unique amenity, for sure. The runway is being built behind the hosts' home on their wooded 33-acre retreat, which is about eight miles from Canton. The five guest rooms have either queen or twin beds with trundles or day beds, a color TV, and VCR with videos. Each room has a different decor, from the bride's room to the cowboy room. The beautiful suite's two-sided fireplace can be seen from the bedroom or the six-foot whirlpool tub.

Like so many in the Canton area, the Thorntons also have transformed some manufactured homes into nicely camouflaged cottages with porches, so a total of 20 can be accommodated at Wind Sock Inn. The three "cottages" face an English garden, with oak trees and hammocks, a water fountain, and covered patio in the middle.

Guests all gather in the Thornton's home, which includes a 1,100-square-foot informal great room with a 13-foot vaulted ceiling, a large stone fireplace—and a pool table. A workout room, a large pool and deck, a ping-pong table, a horseshoe pit, volleyball, and badminton are also available, along with walking trails through the woods. You won't be bored here. Small weddings and other special events and business meetings are often held at The Wind Sock Inn.

Come visit any time of the year, Ann urges, for ongoing area activities include everything from quilt shows and auto swap meets to community festivals.

CLEBURNE

Anglin Queen Anne Guest House

Hosts: Dan and Billie Anne Leach, 723 N. Anglin, Cleburne 76031, (817) 645-5555, or Bed & Breakfast Texas Style (972) 298-8586, 5 guest rooms, 3 baths, continental-plus breakfast, $–$$$, no smoking except on porches, MC, V

Featured in *Bride & Groom* magazine and in demand for weddings and other functions, some say this magnificent mansion is one of the most handsome in North Texas. If you can't spend the night, ask about the nominally priced group tours. Many of the antiques are rare, and you'll enjoy seeing the countless collectibles, including vintage fans that have been spotlighted on TV.

The Anglin Queen Anne was built in 1892 by cattle baron and banker Christopher W. Mertz, whose family let out rooms to guests. The tradition has been continued by the current owners, who spent almost three years on the home's restoration. The results show! Two of the four staircases are favorites with photographers for sittings, and have beautiful grillwork, paneling, and stained glass.

Dominated by a three-story cupola between two second-story porches and a large round veranda with porch posts and gingerbread fretwork, the home has five guest rooms. Ruby's Room has gorgeous antique bird's-eye maple furniture and a private bath. There is an adjoining sitting room with a daybed, fireplace, and TV/VCR. Both rooms can be reserved individually or as Ruby's Suite or a Honeymoon Suite. Fresh flowers, nonalcoholic champagne, and other "surprises" await when reserved for the latter.

Billie and Dan graciously offer to help travelers arrange boarding for pets, or may even permit your pet to stay in a fenced area in back. They also have an extensive library you're welcome to use.

On an acre seven blocks from the courthouse, the Anglin Queen Anne is grand, but comfortable. You'll feel like a queen here—maybe a king.

Cleburne House

Host: Jan Bills, 201 N. Anglin, Cleburne 76031, (817) 641-0085, or Bed & Breakfast Texas Style, (972) 298-8586, 3 bedrooms, 3 baths,

Southern breakfast, $–$$, smoking on porches, credit cards only when booked through reservation service

This three-story Queen Anne Victorian's colorful past includes use as a domino parlor, tearoom, doctor's office, boarding house—and house of ill repute. When the former owners bought the Cleburne House in 1983, they found numbers over every door, even closets! It was built in 1886 of cypress by a Santa Fe Railroad inspector for his bride who became renowned for her hospitality. In fact, Fannie was the talk of the town when she imported ice cream "all the way" from Dallas in an ice cream wagon for one of her celebrated parties.

Two blocks north of the town square, the Cleburne House suggests the elegance of the 19th century, with claw-foot tubs, hardwood floors, stained-glass windows, a beautiful curved staircase, and period furniture. A vintage wedding gown in the hall near one of the guest rooms is in keeping with the romantic ambience.

Two handsomely appointed guest rooms have balconies where you can view the lighted courthouse tower at night. One room has a king-sized bed overlooking a New Orleans-style patio, while you can see the landscaped grounds and herb garden from a room with a queen bed. With its tall oak headboard bed and red claw-foot tub, the Red bedroom is the favorite of honeymooners. Fresh flowers and a fruit basket make guests feel even more special. A Southern breakfast is served in the formal dining room or on the veranda.

There is a Victorian game table in the entry alcove for checkers and chess, but check out Cleburne's antique shops, farmers market, historic district, and the Layland Museum in the 1904 Carnegie Library, listed in the National Registry.

Cleburne's 1896 Railroad House

Host: Quilla Perkins, 421 E. Henderson, Cleburne 76031, (817) 517-5529, fax (817) 517-5615, 5 rooms, 4 private baths, 2 shared baths, full breakfast, $$, no pets, no smoking, MC, V

Make tracks to Cleburne's 1896 Railroad House if you have nostalgic sentiments about railroad days of yore. The B&B, which has the original 11-foot pressed tin ceilings, is filled with railroad memorabilia like an old timey mail bag, railroad lights, and lanterns, which is appropriate, since it was built in 1896 for railroad employees and train travelers. Today, Amtrak stops across the street, so rail travelers are still staying there. Other throwbacks to yesteryear: guest rooms have their original ivory room numbers, and the two hall baths are known as the Ladies' and the Gentlemen's baths.

About a 6,000-square-foot restored building that has a barber shop—and space for a tearoom, perhaps—on the first floor, the Railroad House antique-filled B&Bs are on the second level. (Take the door on the left up to the lobby.) The Locomotive Room has a queen bed and private in-room bath, while the Lantern and Pullman rooms share a hall bath. The Depot has its own private bath in the hall, which is shared when a child or family member is in the adjoining Caboose Room. The latter has a single bed. Quilla puts out cookies, muffins, or fruit for guests as a snack. Breakfast is served from 8:30 to 10:30 a.m., or earlier if you are in town on business. A private office is available if you need to work a while, but take a break on the back decks (one is sheltered by a tin roof).

Cleburne's 1896 Railroad House is within walking distance to the shops and a tearoom in the historic downtown area.

CLIFTON

Heart Cottage

Host: Vivian Ender, Rt. l, Box 217, Clifton 76634, (817) 675-3189, or Bed & Breakfast Texas Style (972) 298-8586, 1 bedroom, 1 bath, country breakfast OYO, $$, smoking outside only, MC, V (only through B&B Texas Style)

Heart Cottage will steal your heart with its stained-glass windows, wooden sunburst trim, and gables. The heart theme is carried out extensively in the picturesque Victorian-inspired cottage, from heart-shaped napkin rings, placemats, picture frames, and frying pans to the hand-painted hearts above all the doors. How many can you count?

Perfect for honeymooners or romantic getaways, Heart Cottage is on gentle rolling farmland about 40 miles from Waco. It has plush carpet, a fully equipped kitchen, a vaulted ceiling, and a double sleeper sofa. There is a skylight above the cozy loft's queen-sized bed, and you can see the stars. (Watch your head going up the steep stairs to the loft.)

Games and a color TV are among amenities. An architectural designer, Vivian did much of the restoration on the home, which once belonged to her grandparents.

Area attractions include the Texas Safari, an exotic wildlife drive through a park, Lake Whitney, and the Bosque Memorial Museum, which features Norwegian artifacts (open weekends only).

Joann's Courtney House

Hosts: Joann and Ken Baucom, 1514 W. 5th Avenue, Clifton 76634, (817) 675-3061, 4 guest rooms, 1 private bath, 1 shared, full breakfast, $$, no pets, smoking on porches only, children 12 and over welcome, no cr

On a manicured one-acre lot in Clifton, which is in the foothills of the Central Texas Hill Country, a beautiful turn-of-the-century home with wraparound verandas welcomes B&B guests. Built in 1905 and shaded by pecan trees, Joann's Courtney House is owned by a couple whose Bosque County ties are strong.

The Victorian home's guest rooms are on the second floor, along with a sitting area where you can watch TV, get a soft drink from the small fridge, or help yourself to coffee. One has a king bed and its own bath, but the rest share a bath, which seems to work out fine, says Joann. The beds in two rooms are doubles, and the other has a king. However, two of the latter rooms adjoin and are often used as a suite.

Breakfast is around 7 a.m. during the week so Joann and Ken can get to work on time, but about 8:30 on weekends. Cinnamon honey waffles and French toast are among her specialties. Fresh fruit in season along with bacon and sausage are standard fare, too, at this hospitable B&B. By the way, ask Joann about her gift shop (another sideline) in an antique mall, if browsing is your bag.

COMMERCE

Bois d' Arc Bed and Breakfast

Hosts: Jim and Frances Stinnett, 2212 Charity Rd., Commerce 75428, (903) 886-7705, 2 guest rooms, 2 baths, gourmet breakfast, $, no smoking, no pets, children over 8 welcome, no cr

If you have a favorite breakfast dish, your hostess will prepare it or treat you to her own specialties like blue corn waffles with spicy apple syrup, apricot scones, huevos rancheros, papas fritas (Mexican hash browns), or the usual bacon and eggs. A small, wood-burning stove adds to the country kitchen atmosphere in this modern-day home.

Nicely decorated, the Blue Room has a double bed, and the Sunflower Room, twin to king bedding. Since many of their guests are drawn by ETSU (now Texas A&M University of Commerce), the hosts have a den with a desk, copy machine, phone, and TV.

There are several antique shops in Commerce along with the Cowhill Express Coffee Company. Nearby is Cooper Lake, which has hiking trails, good fishing, and bald eagles in the winter, a Christmas Tree Farm, and a pick-or-buy blueberry orchard. Attending campus events like the medieval Christmas celebration, the Feast of Carols; the Crawfish Festival in the spring, and the Bois d'Arc Bash as well as the Hopkins County Fair in Sulphur Springs in September are other drawing cards.

Of course, you can always just sit a spell on the bench under the trees in the courtyard at the Bois d'Arc B&B.

The Chapin House

Hosts: Jack and Lois Chapin, 1405 Monroe St., Commerce 75428, (903) 886-6713, 5 rooms, 5 private baths, 1 guest cottage, country breakfast, $, no pets, smoking on balcony and porches only, MC, V

Look for the Dr.'s emblem under the eve in front at the imposing Chapin House, which was built in 1923 by a horse and buggy physician as a surprise for his wife, much to her delight. A storm cellar beneath the sunroom, which has flooring two-feet thick, is another unusual feature. The Chapins have owned this Georgian colonial home, which is within walking distance of the university and the town square, for almost 20 years.

The spacious guest rooms have cable TV, telephones, and sitting areas. Two of the upstairs guests rooms have king-sized beds, one oversized room has two double beds and a sofa, making it ideal if you have children, while a suite across the hall has a double bed. Handicapped accessible, the spacious downstairs suite has a brick floor, tiled bath with a sunken tub, a queen-sized bed, wood-burning fireplace, and TV.

Although your breakfast will be served in their home, you also can stay across the street in the Chapin's one-story cottage. It has gingerbread trim, one bedroom with a king bed and another, a double; a bath, along with a full kitchen, dining room, and living room. On cold winter nights, you'll enjoy the fireplace. Commerce is about 60 miles northeast of Dallas.

CORSICANA

Ashmore Inn

Hosts: Dottie and Dwight Ashmore, 220 N. 14th, Corsicana 75110, (903) 872-7311, fax (903) 872-0732, 4 guest rooms, 4 baths, gourmet breakfast, $$–$$$, no children, pets, or smoking, MC, V, D

Reflecting the grandeur of long ago, Ashmore Inn was renovated and magnificently refurbished when acquired by Dottie and Dwight in 1986, with crystal chandeliers, festive floral wallpapers, and a striking multicolored floral carpet. Because of its elevation, it appears even more imposing. A 15-foot wide veranda extends from the front to one side, while a second-floor balcony is supported by ten large, round white wooden pillars. Protruding from the third floor is a porch where the orchestra sat while playing for balls around the turn of the century.

Owner of the world's largest cotton gin, H. L. Scales spared no expense in building his showplace in 1898, importing many of the more ornate features from Europe. In the north wall at the foot of the winding walnut staircase is a beautiful multicolored beveled glass bay window. The house has six fireplaces.

A massive French walnut buffet that once belonged to a wife of Napoleon and an unusual three-seater museum-quality blue and white

French love seat are among the fine period pieces. The parlor, music room, library, and main dining room have pocket doors that create a spacious open area for functions catered by the Ashmores. (Lunch or dinner for 25 or more, featuring dishes such as stuffed pork chops and raspberry chicken breast, can be arranged, too.)

Ashmore Inn has four nicely appointed rooms and four baths on the second floor. Guests are given a snack and beverage after checking in and a memorable breakfast the next morning.

World famous for the Collin Street Bakery, Corsicana also boasts the Navarro Pecan Company (both can be toured), the Hat Factory, five historic churches within one block, antique shops, and the Richland-Chambers Reservoir.

DALLAS

American Dream B&B

Hosts: Pat and Andre Biczynski, P.O. Box 670275, Dallas 75367, (800) 373-2690 or (214) 357-6536, fax (214) 357-9034, 2 suites, gourmet breakfast, $$, children by special arrangement, no pets, smoking only on patio, MC, V

Look for the American Flag—and you've found the American Dream in a quiet North Dallas neighborhood. The multilingual hosts, who have lived abroad, speak Spanish, French, and Polish fluently, and some Portuguese and German, and especially welcome foreign visitors and those in town on business. Secretarial, fax, and e-mail services are available. In a great location just south of IH-635, the one-story brick home offers easy access to downtown, Las Colinas, the Market Center, major malls, D/FW and Love Field airports, and other area attractions.

The sitting room for one of the queen suites can be converted into sleeping quarters for two, while the luxury master suite has a huge bath with a whirlpool tub and separate shower. A heart-healthy breakfast featuring foods of Texas, landscaping focusing on plants native to the state, and warm, Texas hospitality should make your stay in Big D memorable.

Courtyard On The Trail

Host: Alan Kagan, (972) 553-9700, or contact Bed & Breakfast Texas Style (972) 298-8586, 2 guest rooms, 2 baths, full breakfast, $$$, no children, no pets, no smoking, MC, V

Only a half mile from White Rock Lake where you can walk, jog, or bike around the scenic trails, and just 15 minutes from the West End, Arts Districts, and fine restaurants in downtown Dallas, this stucco Santa Fe style home has eclectic furnishings and lots of wonderful art.

One guest room has a king-sized Biedermeier sleigh bed, French doors leading to the courtyard, and a spectacular marble bathroom. Unwind in the extra large tub—and contemplate the blue sky and beautiful clouds handpainted overhead! The second guest room has a queen canopy bed, a Southwestern flair, and private access to the secluded pool. Select your breakfast from a daily menu; French toast topped with a fruit compote and red raspberry sauce is a specialty. Fresh flowers, wine, and delectables daily, TV, a private phone, and use of a fax are among amenities at Courtyard On The Trail.

The Cloisters

Contact Bed & Breakfast Texas Style, (972) 298-8586, 2 guest rooms, 2 baths, full breakfast, $$, no children, no pets, smoking outdoors only, MC, V

This one-story, tree-shaded country French brick home, which has a sunny garden room and kitchen nook overlooking a small courtyard, is also near White Rock Lake. Across the lake is the Dallas Arboretum and Botanical Garden where your hostess volunteers. She has the proverbial "green thumb," and uses her home-grown zucchini in muffins, which she often serves at breakfast in the formal dining room. The nutrition-oriented hostess, who caters to guests' diets, welcomes you with a beverage; fresh flowers and candy in your room add to the pampered ambience.

Beds in both guest rooms, which have private baths, are doubles. The Rose Room has striking handpainted Mexican and Texas antique furniture, while the oak furniture in the Golden Oak Room has been in the family for over 100 years. (The latter's bath even has two lavatories.) Read, play the piano, or watch TV in the spacious living room.

Tudor Mansion

**Contact Bed & Breakfast Texas Style (972) 298-8586,
1 guest room, 1 bath, gourmet breakfast, $$, no children, no pets,
no smoking, MC, V**

Built in 1933 by a Texas oilman and once owned by a Dallas
mayor, this two-story English Tudor-style home is on a sloping wooded
lot in Kessler Park, an exclusive section of Oak Cliff only minutes from
Downtown Dallas. On the National Register of Historic Places, this
spacious house displays interesting mementos from the genial hosts'
extensive travels.

You'll have drinks and snacks upon arrival, candy beside the queen-
sized bed (the guest room has a private phone), and a printed menu from
which to choose what you want for breakfast. *Huevos rancheros* (a tor-
tilla stacked with refried beans, a poached egg, sour cream, and *salsa*
and topped with grated cheese) is one of Bud's specialties. Swim in
the pool or cross over the bridge to the rustic glider swing where you
can enjoy the woodland garden. Elizabeth is a master gardener, and
it shows!

Upper Lower Greenville Guest House

**Contact Bed & Breakfast Texas Style (972) 298-8586, 1½ guest
rooms, 1½ baths, light continental breakfast, $$$, no pets,
MC, V, AE, Optima**

In The Upper Lower Greenville Guesthouse you are two and three
stories up, nestled in the trees above a detached garage behind the host's
renovated Prairie-style home in a 100-year-old neighborhood. The
ULGG's lower level includes a living room with a Southwestern eclectic decor, a queen-sized sleeper sofa, work space (for business travelers), a full kitchen with a microwave and dishwasher, and a half bath.
The compact loft guest room has a skylight over the queen-sized bed,
and you might wake up to squirrels peering down at you. The guest
house also boasts cable TV, a VCR, a stereo, a hot tub in the tropical
garden, and a balcony with a wicker chair. Relax after a stressful day!

Many of Lower Greenville's noted restaurants and night spots are
within walking distance of this B&B, which is four miles or less to Deep

Ellum, the West End, and White Rock Lake, and only six miles to the Market Center.

DENISON

Ivy Blue

Hosts: Lane and Tammy Segerstrom, 1100 W. Sears, Denison 75020, (888) IVY-BLUE, (903) 463-2479, fax (903) 465-6773, 4 guest rooms, 4 baths, Carriage House (2 suites), Garden House (1 suite), gourmet breakfast, $$, children only in Carriage House, no pets, smoking on designated areas outside, MC, V, AE, D

In the old Silk Stocking area of this North Texas town, which borders Oklahoma, the Ivy Blue is a two-story Victorian home that was built in 1899 out of cypress. Available for special occasions and group tours, the decor is dazzling, with dramatic wallpapers and elegant furnishings that date from the Civil War to turn of the century. The entry way is graced by a striking 10-foot stained-glass panel on the stairway landing. A camera used to take pictures of Presidents Truman, Eisenhower, and Roosevelt and a butcher block owned by Gene Autry in the kitchen are among items of interest in this B&B.

The house has a wraparound porch with a swing, a Victorian garden and gazebo, and a pool encircled by a three-tiered deck. Relax in style! (European massages can be arranged in your room or by the pool.) One guest room has a king bed; the rest, double beds, while all have TV and phones, and some, VCRs. A fax and computer are available. One of the four beautifully furnished guest rooms (the Bridal Suite) in the main house has its own balcony, where you can enjoy a starlit night. The Carriage House has a French country suite with a king bed, full kitchen, a bath with a claw-foot tub, TV, and VCR downstairs, and another suite with a kitchenette on the second floor. The Garden House includes a sunken Jacuzzi tub.

Denison is only four miles from Lake Texoma, which includes a 14-mile hiking trail that hugs the water and more than 100 picnic sites. Ask the hosts about horseback riding, golfing, and rental of Blue Wave runners and adventure tours.

The Molly Cherry

Hosts: Regina and Jim Widener, 200 Molly Cherry Lane, Denison 75020, (903) 465-0575, 1 suite, 2 guest rooms, 2 baths, 4 suites in 2 hideaway cottages, full breakfast, $$–$$$$, no pets, designated smoking areas, all cr

The Molly Cherry is a country retreat—an elegant one, at that—in an urban area. Built in 1872 by a real estate tycoon and gambler, the three-story, turn-of-the-century home is on six wooded acres just off a busy highway, but you'd never know it. To reach the B&B, turn into the parking area by one of the restaurants lining the highway to the long dirt trail that leads to this romantic B&B. If you arrive at night, it's a magical moment because lights from the windows of this Victorian gem shine through the trees like welcoming beacons. You cannot see the restaurants from the house; at the same time, it is nice to have dinner options so close at hand.

An ornate hand-carved tiger oak staircase, nine-foot stained glass double doors, and a beautiful decor are among distinctive features of this wonderful B&B, which has a wraparound porch—and congenial hosts. Regina is a jewel. One of the four rooms in the house is called The Gandy Dancer Room in tribute to the men (called Gandy Dancers) who laid the tracks for the historic Katy Railroad, so important to growth of the town.

A short distance behind The Molly Cherry are two secluded cottages, each with two suites, long front porches (rocking chairs, too), and Victorian decors. Built in 1996, these luxury suites have different features, ranging from fireplaces, private patios, and gorgeous oval-shaped stained-glass "windows," to a garden bath with a two-person, eight-jet Jacuzzi, and mood lighting.

Ideal for business, club, church, and social functions, The Molly Cherry is five minutes away from downtown Denison, where the Wideners own The Gandy Dancer Tearoom as well. About seven miles from Lake Texoma, Denison's attractions include antique and gift shops, Eisenhower's birthplace (a house museum) and State Park, Frontier Village, the Katy Depot and Hagerman National Wildlife Refuge. Explore the area—or relax in the sports pool or hammock on the wooded grounds of The Molly Cherry.

DENTON

Godfrey's Place Inn

Hosts: Marjorie and Dick Waters, 1513 N. Locust, Denton 76201, phone (940) 381-1118, fax (940) 566-0856, or Bed & Breakfast Texas Style (972) 298-8586, 4 guest rooms, 4 baths, heart-healthy gourmet breakfast, $$–$$$, no children, no pets, no smoking, MC, V

Godfrey, the Waters' cat, acts as if he owns the place, so naming the inn after him was only right, you see. This heart-healthy bed and breakfast is a Denton Historic Landmark that was built in 1923 by the first female physician at the Texas College of Industrial Arts (known today as Texas Woman's University), who rented rooms to female students. The Waters used professionals to restore, design, decorate, and landscape their striking Colonial Revival home, and the results show. Original art pieces are attention-getters, too.

Two of the upstairs bedrooms share a tree-top balcony, and a third has its own. All of the beautifully furnished guest rooms have a TV, VCR, and adjustable air mattresses you can make as firm as you like. Other amenities include monogrammed bathrobes (which may be purchased in the small gift shop near the entry way), a video library, and even an exercise room. A telephone and fax are available, too, if you are in town on business. The hosts, who have traveled extensively and live in the carriage house behind their B&B, have published a cookbook featuring some of their heart-healthy recipes, which are often garnished with the edible flowers and herbs they grow year round.

The Texas Storytelling Festival in March and the Denton Jazzfest, featuring University of North Texas students in early fall, are special times in Denton, so make your B&B reservations early. Godfrey's is 15 blocks from the square and across the street from TWU, where you can visit the architecturally acclaimed Little Chapel-in-the-Woods and the botanical gardens, an official state wildflower sanctuary. Art galleries and a collection of gowns worn by wives of presidents of the Republic and governors of Texas, as well as The Courthouse Museum deserve your attention, too.

Of course, so does Godfrey!

Redbud Inn

Hosts: John and Donna Morris, 815 N. Locust St., Denton 76201, (940) 565-6414, (888) 565-6414, fax (940) 565-6515, or Bed & Breakfast Texas Style (972) 298-8586, 2 suites, 3 guest rooms, 3 baths, full breakfast, $–$$$, no pets, no smoking, MC, V, AE, D

In fulfilling a decade-old dream, Donna and John Morris transformed a semi-abandoned Tudor revival home into an appealing English-style bed and breakfast—and did much of the work themselves. It's all been a labor of love! They even restored many of the Victorian-era antiques and fixtures they found in flea markets or in vintage buildings doomed for destruction. The Brass Room, which has a full-sized brass bed and wood-burning brick fireplace, and the Wicker Room, with a queen-sized iron bed, have footed tubs right in the room plus half baths. The two suites have large full baths with claw-foot tubs, sitting rooms, and TV. Donna's breadmaking machine is her pride and joy, and her applesauce bread and biscuits are always a hit at breakfast, which is served in the formal dining room. While you eat, stare at the picture on the wall; you'll be in for a surprise!

Next door (821 N. Locust) is another B&B owned by the couple. Built in 1902, **The Magnolia Inn** has two second-floor suites with a private balcony. The sitting room of one suite is furnished with period furniture collected by John and Donna through the years. On the first floor is Giuseppe's Italian Restaurant, with four dining areas, hardwood floors, and turn-of-the-century antiques. Patio dining is also available under the stars in back. Amenities for the two inns, which are just north of downtown Denton and the courthouse square, include a gazebo-enclosed hot tub and thick fluffy robes.

A Denton landmark, built in 1878, is another inviting B&B option. On Silk Stocking Row at 609 W. Oak St., **The May House** includes a formal library and solarium. Reserve the entire two-bedroom, one-bath cottage, or share it with friends. The courthouse square and University of North Texas are within walking distance. For reservations, call (940) 387-0995 or Bed & Breakfast Texas Style (972) 298-8586.

EDOM

Red Rooster Square Bed & Breakfast

Hosts: Bob and Doris Moore, Rt. 3, Box 3387, Ben Wheeler 75754, (800) 947-0393, (903) 852-6774, 3 guest rooms, 2 baths, full breakfast, $$, no children, no pets, smoking only on porches, no cr

The Red Rooster Square Bed & Breakfast is certainly something for tiny Edom (pop. 300) to crow about!

The brightly painted yellow and white rural-Victorian-style house has a large deck out back and a long porch in front. On three acres just one block off Edom's main street, the Red Rooster primarily is decorated in Early American furniture with a few well-chosen antiques. The downstairs Honeymoon bedroom has a Jacuzzi tub, while the two rooms upstairs each have two twin beds, share a bath, and usually form a suite for four.

Awake to the smell of pine-scented country air and freshly brewed coffee. Start your day with a breakfast served family style—in the nook if you're the only guests, or dining room if there are others.

Edom has drawn tourists for years because of its artists and master craftsmen, whom you can often watch at work. The Edom Art Fair each September is a quality event. A herb and gift center, Blue Moon Gardens; Canton, Tyler, and the Blueberry Hill Farm, where you can pick your own blueberries in season, are among area attractions.

If you stay at the Red Rooster, you'll have something to crow about, too!

Wild Briar, the Country Inn at Edom

Hosts: Max and Mary Scott, FM 2339, P.O. Box 21, Ben Wheeler 75754, (903) 852-3975, 6 guest rooms, 6 baths, full breakfast and dinner, $$$, no pets, no smoking (except in snug), no cr

A winding lane leads to Wild Briar, a moss-covered brick manor named for the wild berry vines on its 23 wooded acres. Opened by native East Texans Max and Mary Scott in 1987 after becoming captivated with country inns in Great Britain and France, Wild Briar echoes favorite features found abroad, with charming results. Instead of a living room, Wild Briar has a "gathering room," and instead of a den, a "snug," with a patterned carpet and antique tin ceiling. The dining room resembles an English pub.

The guest rooms in the 6,000-square-foot country inn even have names that reflect the Scott's travels. For instance, a room called Bonthddu (pronounced Bone-thee) is named for Bonthddu Hall, a castle-like hotel with beautiful gardens in Wales where the Scotts celebrated an anniversary. They hope you'll find their Bonthddu special, too. A wildflower painting by Texana artist George Boutwell adds a Texas touch. Five rooms have queen beds; one, twins.

Enjoy a full breakfast that includes biscuits and gravy and maybe Mary's quiche or strawberry bread in the garden room, which has rattan and glass furniture and stained-glass transoms that match pottery brought from England.

Believe it or not, a sumptuous dinner is included at no extra charge, but make reservations. Save room for the grand finale, like chocolate mousse or toasted coconut pie. Even if you're not staying at Wild Briar, you can have dinner with advance reservations ($17.50). The gracious couple also host special functions like family reunions and weddings. "Nice" children are occasionally welcome.

Wild Briar, which has a separate craft shop, is an ideal base for First Monday Trade Days in Canton, the Rose Festival in Tyler, the Kilgore Oil Museum, or the Caddo Indian Mounds.

ELIASVILLE

Andrews House

Hosts: Mike and Melba Riggs, Box 775, Eliasville 76481, (817) 362-4243, or Bed & Breakfast Texas Style (972) 298-8586, 2 guest rooms, 1 bath, continental breakfast OYO or country breakfast, $$, all cr

Eliasville was an oil boom town in 1917 with more than 10,000 people, but little remains today except a cafe and a general store. Population: 200. It's pretty country, though, with rolling hills and woods. Located about 40 miles west of Mineral Wells, the rural community's "attraction" is a grist mill, which has a historical marker.

The Andrews House was the home of W. A. Andrews who ran the grist mill. The remote B&B was built in the early 1900s on a bluff about

300 feet from the hosts' home. The Gothic-style frame house draws a variety of B&B guests, from honeymooners to hunters who really want to "get away from it all." It's cozy and quaint with special touches such as stenciled floors, lace curtains, and unusual antiques. In the kitchen is a vintage Maytag refrigerator with the motor on top. The Paisley Room and Rose Room have a shared bath. The entire house can be rented. If you want to explore the countryside, bikes are available.

The most popular area attractions include Possum Kingdom Lake and a registered National Landmark, Fort Belknap, both less than 20 minutes from the Andrews House.

FORT WORTH

Azalea Plantation

Innkeepers: Martha and Richard Linnartz, 1400 Robinwood Dr., Fort Worth 76111, (800) 68-RELAX, (817) 838-5882, 2 guest rooms, 2 baths, 1 cottage with 2 suites, full breakfast buffet style (weekends), continental plus (weekdays), $$–$$$, no pets, outside smoking only, MC, V, AE, D

When the magnolias and azaleas are in bloom, this plantation-style home is especially beautiful! On almost two tree-covered acres and built in 1948, the white-columned B&B is enhanced by terraced grounds, a fountain, a gazebo and wooden swing. It has a country feeling, yet the Azalea Plantation is only 10 minutes from the Stockyards Historic District and downtown's Sundance Square. Fine china, delicate crystal and unique antiques are displayed throughout the common areas of this lovely home. One guest room has a Cape Cod ambience, and the other, a romantic Victorian, but both have king-sized beds and private verandas.

The quaint upstairs suite of the nearby cottage includes two bedrooms, a full bath, and a cozy parlor. It's brimming with antique quilts, elegant bed linens, and an enchanting collection of cherubs. A Texas-quilted queen bed and separate parlor with a twin bed and wicker furnishings are highlights of the lower suite.

Turn-down service with mints, terry robes, and complimentary soaps and bubble bath are amenities. Every room has a TV; free fax and copier service is available, along with a VCR and an assortment of games, such as croquet and horseshoes. Honeymoon and anniversary packages are available at the Azalea Plantation—along with old-fashioned Southern hospitality.

Etta's Place

Hosts: Bonnie and Vaughn Franks, Innkeepers, 200 W. Third St., Fort Worth 76102, (817) 654-0267, fax (817) 878-2560, 4 suites, 6 rooms, choice of continental or full breakfast, $$$–$$$$, children and pets welcome, smoking on balconies, all cr

The Fort Worth Water Gardens and Convention Center are on a site once known as Hell's Half Acre. For about four months, the infamous outlaw, Butch Cassidy, and his partner, the Sundance Kid, lived there. Fort Worth's newest B&B is named for Sundance Kid's girlfriend, Etta Place, rumored to be either a school teacher or a woman of the night. This unusual bed and breakfast is in a five-story building with an art deco facade in Sundance Square, which now encompasses 20 blocks. The Franks, who own the heralded Bonnynook B&B in Waxahachie, now also are the resident innkeepers at Etta's Place, and have been involved with its planning from the start.

You'll enjoy the first-floor common areas, which include a library that resembles an English club, two dining rooms (one has an art gallery), a game room in a loft overlooking a music room with a Steinway grand piano, and two patios. A well-stocked coffee nook and a spacious garden-covered, roof-top patio are other amenities B&B buffs will enjoy. (Etta's Place is the place for meetings, too.)

One guest room is handicapped accessible; all suites have full kitchens. Some of the antique chairs, desks, and beds in the guest rooms are reproductions of Texas heirlooms. Etta's Place has a rustic, but elegant decor, and it's in a great location, near a new outlet mall in the Old Tandy Center, the new Symphony Hall, and the Caravan of Dreams (a club which features live music, especially jazz).

Miss Molly's Hotel

Host: Mark Hancock, 109½ West Exchange Avenue, Fort Worth 76106, (800) 996-6559, (817) 626-1522, fax (817) 625-2723, 8 rooms, 4 baths, continental plus breakfast, $–$$$, no pets or smokers, MC, V

Located in the heart of the Fort Worth Stockyards' Historic District above the Star Cafe, Miss Molly's is a real charmer. It's in a 1910 building that was first used as a prim and proper boarding house, then as a bawdy house run by Miss Josie. Miss Josie sure would be thrilled if she could see the Victorian room named in her honor! With a draped fabric ceiling, elaborate wall covering, dramatic window dressing, and an elevated private bath, the room is among the most beautiful B&B rooms in the state.

The other seven guest rooms are attractive, also, but smaller, and more casual with a Western flair, and share three baths down the hall. Each pays tribute to those who played significant roles in development of the Stockyards: the rodeo performer, cattleman, cowboy, oilman, gunslinger, and railroad worker. The baths have claw-foot tubs with showers, pedestal sinks, and pull chain toilets. Breakfast is served in the parlor beneath a stained-glass skylight.

The White Elephant Saloon, Billy Bob's Texas, and the Stockyards Hotel are within walking distance of Miss Molly's. The Tarantula steam train is another Stockyard attraction.

Reflecting on the history of his B&B, Mark says, "We operate legally now, but still with discretion!"

Miss Molly, by the way, was not a madame, but the name the Longhorn steers were called by ranchers during cattle drives!

The Texas White House

Hosts: Grover and Jamie McMains, 1417 Eighth Ave., Fort Worth 76104, (800) 279-6491, (817) 923-3597, fax (817) 923-0410, 3 guest rooms, 3 baths, gourmet breakfast, $$–$$$, no children, no pets, smoking on front porch, MC, V, AE, D

Texas has its own White House! Built in 1910 and owned by one family until 1967 (one son became Fort Worth's mayor), this historic landmark is a classic example of a hipped-cottage. Relax with your morning coffee or afternoon snacks on the large, wraparound front porch, in the parlor, or by the fireplace in the living room. Boasting gleaming hardwood floors, the Texas White House has country-style furnishings and simple elegance. Lone Star, Land of Contrast, and Tejas are the appropriate names of the guest rooms, which have private baths and are on the second floor. A TV, phone, secretarial services—even a feather bed—are available upon request. Business conferences, · small weddings, and other functions are often held here.

Centrally located, The Texas White House is only five minutes to downtown, the Cultural District, TCU, the Botanical Gardens, and Fort Worth Zoo.

GAINESVILLE

Rose House

Hosts: Kay and Guy George, 321 So. Dixon, Gainesville, Texas 76240, (817) 665-1010, 6 guest rooms, 5 private baths, 1 shared bath, full breakfast, $$, MC, V, AE

This is a heavenly place! Angels and cherubs are everywhere! Biscotties and coffee at 7 a.m. and a full breakfast a little later, along with afternoon High Tea with a lemonade punch, smoked turkey sandwiches, and scones—a feast in itself—will be among highpoints of your stay at the hospitable Rose House. Fresh flowers, nightly turn-down service, and an evening decanter of peach brandy, which Guy himself makes as a special treat for guests, along with Victorian night shirts and gowns, terry cloth robes, and candles for your bath—even your own rubber ducky—add to the amiable ambience. All of the guest rooms are bright and cheery with custom decors; one has its own sun porch.

Built in 1898 by R. S. Rose, a cotton broker, the antique-filled Queen Anne Victorian home has a wraparound porch with rockers and swings, hardwood floors, three coal-burning fireplaces, and a player piano in the entry hall. One of the parlors is a game room with a hand-crank record player, a Victorian game table, and an antique pool table. The back deck is "decked out" for your enjoyment.

Chances are, Guy will give you a guided tour of town in his beloved Model A Ford convertible, but you can walk along the tree-shaded streets from the Rose House, which is in Gainesville's historic district, to restaurants, the Morton Museum, and Butterfield Stage Playhouse in the nearby square. Gainesville Factory Shops and the Frank Buck Zoo are not far, either, from this charming B&B.

For a more rural setting in the Lake Texoma area, consider **Alexander Bed and Breakfast,** a 65-acre wooded retreat south of Whitesboro with four second-floor bedrooms with delightful decors and private baths and a third-floor conference area for retreats or meetings with a kitchenette, TV, bath, and three futon couch-beds in the host's home, a three-story Queen Anne reproduction. A full breakfast is served.

In the woods nearby, Pamela and Jim Alexander also have a two-story, three-bedroom Guest Cottage with a wood-burning stove, a fully equipped kitchen, a large living/dining area, a bath and a half, and a large screened-in porch with a hammock. Contact the Alexanders at (800) 887-8794, (903) 564-7440, or Bed & Breakfast Texas Style (972) 298-8586.

GALLATIN

Ronda's Rest N Roost

Hostess: Ronda Hanson, 4th Street, Gallatin (Rt. 84 west of Rusk) 75785, (903) 683-4696, 1 bedroom cottage, continental plus breakfast, $$$–$$$$, no children, no cr

There's no way to get around it; you can't imagine why anyone would come to Gallatin, and, even if they come, you still can't believe this B&B is where it is—down a little path behind some houses that dead-ends into a huge tree and an herb garden. The rustic cabin, which is almost buried in the bush, is so funny, it's great. There's 1930s furniture you haven't seen people using since that time, including an old Roper stove and 1940s fridge that actually works. A SunCrest Clock adorns the kitchen, which has a tin washtub for a sink. A huge bedroom and bathroom, with claw-foot tub and painted floors, with a hot tub on a porch out back buried in foliage (grape vines and honeysuckle) offers privacy beyond comprehension. Ronda encourages that by dropping a basket of homemade, old-fashioned cinnamon rolls, buttermilk biscuits and gravy, eggs and deer sausage off at your door (and rings the bell to let you know breakfast is ready). There's bass and catfish in the pond down the path, horses for riding, and coffee cups and chocolates for you to enjoy or take home should you wish to leave, but, so far, everyone who has come to stay just stays and stays and stays. Maybe they become attached to Bonnie and Clyde (the rooster).

Ronda's Dad said she had to have a roost if she was going to have a Rest N Roost. Why, you ask, would you come to Gallatin? There's a wildlife park down the road, and there are two stores that cook three meals a day, Ronda tells us. And, every April and September, Ronda's uncle is trail boss to a trail ride that attracts a bunch of people. And, believe it or not, they have a Christmas parade (in which Ronda won the float contest with her dogs wearing hats seated on the Roost). There's no end to surprises in Gallatin, but, mostly, people come to hide away, which makes Ronda's the funkiest hideaway in Texas.

GARLAND

Catnap Creek

Contact Bed & Breakfast Texas Style (972) 298-8586, 1 bedroom, 1 bath, continental breakfast weekdays, full on weekends, $, no children, no pets, no smoking, MC, V

You'll fall in love with the backyard of this B&B in Garland (a suburb northeast of Dallas). A deck extends across the back of the traditional, one-story brick house, then the bank slopes 30 feet to a trickling rocky creek bed, which becomes a rushing stream with enough rainfall. The "yard" is so heavily wooded that you would hardly know civilization is so near (next door, in fact). There is even a covered patio where you can eat breakfast when the weather is nice. About a dozen windows in the breakfast nook and airy kitchen bring the outdoors in. Because the congenial hosts have three cats for pets, Catnap Creek is an appropriate name for this B&B. You'll also see cats on towels, pillows, plates, pictures—most everywhere you look.

Catnap Creek is conveniently located in the northern part of Garland only minutes from the Telecom Corridor in adjoining Richardson as well as to major freeways. Though often overlooked, sprawling Garland has a quaint downtown with a fountain, antique and craft shops, and Heritage Park that includes a museum in a former Santa Fe Railroad Station. Just off the square is The Big G Jamboree Theatre, which features western, gospel, and blues groups each Saturday night and the Garland Center for the Performing Arts, most noted for its top-notch musicals.

GILMER

Corner Cottage Bed and Breakfast

Host: Jeannie Glaze, 219 Butler, Gilmer 75644, (800) 440-5223, (903) 843-2466, (903) 843-3249, 3 guest rooms, 3 baths, full breakfast, $$, no pets, no smoking, MC, V, D

This comfortable, cozy cottage, a white-framed house with a wrap-around porch and an old iron fence, is within easy walking distance of historic downtown Gilmer, where you'll find brick-paved streets, a town square around the courthouse, and antique and craft shops, including one (the Corner Store Antiques) owned by Jeannie. Each of the guest rooms in the Victorian cottage was named for her nieces (two are former Yamboree queens). A full southern breakfast is served. You won't want to miss her special Sunday breakfast featuring her made-from-scratch sweet potato pie, either!

Lodging is also offered in the unhosted **Machen Lane Farmhouse,** an original East Texas farmhouse near the new Lake Gilmer, on the historic Cherokee Trace, which is part of the Trail of Tears northwest of Gilmer. It has a screened-in back porch with a double bed, three guest rooms, and one bath, along with a full kitchen, a living room, dining room, a TV, VCR, and microwave. Located 1.5 miles west of Gilmer, the farmhouse is available for small functions. There are picnic tables under huge old pecan trees.

Though noted for its East Texas Yamboree each fall and Cherokee Rose Festival in May, Gilmer is relatively undiscovered by tourists. However, this East Texas town is a good base to tour nearby attractions like Lake O' the Pines, which is 15 minutes away. The Historic Upshur Museum in the old Post Office building on the square is of interest, too.

Sarah's

Hosts: Deborah and Joe Bell, 104 N. Montgomery, Gilmer 75644, (903) 843-6203, 5 guest rooms, 1 private and 2 shared baths, full breakfast, $$–$$$, well-behaved children welcome, no pets, smoking outside only, MC, V

Sarah's is an 8,000-square-foot, three-story red brick, Italianate Prairie-style house with a veranda on three sides, a full attic and basement—and sound-proof rooms, thanks to six inches of concrete between walls and the floors. No wonder it was considered the strongest house west of the Mississippi when constructed (between 1911 and 1916, and why it took so long to build is another story).

Four rooms are on the second floor and all have hardwood floors, fireplaces, and are furnished with antiques; one guest room is downstairs. Three rooms have full-sized beds, one, a queen; and another, twin beds. For the convenience of guests, since most have shared baths, two robes are in each bedroom. Sweet potato pancakes have become the specialty of the house, but the freshly baked cookies served in the evening are a hit, too. The house lends itself well to weddings and such, so catering keeps Deborah on the go as well. She also does special candlelight dinners upon request. Bring your swimsuit when you stay at Sarah's, because a pool and cabanas are in back of the acre lot, which is about two blocks from the town square.

GLADEWATER

Honeycomb Suites

Hosts: Bill and Susan Morgan, 111 N. Main, Gladewater 75647, (800) 594-2253, (903) 845-4430, fax (903) 845-2448, 7 suites, gourmet breakfast, $$–$$$$, no children, no pets, no smoking, MC, V, AE, D

If you are into antiques, you'll be happy at the Honeycomb Suites, for there are more than 200 dealers within walking distance, along with several arts and crafts malls. This luxurious East Texas B&B is also the place for a romantic rendezvous, for four suites have whirlpool tubs for two, while one has a lace-trimmed, mirrored canopy over an antique queen bed. The hosts have created a special ambience for each suite, from the Gentlemen's Quarters' rich, bold-colored fabrics to the floral fabrics and rose tulle netting cascading from the ceiling around the bed in another suite.

Five suites are above the Glory Bee Baking Co., which the Morgans also own, in the center of town. (One of the last remaining "from scratch" bakeries in the region, specialties include Bodacious Brownie Chunk Cheesecake—absolutely exquisite—and Blueberry Chess Pie.) Two new suites are in a brownstone around the corner: the Hideaway, a spacious second floor honeymoon suite, and the nautical-themed Captain's Quarters below. Both suites have queen beds, a coffee maker, microwave oven, and refrigerator. All the suites have color TV.

"This is a place," the hosts proclaim, "where memories are made . . . and dreams come true," and two special packages are designed to help those dreams along. Both the two-day romance and the vow renewal packages include fresh flowers, a horse-drawn carriage ride, and a candlelight dinner, along with other perks. Renew your vows, for instance, and the Morgans will also provide a garden ceremony under a white canopy, a personalized mini-wedding cake, a souvenir photo album—and more. The Morgans, who have a cozy restaurant adjoining their bakery, also offer their romantic carriage and candle-light dinners each Saturday year round (by reservation) to guests and the public (on a limited basis). During the holidays, B&B guests are given a coupon to take the carriage ride in nearby Marshall for its mag-ical Wonderland of Lights Festival.

Gladewater, which celebrates Christmas Tyme in Gusherville from Thanksgiving through the holidays, has another very nice B&B one block off Main Street. **Primrose Lane,** Linda Patton's late '30s home, has two bedrooms with period furniture, private entrances, and a shared bath. A '30s wedding coat and a porcelain doll are attention get-ters. For reservations, call (800) 293-0195. Children are welcome.

GLEN ROSE

Hummingbird Lodge

Hosts: Richard and Sherry Fowlkes, P.O. Box 128, Glen Rose 76043, (817) 897-2787, fax (817) 897-3459, 6 rooms, 6 baths, continental plus buffet, $$–$$$, no children under 18, no pets, no smoking, MC, V

Over four miles of walking trails, a fishing pond stocked with black bass and channel catfish, two seasonally flowing streams, and a waterfall will be yours to enjoy at this 140-acre, two-story rustic con-temporary retreat in the hills of Somervell County. You'll see lots of white tail deer and other wildlife—hummingbirds, too, which was the inspiration for the B&B's name. Built on the side of a hill, the Lodge has several decks and a covered balcony offering scenic vistas. You can also see for miles from the dining and living rooms, which have wood-burning fireplaces and TVs. A short walk takes you to a hot tub in a secluded wooded area.

Pine walls, flooring, and ceilings contribute to the lodge-like ambience of this B&B, which is furnished with antiques, early Texas furniture, and original art. Guest rooms have either a king or queen-sized beds and sitting areas. Four studio rooms also have a small refrigerator and a sofa that makes into a single bed. The hosts say Hummingbird Lodge, which is about six miles west of Glen Rose and only five minutes from Fossil Rim Wildlife Center, can comfortably accommodate up to 16. It's ideal for corporate and group meetings and retreats.

The Lodge at Fossil Rim and The Foothills Safari Camp

Hosts: Debra Haynes, Resident Owner of Nature Escapes; Billie Kinnard, Manager, Route 1, Box 210, Glen Rose 76043, (817) 897-4933, fax (817) 897-4933, 1 suite, 4 guest rooms, 3 private baths, 1 shared, in Lodge; 7 African safari tents, 7 baths, continental breakfast and gourmet brunch, $$$$, children welcome, no pets, smoking outside, all cr

Whether you stay in The Lodge at Fossil Rim or in the more rustic Foothills Safari Camp, you'll have a unique experience at Nature Escapes at the Fossil Rim Wildlife Resort—probably the only B&B accommodations in a wildlife preserve. Home to over 60 species of wildlife, the 2,700-acre preserve has nearly 1,100 exotic and endangered free-roaming animals. Both the Lodge (one guest room has a queen bed, the rest, king and all are beautifully furnished with massive antiques; some include patios, Jacuzzis, or fireplaces) and Safari Camp have glass-walled dining rooms with panoramic views, well-stocked bars, and custom decors, so you won't be roughing it at either B&B. Both of the two-acre compounds are encircled by protective fences. From the Lodge, you can see wildlife grazing in a pasture; beyond that is a pool and a waterfall.

If you stay at The Lodge, start your day with a light breakfast, take the two-hour 8 a.m. tour of the preserve, then return for a delicious brunch. At night, relax in the common area on the main floor (second floor), which has a massive stone fireplace, a beamed cathedral ceiling, and beautiful stained-glass window, or in the first-floor TV room, which has a full-service bar.

The seven tents (wood cabins covered with canvas) are about 40 feet apart at **The Foothills Safari Camp,** which is a mile from The Lodge and deeper into the wildlife park. The cabins are smaller than the guest rooms at The Lodge, but each has twin beds, a private bath, central air and heat, and ceiling fans. A professional chef serves brunch inside a second glass-walled dining pavilion or on a veranda overlooking another wildlife-filled meadow and a watering hole where animals come to water in the afternoon. If the wind is just right, you can hear the wolves howling at night.

Ye Ole' Maple Inn

Hosts: Roberta and David Maple, Box 114, 1509 Van Zandt, Glen Rose 76043, (817) 897-3456, 2 guest rooms, 2 baths, full breakfast, $$, no children, pets, or smoking , MC, V, AE

With its three-course gourmet breakfasts, period decor, and wonderful amenities, the marvelous **Inn on the River** on the banks of the beautiful Paluxy River long has been one of the state's outstanding historic inns.

But Glen Rose now has another inviting, but much more modern and modest, lodging option: **Ye Ole' Maple Inn.** Both guest rooms also have a view of the Paluxy River, which is across the street. Enclosed by a white picket fence and framed by 200-year-old pecan trees, the house, which was built about 1950, has an inviting front porch with a swing and chairs. Just put up your feet and relax! Something sinful like chocolate marshmallow mousse pie will be an evening treat.

Mementos of the couple's travels, such as a grandfather clock from Germany and candleholders from Turkey, will catch your eye. A pre-Civil War brass clock on the dining room wall and a lovely collection of early 20th-century salt cellars are of interest, too.

Dinosaur Valley State Park, the Fossil Rim Wildlife Center, and the Somervell County Historical Museum long have been luring visitors to Glen Rose. The Texas Amphitheatre and the impressive pageant, *The Promise,* is a more recent attraction for the scenic area, which is only about an hour and a half from Dallas or Fort Worth.

GRAHAM

Victorian Memories

**Host: Judy Smith, HC 60, Box 406, Graham 76450,
(817) 549-4005, or contact Bed & Breakfast Texas Style,
(972) 298-8586, 2 guest rooms, 2 baths, continental breakfast
OYO, $$–$$$, no smoking, no cr**

That old adage "good things come in small packages" takes on new meaning when applied to this B&B. It's tiny, but it's nice! Lovingly preserved with its stained glass, wood floors, and high ceilings, this B&B owner refers to it as "an enchanting way to add charm to your stay." Built by one of Graham's pioneer families in 1885, the home's Folk Victorian influence is felt throughout. An entranceway embellished with English ivy, floral wreaths, quilts, and antiques, and a sunny sun room filled with plants, flowers, and wicker furniture, contributes to its charm. The guest rooms are cozy, and the cottage has a fully equipped kitchen and dining area, where a continental breakfast will be left for you. One of two bathrooms has a claw-foot tub.

The county seat of Young County and considered part of the Panhandle, Graham was founded in 1872, but the area was an Indian reservation in the 1850s. About 11 miles away is Fort Belknap, which has two museums, some restored buildings, and a grape arbor where you can picnic. Possum Kingdom Lake State Park, one of the state's recreational hot spots, is about 20 miles southeast of Graham, which boasts it has "America's largest downtown square." Located two blocks south of town, you'll have fond memories of your stay at The Victorian Memories Bed and Breakfast.

GRANBURY

Arbor House, a Lakeside Inn

**Hosts: Mike and Helen Pemberton, 530 E. Pearl St., Granbury
76048, (817) 573-0073, (800) 641-0073, 7 guest rooms,
7 baths, full breakfast, $$$$, children over 12 with advance notice,
no pets, smoking only on porches and in gazebo, MC, V**

From the upstairs balcony and bedrooms of the Arbor House, you can view beautiful Lake Granbury and the city beach, which is just across the street. At the same time, it is only four blocks from the boutiques, art galleries, and restaurants on the historic town square. Though only built in 1996, the Arbor House offers the old-fashioned hospitality and ambience of yesteryear. In the entry hall of this impressive two-story Queen Anne Victorian lakeside inn is a 13-foot high, hand-painted mural of an arched wisteria arbor, a pond, and the Arbor House on one wall.

Two of the beautifully decorated guest rooms have full-sized sleeper sofas and one, a rollaway. All the guest rooms have private marble bathrooms, some with jet tubs. One of the first-floor rooms is wheelchair accessible and can be set up with a king or twin beds. Victoria's suite is really special, with a crystal chandelier and a sitting area in a coned turret. A refrigerator in the kitchen contains ice cream, soda, juice, and sandwich fixings for guests, so help yourself. TV and phone lines are available, too.

Well-suited for special occasions, from reunions to rehearsal dinners, the entire house can be reserved. The Arbor House has pleasant walkways, groomed floral and herb gardens, a gazebo—and talented hosts whose personalized touches add to its charm!

If you are lucky, you'll get to sample some of Mike's cinnamon rolls, which reportedly are "the best."

Doyle House on the Lake

Hosts: Patrick and Linda Stoll, 205 W. Doyle, Granbury 76048, (817) 573-6492, 1 suite, carriage house, pool cottage, continental plus (weekdays), gourmet breakfast (weekends), $$–$$$, no pets or smoking, all cr

Framed by a white picket fence, this sprawling one-story home (painted white, of course) has a manicured lawn from the street to the edge of the property, which covers several acres. Built on a bluff around 1880 by Dr. Doyle, a prominent Hood County physician, the back of the house provides a panoramic view of Lake Granbury. You have several choices here. Emily's Room in the Doyle House is the most elegant, with a king-sized bed, cherry and mahogany furniture, and a private sitting room, Jacuzzi, and entrance. The carriage house has its own entrance, too, along with a queen-sized bed, a trundle bed in a separate room, and a "Shaker" decor.

The cozy cottage by the pool has the best view of the grounds and water, a queen-sized bed (and a daybed), and a living area. Take a few steps and you're in the pool! Both the cottage and carriage house have private baths, a microwave, refrigerator, and coffee maker, while all three rooms have a radio and TV. A barbecue pit, a dinner bell, and a swing are near the bluff's edge, while the Stoll's boat house and fishing platform are down below. The hosts serve breakfast in their home, which is just a few blocks from the courthouse square.

Besides the art galleries and boutiques around the square, Granbury now has an antique mall with more than 75 vendors. A narrated tour on the Granbury Queen Riverboat or a sidetrip to nearby Glen Rose to see *The Promise,* or other entertainment at the Texas Amphitheater, are also hard to beat options.

Of course, you can just relax and enjoy your beautiful B&B by the lake!

Pearl Street Inn

Host: Danette D. Hebda, 319 W. Pearl St., Granbury 76048, (888) 732-7578, (817) 579-7465, 1 suite, 4 guest rooms, four baths, gourmet breakfast, $$–$$$, no children under 10, no pets, no smoking, no cr

You'll have a front row seat to the town's parades from the Pearl Street Inn's porch, notable for its large square supports and a beautiful wisteria bush. Sit a spell on a side-screened porch, or maybe play a game or two. The closet in the den has puzzles and board games, while a refurbished inlaid wardrobe conceals a TV, VCR, and stereo system.

On a corner lot three blocks from the square, this 1912 two-story Prairie-style home is known as the B. M. Estes House. Estes, who practiced law for 64 years, once served as Granbury's mayor. A guest room is named in his honor. Furnished with a king-sized antique bed, the Estes Room has a claw-foot tub and a pull-chain, high-tank water closet— one of the first second-story bathrooms in Granbury!

A folding screen separates the antique tub and water closet from the full-sized, nine-foot tall Belgian Eastlake bed and built-in dresser in the Pink Rose Room. (The clock tower on the square is visible from the side windows.) Dee Dee's Room on the main floor has a shower-only bath and a boldly colored art nouveau motif. All of the guest rooms are spacious.

Ask Danette about personalized dinners for six or more and her Enchanted Evening Package, which includes a romantic board game momento.

And give Ralph, the resident cocker spaniel, a pat or two before you leave!

The Iron Horse Inn

Hosts: Judy and Bob Atkinson, 616 Thorp Springs Road, Granbury 76048, (817) 579-5535, 4 suites, 2 guest rooms, 2 baths, gourmet breakfast, $$–$$$$, no small children, no pets, smoking on front porch, all cr

Three-hundred-year-old live oak and pecan trees grace the acre ground of this large, 7,000-square-foot Craftsman-style home. Built in 1905 by Daniel Cogdell, who brought the train to Hood County in the late 1800s, this estate features ornate mill work and intricate leaded glass held in place by copperwork. Pristinely restored, the home has two comfortable living rooms, a huge dining room, and a great front porch, where guests can enjoy the sunset in comfortable wicker chairs. A gourmet breakfast is served each morning, and complimentary wine, each evening.

The guest rooms and suites have unique themes, including the Stateroom (reminiscent of a 1920's ocean liner, and highlights include nautical prints, and a ship's mahogany door with a port hole). The Cogdell Suite includes a beautifully canopied bed, a solarium with 13 original windows on three sides, a skylight, and a six-foot claw-foot tub. Weddings, receptions, reunions and other functions are often held in The Iron Horse Inn, which is especially beautiful at Christmas, with decorated trees in each room.

Check with the Granbury Visitors Bureau, (800) 950-2212, for other listings like the memorabilia-filled **Victorian Rose,** an 1870's home at 404 W. Bridge St. with a wraparound porch, sun room, gorgeous stained-glass windows, and lavender exterior (800) 430-7673; and a long-standing B&B, the **Dabney House,** 106 S. Jones, a Craftsman-style country manor that gives discounted rates to peace officers and fire fighters. John and Gwen Hurley will be happy to tell you more about their B&B, special occasion and picnic baskets, and candlelight romance dinners. Call (800) 566-1260.

Another option is a wooded country retreat on 24 acres only 10 minutes from the Granbury courthouse. **Oak Tree Farm B&B** not only can accommodate 10 guests (children over 12, too), but offers small conference facilities as well. Your hosts are identical twin sisters, Jeanne Bennett and Jeanette Carmichael, and the latter's husband, Michael, who built their homes on the property a few years ago just for this purpose. Some beautiful antiques and collections reflect their travels. Choose between a gourmet or country breakfast, which may be served as a buffet for a group. For information, call (800) 326-5595.

The Captain's House

Hosts: Bob and Julia Pannell, 123 W. Doyle St., Granbury 76048, (817) 579-6664 or (817) 579-LAKE, 2 suites, 1 guest room, private baths, 1 cottage, continental plus breakfast and choice of brunch or lunch, $$$, no children, no pets, no smoking inside, no cr

Sit at the water's edge, fish from your own "fishing rock," or enjoy Lake Granbury from the spacious second-floor balcony that extends across the back of this beautifully furnished historic Queen Anne Victorian B&B. Built in the 1870s by James H. Doyle, a respected leader who was affectionately called "Captain," The Captain's House has unusual touches such as handpainted birds on balconies and some furniture made by the host's ancestors. All of the romantic guest accommodations open to the Common Room, where you can watch TV, read books dating to the 1800s, or visit with other guests.

A delightful hostess who wears a ruffled Victorian skirt, Julia gladly makes arrangements for special dinners, flowers, the Granbury Opera House, or whatever in advance for guests. Homemade desserts, chocolates, and freshen-up drinks are provided, along with a full continental breakfast, which is brought on a tray to each room. But guests also have the option of brunch or lunch at the Nuttshell Bakery on the square—or four loaves of homemade bread to take home! A 20 percent off gift certificate for the ladies to a boutique (Jeannine's) is another unique touch.

The hosts offer the same amenities and personal attention in a second beautifully decorated B&B, an unhosted 1920s bungalow with two spacious suites that can each sleep four. **The Cottage** is on a large, tree-covered corner lot near the square at 204 South Travis. You'll be pampered here, too!

HAMILTON

Hamilton Guest Hotel

Hosts: Christian Roff, Resident Owner; Steve Moore, Manager, 109 N. Rice, Hamilton 76531, (800) 876-2502, (817) 386-8977, or Bed & Breakfast Texas Style, (972) 298-8586, 6 guest rooms, 2 baths, $–$$, continental plus breakfast OYO, children and domesticated pets welcome, no smoking, all cr

Located at the northern rim of the Texas Hill Country, this quaint, turn-of-the-century inn on the square has been a stopping place for travelers as well as hunters. B&B buffs enjoy it, too, especially since it's close to Glen Rose and a golf course is nearby. Filled with family quilts, books, art, and some antiques, the six guest rooms each have a different decor, access to a sitting room, and individual antique locks and keys from the Texas Hotel in Fort Worth. Sharing only two bathrooms—hand-held shower fixtures are in both claw-foot tubs—doesn't faze many guests. A hearty continental self-serve breakfast is available by 7:30 each morning in a sky-lit area in the lobby.

The lobby will get your attention with shops that sell teas and coffees from around the world, linens, and gifts along with an apothecary and tea garden.

What's really nice is that both children and pets are welcome here—both on their best behavior, of course.

HICO

Indian Mountain Bed and Breakfast

Host: Val Fletcher Taylor, Rt. 1, Box 162A, Hico, Texas 76457, (817) 796-4060, fax (817) 796-4090, or Bed & Breakfast Texas Style, (972) 298-8586, 3 bedrooms, 2 full baths, 2 half baths, country breakfast, $$–$$$, no pets, smokers on porches or outside, MC, V

This is probably the only B&B in Texas on land that was once a sacred ceremonial ground for Native Americans. Buying the property was the last thing on Val's mind when she initially went to see Indian Mountain in 1990, but she immediately knew it was meant for her (a story in itself that maybe she'll relate). On 65 acres north of Highway 220, between Hico and Glen Rose, Indian Mountain B&B is also the site for seminars, retreats, reunions, and weddings. A writer and a teacher, Val often brings in well-known writers for workshops, too.

Built of natural cedar with a second-floor open mezzanine encircling a spacious, living area below, a high-beamed, yellow pine ceiling, 62 windows, and glass doors that bring the outdoors in, along with lots of covered porches and balconies, make her rustic home distinctive. Primarily heated by wood stoves, the unusual hillside hideaway has a Southwestern decor. Indian artifacts and handpainted drums, saddles, and blankets are interesting accents. "Victorian it is not," quips the host. A stone swimming pool, a cattle pond, picnic tables, and old-fashioned swings add to the relaxed ambience. Val even can arrange a trail ride or two.

Close to Glen Rose and an easy drive from Dallas and Fort Worth, Hico (pronounced to rhyme with "eye") itself is attracting tourists now. A bustling town in the 1800s, it died when the trains left, but its deserted stone relics of yesteryear are being transformed into boutiques and restaurants. Hico even has a gazebo, horse-drawn carriage rides, and free concerts on Saturday night.

And, of course, Indian Mountain B&B!

HILLSBORO

Hillsboro House

Hosts: Sabrina and Steve Warren, 301 E. Franklin, Hillsboro 76645, (817) 582-0211, (800) 566-3740 or Bed & Breakfast Texas Style, (972) 298-8586, 5 rooms, 5 baths, 1 suite, country breakfast, $–$$, no pets or smoking, MC, V

Just around the corner from the Tarlton House and only two blocks east of the Courthouse Square is a second B&B, the Hillsboro House, which has hardwood floors and a beveled glass entry door. The Warrens have done extensive renovation of their two-story Prairie-style home since it opened in mid-'96, including the addition of a second dining area, but plan even more.

Built in 1894, the Hillsboro House boasts a wraparound porch plus a private balcony adjoining the Yellow Room that has a queen-sized bed with wicker headboard and nightstand, a mirrored oak armoire, and bath with a five-foot claw-foot tub/shower. The Peach Room also has a queen canopy bed, while the Rose and Emerald Rooms have doubles. There is a king-sized bed with a knotted pine headboard in the King Room, which can be used as a suite with an adjoining sitting room. Light and airy, the latter has nine windows, a twin daybed and trundle bed. All guest rooms have ceiling fans and cable television. The Warrens hope you'll make their Hillsboro House your home, at least for a little while!

Tarlton House of 1895

Hosts: Tricia and Rick White, 211 N. Pleasant, Hillsboro 76645, 1 (800) 823-7216, (817) 582-7216, 8 guest rooms, 8 baths, country breakfast, $$$–$$$$, no pets, no smoking, MC, V, D, AE

Besides its beautiful ambience, the Tarlton House of 1895 now offers customized packages on stress relief (including a masseuse), golfing, food, fashion, murder mysteries, and more. Just let Tricia know what you have in mind. (It didn't take this London native long to learn what Texas hospitality is all about.)

One of the state's better known B&B's, the 7,000-square-foot Queen Anne Victorian has a dazzling oversized front door with 123 pieces of beveled glass that send rainbows of color cascading through the entryway when struck by the sun.

On both the National and Texas historical registries, the Tarlton House has 12-foot ceilings, East Texas pine floors, four gem-colored stained-glass windows, and seven coal fireplaces with hand-carved mantels and Italian tile trim. Furnished with luxurious oriental rugs, antiques, and collectibles, the three-story house has eight well-appointed guest rooms. All have king-sized beds except the Green Duck Loft, which has a double, and is often used with a king room as a suite. Breakfast is served at 9, but early risers enjoy drinking coffee on the swing and rocking chairs on the front porch.

The Tarlton House is only a few blocks from Bond's Alley, antique shops, and heralded historic courthouse, which has been rebuilt after being ravaged by a fire a few years ago. Near Hillsboro, also noted for the Southwest Outlet Mall, are two lakes, Aquilla and Whitney. The Lighthouse, a restaurant on a bluff at the latter, is popular with B&B guests wishing to make the short drive.

JEFFERSON

Gingerbread House and Honey-Do Inn

Hosts: Douglas and Norma Horn, 601 E. Jefferson Street, Jefferson 75657, (903) 665-8994, 1 guest room, 1 bath, 3 suites, full breakfast, $$, smoking only on porches, no pets, MC, V

Come spend one night or seven in the Horns' Gingerbread House and Honey-Do Inn in the Historic District overlooking Lions Park. Not as pricey as some of the other places around, the Honey-Do Inn has two appealing suites on the second floor with queen beds, and one on the first with a king bed. The larger upstairs suite has two bedrooms, a sitting area, a kitchenette, and a private bath.

Our favorite, though, is a lovely room in their home. The early Victorian walnut double bed has an ornate eight-foot-tall headboard that matches a marble-topped dresser and washstand. The room has an adjoining bath. Breakfasts are sumptuous at the Horns, and elegantly served on fine china and crystal. Their freshly baked gingerbread is still a special treat! It's the warm hospitality of the Horns themselves, however, that brings back guests time and again.

The renowned Jefferson Historical Museum opposite the famed Excelsior Hotel, which you can tour; restaurants like the Mint Tulip, the Bakery, and The Grove, and of course, the Stillwater Inn; and historical tours by boat, horse-drawn wagons, water, train, and trolley, and tons of antique shops, make Jefferson one of the state's most popular historical getaways year-round.

Kennedy Manor

Hosts: Mary Bill and Larry Royder, 217 W. Lafayette, Jefferson 75657, (903) 665-2528, fax (903) 665-6191, 6 guest rooms, 6 baths, gourmet breakfast, $$–$$$, no children under 10, no pets, no smoking, MC, V

Mary Bill seems to the Manor born. Though she and her husband only acquired what was known in recent years as Roseville Manor in 1996, she quickly showed she had the knack for making guests feel at home—and a true love for the house. Originally constructed as a one-story Greek Revival, the circa 1860 frame home's second story and wraparound porches were added about the turn of the century. Restored in 1989, the elegantly furnished B&B has wide porches, beautiful woodwork, ornate ceilings, and antique stained glass, along with a beautiful courtyard in back. (It's no wonder so many weddings and other functions are held here.)

In the Historic District, Kennedy Manor has two guest rooms downstairs and four more on the second floor, all with antiques, ceiling fans, a phone, and private bath. If you're an early riser, help yourself to coffee in the hospitality room, then join other guests at the banquet-sized dining room table for a sumptuous breakfast. A social hour each afternoon with refreshments is a chance to mingle, too. The library and parlor (feel free to play the grand piano or pump organ) are also yours to enjoy. Ask Mary Bill to tell you about the history of the house and why she chose Kennedy Manor as the name of her wonderful B&B.

Other outstanding B&Bs include the picturesque **Hale House,** 702 S. Line, (903) 665-8877, with six antique-furnished guest rooms and a gazebo, and **Cottonwood Inn,** 209 N. Market, (903) 665-2080.

The latter has wood-burning fireplaces, beautiful antiques, and a lot of charm. **The Terry McKinnon House,** a Gothic Revival charmer at 109 W. Henderson, has three guest rooms with queen beds and a fourth with a king (903) 665-1933. A reproduction designed in the Greek Revival style, **The Steamboat Inn,** 114 N. Marshall, (903) 665-8946, has a fireplace and claw-foot tub in each of the four spacious guest rooms, which are named for steamboats that docked in Jefferson. You'll also love **The Governor's House,** 321 N. Walnut, (800) 891-7933. Once owned by a Texas governor, the antique-furnished, Classic Greek Revival home's gourmet breakfast is served in style. Whatever you chose, you can hardly go wrong in Jefferson, which has more than 60 B&Bs!

McKay House

Innkeepers: Alma Anne and Joseph Parker, 306 E. Delta, Jefferson 75657, (903) 665-7322, or Book-A-Bed-Ahead (903) 665-3956, 3 suites, 4 guest rooms, all private baths, gourmet breakfast, $$–$$$$, no pets or smoking, MC, V

Jefferson has a lot of very special B&Bs, but none more so than the McKay House. You really feel a kinship with the past when you put on your Victorian nightgown and sleep shirt or wear a vintage hat to breakfast where Alma Anne tells historical tidbits about the town and the McKay House itself. Notables who have experienced the hospitality here include Lady Bird Johnson, *Roots* author Alex Hailey, and movie producer Martin Jurow, say owners Tom and Peggy Taylor, who did a great job on its restoration.

Built in 1851 by Dan Alley, Jefferson's co-founder, this restored Greek Revival cottage has both state and national markers. For 85 years, the house was occupied by the McKay family. McKay was a defense attorney in the famous "Diamond Bessie Murder Trial," which is reenacted during the Pilgrimage and home tour the first weekend in May.

Documented Schumacher wallpapers, an ornate 1880s staircase, fireplaces, and antique furnishings contribute to the McKay House mystique. Amenities include fresh flowers, lemonade, and homemade tea cakes. One second-floor suite with Eastlake furnishings and twin tubs and another with a step-down sitting area, oak furnishings, and a stained-glass skylight in the shower are especially inviting. Two more of the distinctive guest rooms are in the hundred-year-old Sunday House in back.

A delicious "Gentleman's Breakfast" is served in the glassed Conservatory. Guests rave about the food—and their stay at the magical McKay House, which was chosen "one of the ten most romantic inns in the USA" by a national publication.

The Captain's Castle

Hosts: Buck and Barbara Hooker, 403 E. Walker, Jefferson 75657, (800) 650-2330 or (903) 665-2330, 3 guest rooms, 3 baths, Carriage House, 3 rooms, private baths, and Cottage, 1 suite, private bath, full breakfast, $$–$$$, no pets or smokers, but children over 12 are welcome in the Carriage House, MC, V

Buck says Barbara is the captain; he is first mate!

One of Jefferson's most beautiful homes, Captain's Castle has a novel history. In the late 1870s, Captain Thomas J. Rogers, a Confederate officer and local banker, enlarged his one-story home (on Captain's Castle's present site) by adding an imposing landmark, a house built in Tennessee Planters-style architecture. Oxen pulled the huge house on log rollers from the waterfront across town. The added portion, supposedly, was one of Jefferson's most infamous bawdy houses during the town's river boat heyday.

Listed in the National Register of Historic Places, Captain's Castle also has a Texas Historical Medallion. The three guest rooms in the main house have sitting areas and period and European antiques. Muffins and coffee are brought to the rooms at 8 a.m., then a full breakfast is served at 9 in the dining room. Those who stay in the Carriage House (the three rooms have queen beds) or Cottage (it has a king and a daybed) breakfast in the glassed-in, temperature-controlled gazebo. There are TVs in all the rooms and swings and chairs on porches for guests' added enjoyment.

The Captain would be pleased!

Pride House

Hostesses: Carol Abernathy, Christel Frederick, 409 E. Broadway, Jefferson 75657, (903) 665-2675 or (800) 894-3526, 6 guest rooms, 6 baths, 1 guest cottage, gourmet breakfast, $$–$$$, no pets, children in the Dependency only, MC, V

Jefferson's pride and joy—one of them, anyway—is still the Pride House, a gabled Victorian home with original stained-glass windows in every room, ornate woodwork, and a wraparound porch. Furnished with Eastlake Victorian family treasures as well as other period pieces, the Pride House has a Texas Historical Marker. A back porch serves as a breakfast, game, and visiting center. Books, periodicals, and games are scattered everywhere.

The first bed and breakfast in Texas, Sandy Spalding restored the imposing two-story B&B, which was built in 1888, then sold the house to her mother, Ruthmary Jordan (her poached pears in cream and praline sauce are legendary). Its hospitable ambience continues, although Sandy now owns the house once again.

Oversized beds, eyelet pillow shams and dust ruffles, wonderful wallpaper, armoires, and pedestal lavatories contribute to the charm of the six guest rooms in the Pride House. The rooms have been renamed for the family's steamers that once were involved in Jefferson trade. Copies of the *S&D Reflector,* put out by the Sons & Daughters of Steamboat Pioneers, are in every room, while a massive ornate mirror from one of the steamers is in the parlor.

In back of the Pride House is the two-story Dependency, originally a two-room cottage for servants that has three guest rooms and one suite, with decors ranging from Victorian to a more country, primitive look. All have exterior entrances, porches or balconies, private baths, and a common kitchen with old-timey touches.

Find out for yourself why everyone fusses over the Pride House!

Near the Pride House at 203 E. Broadway is another outstanding bed and breakfast, the **Stillwater Inn,** which has gained acclaim for its superb restaurant as well. Bill Stewart was a sous-chef at the Adolphus Hotel in Dallas before he and Sharon brought fine dining to Jefferson in 1984.

Dramatically pitched ceilings, stained-glass windows, and skylights highlight the three upstairs guest rooms, which have queen beds, private baths, and TV. As you'd expect, the full breakfast is memorable, too. An adjoining cottage is also available if you prefer more privacy. (To accommodate groups, a carriage house now offers seated dining for 60.) Reservations: (903) 665-8415, fax (903) 665-8416.

The Seasons Guest House

Hosts: Kirby and Cindy Childress, 409 S. Alley St., P.O. Box 686, Jefferson 75657, (903) 665-1218, 3 suites, gourmet breakfast, $$$$, no pets, no smoking, MC, V

Touring the heralded House of the Seasons has long been a highlight for tourists to Jefferson. Built in 1872 when Jefferson was Texas' largest inland port, the gorgeous Greek Revival home, which is considered Victorian in style with certain Italianate characteristics, is renowned because of its cupola. Each wall contains a different color of stained glass, creating the illusion of a different season. Christmas tours of this unique home are especially popular.

Complimentary tours are given bed and breakfast guests who are served a full breakfast in the dining room. The three luxurious suites in the Seasons Guest House are in the reconstructed carriage house behind The House of the Seasons. Strikingly decorated with family antiques and heirlooms, they include private entrances, whirlpool tubs for two, and a TV. The Seasons Guest House is a guest house for all seasons.

Twin Oaks Country Inn

Hosts: Carol and Vernon Randle, P. O. Box 555, Hwy. 134, Jefferson 75657, (800) 905-7751, (903) 665-3535, fax (903) 665-1800, 5 guest rooms, 5 baths, 1 bungalow, hearty plantation breakfast, $$–$$$, no children under 12, no pets, no smoking, MC, V, D, AE

The Twin Oaks Plantation is another impressive home that is open for tours in addition to offering bed and breakfast lodging in separate quarters. On Hwy. 134 on the outskirts of Jefferson, the Randle's majestic Southern colonial home is actually a 26-year-old reproduction of an historic Mississippi plantation. Beautifully furnished with rare 18th- and 19th-century antiques and family heirlooms, it is on a Pre-Civil War Plantation site. (A Civil War-era well lined with a double wall of slave-made bricks is of interest on the grounds.)

In 1995, the Randles saved a Victorian home more than a century old in Marshall from the wrecking ball, and relocated it on their seven-acre site for a bed and breakfast. The restored Twin Oaks Country Inn has five elegant guest rooms with adjoining baths, private entries, and TV. A fully furnished poolside bungalow with a king-sized white iron bed and a large picture window is also available. (Watch the deer come up to graze.) A hearty plantation breakfast (a sausage and cheese casserole, apple dumplings, and cheese grits are menu samples) is served at 9 a.m. in the inn.

LAKE O' THE PINES

Holcomb Lodge

Innkeepers: Lex and Glenda Holcomb, 1211 Pine Hill Drive, Jefferson 75657, (903) 665-3236 or three Jefferson reservation services, 2 bedrooms, 1 bath, continental breakfast OYO, $$, no smoking, no pets, no cr

You might say this B&B is for the birds! A bird feeder and bird houses let feathered friends enjoy the place, too, and the bald eagle still winters at Lake O' the Pines. On a winding, tree-lined street, Holcomb Lodge is a half mile from a boat dock, park, fishing pier, beach, and two marinas on scenic Lake O' the Pines. Rent a boat (or bring your own), go water-skiing or swim, take hikes or bike around the lake. Because the bath is shared, the cabin would be reserved by one couple or family or friends. (A nominal fee is charged for more than two.) Both bedrooms have full beds, with a queen-sized sleeper sofa in the living room, which has a fireplace.

Owned by Lex's mom, Bobbie Holcomb (a good artist you'll discover), the 1,000-square-foot cabin has a long redwood deck in front with a swing, hammock, and grill. A picnic table is under some towering pine trees. Equipped with everything from pots and pans to bubble bath, Holcomb Lodge has central air and heat, a TV, radio, microwave, and dishwasher—all the comforts of home. And yes, bring the kids (we know they're well-behaved). Breakfast fixings will be in the refrigerator. Fresh catfish and homemade pies are specialties of a nearby restaurant, but many prefer going into Jefferson eight miles away for dinner.

McKenzie Manor

Hosts: Fred and Anne McKenzie, Woodland Shores, Route 1, Box 440, Avinger 75630, (903) 755-2240, or Book-A-Bed-Ahead, (800) 468-2627, 7 guest rooms, 6 baths, country breakfast, $$–$$$, no pets, smoking outside only, MC, V

Seventeen miles west of Jefferson, on the north shore of Lake O' the Pines, is a rustic rock lodge that is ideal for retreats, reunions, and receptions, as well as a scenic getaway for B&B buffs. McKenzie Manor, a family home for four generations, has seven bedrooms, a large meeting room, vaulted ceilings, a rock fireplace, and stained-glass windows. Most of the guest rooms have private entrances and balconies; all have private baths, sitting areas, lovely antiques, and family possessions. (Private suites are available.)

Relax in the gazebo or by the rock fireplace. Borrow a book from Fred, a historian, or perhaps read one he himself has written, *Avinger, Texas USA*. Nature trails beckon. Rent a canoe at a nearby marina or sign up for a boat tour of the lake. An airstrip is on the property only minutes away.

Leave time to visit with the McKenzies, by the way. Some say that's the best part of their visit here!

Another family home that welcomes bed and breakfast guests is in Jefferson at 201 S. Alley in the Historic District. The McKenzies' daughter, Carol Harrell and her husband, Paul, are the hosts of **Anne's Arbor,** a five-bedroom, restored Louisiana-style home that is ideal for families or couples traveling together. (One three-bedroom suite shares a bath.) For the business-minded, fax, phone, and copying facilities are available. Call (903) 665-3180 for reservations.

LAKE TEXOMA

Yacht-O-Fun

Hosts: Diana and Buddy Greer, P. O. Box 1480, Pottsboro 75076, (903) 786-8188, fax (903) 876-8288, 2 staterooms, 1½ baths, gourmet brunch, $$$$, no children, pets, or smoking, no cr

What could be more romantic than spending the night on the luxurious 51-foot Yacht-O-Fun, probably Texas' most unique B&B. The elegant master stateroom has a full bath with a tub, a queen-sized bed, and matching coverlet and curtains. At the opposite end of the sleek yacht is a guest room just big enough for the built-in three-quarters bed, a small closet, and tiny bathroom with a hand-held shower. The Greers also have a one-bedroom condo with a king bed, a queen sofa bed, and full kitchen at nearby Tanglewood Resort, if this is preferable. (They can even set you up with a round of golf there, if you wish.)

Your B&B adventure begins with an evening cruise around Lake Texoma. Buddy, a licensed Coast Guard captain, cuts the motor, and the yacht drifts silently beneath the star-studded sky. Moonlight casts an orange glow on the becalmed water while mood music adds to the unforgettable ambience.

Instead of anchoring on the open water, the boat docks at Loe's Highport Marina, which you can explore at night. The premier marina on Lake Texoma, Loe's has a cafe, volleyball and basketball courts, horseshoes, a piano bar and dance floor, and more. Tanglewood Resort has a first-rate restaurant and a club with a panoramic view of the marina.

Wake up aboard the Yacht-O-Fun to the aroma of brewing coffee. After again cruising around Lake Texoma, which has white cliffs, sandy beaches, and islands, Buddy heads for a secluded sandy cove where brunch is served. A former caterer, Diana's varied brunches might include canteloupe soup, seafood quiche, and twice-baked potatoes.

Willing to schedule any kind of cruise desired, for individuals and groups, from hot dog roasts on the sandy beach to day-long charters, the Greers particularly enjoy their B&B guests. And nothing beats being lulled to sleep by the water slapping against the fabulous Yacht-O-Fun!

MARSHALL

Heart's Hill

Hosts: Linda and Richard Spruill, 512 E. Austin St., Marshall 75670, (903) 935-6628, fax (903) 935-6932, 3 guest rooms, private baths, gourmet breakfast, carriage house, continental plus OYO, $$–$$$, no children, no pets, no smoking, no cr

With more than 150 turn-of-the-century homes, attractions like the famed Marshall Pottery and at least ten other potteries, the Michelson Reves Museum of Art, and Franks Doll Museum, Marshall has become one of East Texas' top tourist meccas. It also has some wonderful B&Bs like Heart's Hill!

A towering semi-circular turret with a pillared gallery gives Heart's Hill a dramatic look. Constructed in 1900, this elegant, antique-filled Victorian home has an inlaid floor in the turret parlor, hand-tooled fretwork over doors, fireplaces with original Italian tile, and other distinctive architectural features. Beautifully decorated, Heart's Hill has a romantic ambience. All three spacious upstairs rooms have fireplaces, and are off a large central hallway, where guests can watch TV, get a cup of coffee or soft drink, or just visit with each other. You can also relax in the sun room porch.

The Turret Room has an antique iron frame double bed, the Ivy Room has a king-sized canopy bed with a feather mattress, and the Sister's Room across the hall has antique twin beds. A spiral staircase leads to a loft bedroom and a sitting area in the carriage house, which also has a kitchenette, a bath with period fixtures, and private access to a brick patio with a spa. (The spa is available to all guests.) The Spruills cater special dinners and business functions at their beautiful home.

Remember to make your reservation early for the Wonderland of Lights Festival, but the Fire Ant Festival—a chili cook-off, an arts and crafts display, and a fire ant calling contest are highlights in October—and Stagecoach Days in May are other events that attract lots of tourists, much to the delight of B&Bs like Heart's Hill.

History House for Guests

Host: Anne Dennis, 308 W. Houston, Marshall 75670, (903) 938-9171, 2 guest rooms, 1 bath, continental breakfast OYO, $, no pets, no smoking, no cr

Anne Dennis has applied the same talent and creativity in decorating the History House for Guests as she has in the projects she has undertaken to promote her town. One of these projects is *Marshall Yesterday,* a historical review for children and adults, which Anne wrote, hand-lettered, and illustrated. Her holiday notepaper depicting carolers in front of the Harrison County Courthouse Museum during the Wonderland of Lights Festival is charming, too.

You'll have a grand view of the glowing courthouse and historic town square during this heralded festival from the balcony of this B&B, which is located above her husband's law offices in a quaint-looking, two-story home. Remember to make your reservation to stay here— or at any of the other bed and breakfasts in Marshall—during the holidays far in advance!

Located above her husband's law offices in a quaint-looking, two-story home, the History House has a Southwest decor. One guest room has a king-sized bed, and a second, two single beds, but up to six can be accommodated because the living room has a queen sleeper sofa. Breakfast fixings are in the refrigerator. Laundry facilities are also available, along with reading material and games.

Incidentally, during the Wonderland of Lights Festival, when the town is aglow with more than six million tiny white lights, you can even take carriage rides around the Courthouse or go ice skating on the outdoor rink on the square. Narrated bus tours of the light displays are available each evening from information centers. Candlelight home tours are held on Friday and Saturday evenings. It's a magical time in Marshall.

Three Oaks

Hosts: Laurie and Tony Overhultz, 609 N. Washington, Marshall 75670, (800) 710-9789, (903) 935-6777, 1 suite, 3 guest rooms, private baths, continental breakfast weekdays, full breakfast weekend, $$$, no pets, smoking only on porch, MC, V

Three Oaks is in the Ginocchio Historic District, next door to the home of Charles Ginocchio, who built the historic Ginocchio Hotel, which is famed for its magnificent curly pine staircase, and only one block from the hotel and the T&P Depot. The latter was saved from the wrecking ball because of the undaunted efforts of townspeople. If you have the time and inclination to arrive by rail, Amtrak comes to and through Marshall six days a week.

The ambience at Three Oaks is ideal for intimate weddings, small receptions, showers, luncheons, or formal dinners, as well as for bed and breakfast. Listed in the National Register of Historic Places, the 13-room Victorian home, which was built in 1895, still boasts the original leaded glass transoms, seven handcarved fireplaces, egg and dart trim, beamed ceilings, cut glass French doors, and gleaming oak flooring.

Handsomely embellished with fine period antiques that came up the Red River by steamboat, the B&B's ornate solid cherry Eastlake bedroom suite with red marble once belonged to ancestors of Paul G. Whaley, who built this Queen Anne gem. The massive bed has a headboard over six feet tall! The Victorian Room has both a king-sized bed and a double bed that are separated by lace privacy panels. Children are welcome at Three Oaks; there is a baby bed in the alcove adjoining the Ginocchio Room.

When refreshments are served in the afternoon, it's nice to sit a spell on the porch and to contemplate that the three towering burr oaks providing shade have grown from acorns brought from the old country!

Wisteria Garden

Hosts: Mary Lynn and John Vassar, 215 E. Rusk, Marshall 75670, (903) 938-7611, 5 guest rooms, 5 baths, full breakfast, $$, no pets unless in a carrier, smoking only on balconies and deck, MC, V, AE

This beautiful white, antique-filled three-story Queen Anne was the first house in Marshall to have gas and the second one to have electricity. Most of the light fixtures are originals. There are two verandas in front and two in back with swings, as well as a backyard deck and gazebo. Wisteria Garden is an appropriate name for this B&B, since a 100-year-old wisteria bush is entwined around two towering oak trees in front.

Formerly a B&B known as the Wood-Boone-Home, the previous owners found love letters—written between 1880 and 1884—in a metal box hidden in a wall during the home's renovation. Now in a scrapbook in the entry hall, the letters were written by Sam Wood and the love of his life, Mattie Calloway. Because Sam was a Yankee, her father was against their romance, but love prevailed, and they married in 1884, a month after he built the house. Two more stories were later added because their seven children needed more room. Either the Woods or their descendants owned the house until 1988.

The Wisteria Garden has beautiful furnishings, like the full French bed inlaid with brass, a 120-year-old queen-sized sleigh bed, and an eye-catching 12-foot dining room table that had been John's great-great grandfather's. An eight-drawer surveyor's chest for maps from John's family on display in the Eastlake Room is of special interest, too. All rooms have TV, but guests are welcome to watch TV or videos in the den. No one ever has to wait in line to use a bathroom here, since the Wisteria Garden has seven and a half bathrooms! If a downstairs bedroom is needed, a second parlor can be used.

The couple's hospitality is out to one and all, and they even have a baby bed on hand. A dietician who accommodates special diets, Mary Lynn enjoys catering and preparing candlelight dinners for special occasions upon request. Honeymooners are treated to breakfast in bed. Continental breakfasts and corporate rates are available for those in town on business. On weekends, breakfast is at 8:30, and Mary Lynn tells the history of the house and the family who lived there so long. As a special treat at night, cappuccino and dessert are served between 8:30 and 9. She and John enjoy their guests, and you'll enjoy them!

McKINNEY

Dowell House c. 1870

Hosts: Fred and Diane Mueller, 1104 S. Tennessee, McKinney 75069, 1 (800) 373-0551, or phone and fax (972) 562-2456 (Dallas Metro), 2 guest rooms, 2 baths, continental breakfast (weekdays), full (weekends), $$, no children under 12, no pets, no smoking inside, no cr

Ask almost anyone in town for directions to "the Benji House" and you'll find yourself at this appealing bed and breakfast. Part of the first Benji movie was filmed in the Dowell House c. 1870 about 20 years ago, primarily in the great hall, which has hardwood floors, handmade lighting fixtures of solid brass and etched glass, and 12-foot ceilings. Focal points are a dramatic staircase with elaborately paneled wainscoting, an oak pump organ, and an Eastlake-style secretary containing a cobalt glass collection.

On an acre-and-a-half corner lot, the huge colonial blue Federal-style house is even more appealing because of an apple tree, a hammock, a two-seat swing, glassed-in sun porch, and an adjoining deck. Relax a bit. The Peach Room, which has a queen bed, a white marble-hearthed fireplace, turn-of-the-century furniture, and half bath, shares a tub/shower with the airy yellow room across the hall. Amenities include thick terry robes and toiletries. A fax and phone are available.

You'll be welcomed with a glass of wine, champagne, or mineral water. Breakfast is served on fine china and crystal in the formal dining room, which has a Czechoslovakian crystal chandelier similar to one in the living room. The floor is laid in an "everlasting square" parquet pattern of alternating oak and walnut planks.

The Muellers happily host weddings, receptions, mystery dinners, and other functions. (Ask about Ladies' Getaway Weekends.) McKinney is noted for its antique and outlet shops, chocolate chip pie at the Pantry, Chestnut Square (a collection of historic homes), and laid-back charm.

Two or three blocks from Chestnut Square is another bed and breakfast, **The Bingham House,** at 800 S. Chestnut, which opened in 1996. Bill and Karen Lynch have four guest rooms with private baths, a gazebo, and hot tub and serve a full plantation breakfast. Built in 1883, the two-story L-shaped Italianate Georgian wood house has eight double sets of double columns 25 feet high and a unique cantilevered front balcony that has no obvious support. It was on the '96 Christmas Tour of Homes. Contact the Lynches at (972) 529-1883.

MINEOLA

Fall Creek Farm

Hosts: Mike and Carol Fall, Rt. 3, Box 289D, Mineola 75773, (903) 768-2449, fax (768-2079), 3 suites, 2 rooms, 2 private baths, full breakfast buffet, $$–$$$, no pets, no smoking indoors, MC, V

To appreciate the warmth and charm of this 10-acre Piney Woods retreat, which is seven miles north of Mineola (near Quitman), you have to see the inside! Carol has done a splendid job of mixing and matching unusual fabrics and colors. It's light, bright, airy, and warm—and quite a surprise, because the two-story brick and frame house itself, which was built in 1980, is rather traditional. There are lots of delightful areas to just sit and relax, especially the sunny sitting room that has a striking black and white diamond-patterned floor and papered ceiling and walls; it's just off the big open kitchen.

Staying here is perfect not only for couples, but for two to four friends traveling together, since all of the rooms and suites have two (or more) beds—and personality-plus, just like Carol. One spacious room with two queen-sized beds has a balcony that overlooks the countryside. There is a pool and hot tub in back along with a pavilion under a huge old oak tree where you can picnic or swing. If you like to fish, Lake Fork is 10 minutes away. Groups up to 20 can be accommodated.

Lott Home Cottages

Hosts: Mark and Sharon Chamblee, 311 E. Kilpatrick, Mineola 75773, (903) 569-0341, 2 cottages, full breakfast, $$$, no small children, no pets, no smoking, MC, V, D

Mark and Sharon Chamblee, who have a beautiful B&B in Tyler (the Bed of Roses Country Inn), fell in love with the Lott Home and are meticulously restoring their "dream house," which will eventually have rooms for bed and breakfast guests as well. Built in 1918, the two-story Prairie-style home was bought ten years later by Howard and Vivian Lott, who were instrumental in the growth of Mineola and Wood County. Behind the Lott house is the original two-story carriage house, which has been converted into upper and lower cottage suites.

Miss Vivian's Canning Room is a romantic suite with a Grecian Jacuzzi tub for two and a gas log fireplace. The suite includes the original antique iron bed that belonged to the Lotts. Equally charming, the second floor Garden Gate suite has the original pine floors, a footed tub, and a balcony with wooden rockers. Both suites have TVs, period furnishings, queen-sized beds, small refrigerators stocked with juices and snacks, and cozy kitchens where you'll breakfast, unless you prefer eating in the dining room of the Lott house.

The lovely grounds include a patio with an outdoor fireplace, where you can roast marshmallows in cold weather. Fresh roses (in season) upon arrival is a special amenity provided by the hosts, who have a garden center, Chamblee's Rose-Arama, in Tyler. Ask about special packages.

Munzesheimer Manor

Hosts: Bob and Sherry Murray, 202 N. Newsom, Mineola 75573, (903) 569-6634, 7 guest rooms, 7 baths, 2 cottages, gourmet family-style breakfast, $$–$$$, no pets or smoking, MC, V, D

Come meet the Murrays and enjoy the hospitality of Munzesheimer Manor! Easier to pronounce than to spell, Munzesheimer Manor is a Princess Anne-style structure that is ideal for a respite from the workaday world—and special events such as weddings. English and American antiques abound in the 17-room inn, which includes seven fireplaces (three are in guest rooms) with exquisite mantels, high ceilings, bay windows, and a wraparound porch.

Built of cedar and pine at the turn of the century by a German immigrant for his bride, the 4,000-square-foot Victorian home has two parlors, a formal dining room, and lots of charm. Most of the guest rooms have queen or full beds. Besides the four guest rooms in Munzesheimer Manor, two more rooms are in a cottage (the Home Terminal), which is furnished with memorabilia commemorating Mineola's roots as a railroad town. Another cottage is the Tack Room, which includes a hayloft, now a raised bathing platform. Once the site of a horse stable, it is popular with bridal couples because of its feather bed.

Victorian gowns and nightshirts are provided by these special hosts, along with fresh flowers, turn down with chocolate mints, and custom soaps. And how about German pancakes, blueberry or pear soup, and morning glory muffins for breakfast?

If you're in Mineola on Saturday night, take in John DeFoore's Piney Woods Pick'n Parlor, which offers live musical concerts by performers like Ray Wylie Hubbard, The Dixie Chicks, and Alan Dameron. The Pick'n Parlor is on the third-floor ballroom of a nearby local landmark, the restored **Beckham Hotel,** which also contains a full-service restaurant, antique shops, an art gallery, and several period suites and rooms. (A continental breakfast is provided.)

Noble Manor

Hosts: Rick and Shirley Gordon, 411 E. Kilpatrick, Mineola 75773, (903) 569-5720, fax (903) 569-0472, 9 guest rooms, 9 baths, Brooks House, Cupid's Cottage, full breakfast, $$–$$$, no smoking, no pets, MC, V, AE

This 19-room Greek Revival mansion was begun in 1910, but took three years to complete, the same length of time it took for its restoration and refurbishment! Resplendent once again, Noble Manor has gleaming hardwood floors, vintage chandeliers, a grand entrance hall, antique furnishings, and an elegant ambience. A wraparound porch on the second floor has comfortable seating. There are three luxurious suites and two rooms in Noble Manor itself, all with private baths.

The Brooks House nearby has three more suites, two with two-person Jacuzzi tubs and the third, with a claw-foot tub. Each has a private entry. Ten can be comfortable here. Nestled under the trees, not far from the main house, is a pink and white Cupid's Cottage, with a fenced yard and hot tub. Once a servant's quarters, the refurbished little house has a tin roof, stained-glass windows, his and hers claw-foot tubs, and antique cherub light fixtures. A queen-sized, hand-carved cherub sleigh bed from the 1800s is striking. Breakfast is a four-course feast!

The Homestead

Hosts: Margaret and Douglas Hoke, 123 N. Line, Mineola 75773, (903) 569-9913, 3 guest rooms, 2 shared baths, full breakfast, $–$$, no children, no pets, no smokers, no cr

Ancient pecan trees tower over this turn-of-the-century Queen Anne-style home, which has a turreted roof, multiple gables, a wraparound veranda, and second-floor porches. Used as a rooming house for railroad men in the 1930s, the Homestead has two historical markers. The grounds are lovely and yours to enjoy (and perfect for parties or weddings, too), with daylily gardens and gazebos. There is a goldfish pond in the North Garden, where a house once stood that was the birthplace of Governor Jim Hogg's only daughter, Ima.

A divided stairway with huge, hand-carved newel posts is the focal point of the L-shaped entry hall. The three guest rooms are upstairs and have elaborate chintz canopy bed and window treatments. One bathroom with a vintage tub is upstairs; a second bath is downstairs. Guests are called to breakfast by a brass dinner bell. Breakfast is usually served in the large formal dining room, or in the butler's pantry by candlelight on a honeymoon or anniversary.

Mineola, which traces its roots to 1873, when the Texas & Pacific Railroad became the first line to pass through the area, is about 25 miles north of Tyler and a half hour from Canton. Mineola has lots of antique shops, a little theater, and a tearoom. Kitchens Hardware is widely known for its sandwiches and ambience.

MOUNT PLEASANT

Gardenside Bed & Breakfast

**Hosts: Jim and Nadene Capel, Rt. 7, Box 695,
Mount Pleasant 75455, (903) 575-9000, 2-room guest house,
Hollywood bath, full breakfast, $, no pets, children 13 and older,
smoking outside only, MC, V**

From a green-and-white elevated wooden deck in the courtyard, the hilltop colonial-style guest cottage overlooks Tankersley Lake and Gardens, which the Capels formerly owned. (In fact, this B&B used to be called Tankersley Gardens.) You can still tour the lush five-acre garden, which even has a lovely chapel with ornate oak pews, stained-glass windows, and antique pump organ. Some couples marry there, then start their honeymoon in the B&B next door.

Separated from the main house by a patio and pool, the comfortable furnished cottage has queen-sized beds, a sitting room with a microwave, refrigerator, TV and phone. Though the guest rooms share the tub and shower, each has its own commode and lavatory. Unless traveling with friends, you'll have the place to yourselves.

A goodie basket, soft drinks, and coffee are furnished. If you want privacy, a continental breakfast will be brought to you on a tray, but many guests enjoy eating in the garden room of the Capels' home, where a more sumptuous breakfast includes frozen fruit slush and fancy egg scramble.

Picturesque area lakes and state parks offer some of the best fishing and water recreation around. In Mount Pleasant, Antiques and Uniques (home of the Main Street Bakery, which makes the acclaimed Laura's Cheesecakes), Walker's (a gift shop and restaurant), and Sincerely Yours (a catalog outlet store with a tea room and bakery) are attention getters.

MOUNT VERNON

Miss Ikie's

Hosts: Bob and Ikie Richards, 110 Oak St., Mount Vernon 75457, (903) 537-7002, 1 suite, 5 guest rooms, 4 private baths, 1 shared bath, 1 guest house, full breakfast, $$–$$$, no children, no pets, no smoking, MC, V

The origin for the catchy name of this outstanding B&B is readily apparent because Ikie and her husband, Bob, are your hosts. Known also as the Dutton-Teague house (both the Duttons and Teagues were among early owners) and built in 1882, Miss Ikie's has been lovingly restored and furnished with family heirlooms. You'll enjoy the interesting hosts, who have traveled around the world while working on international flights for American Airlines. Bob was a pilot until retiring recently; Ikie is still an international flight attendant, but has plenty of time to devote to their guests.

On two-and-a-half acres, the Prairie-style home has a covered veranda across the front and side, hardwood floors, and lots of stained glass. You can watch TV in the sitting room or enjoy the landscaped grounds. A white picket fence wraps around part of the couple's property, including a pond and a gazebo under a cluster of huge oak trees. Besides a spacious suite, which contains a desk, writing table and a fireplace, and the five guest rooms in the main house, the Richards have a one-story guest house with two bedrooms, two baths, a fully furnished kitchen, and a parlor across the street. Although it has a Victorian look, it is not a historic home. Breakfast is across the way at Miss Ikie's, unless you prefer otherwise. French toast and quiche are among breakfast favorites, but the hosts are happy to fill special requests. Talented Bob even might play a tune on the 10-foot concert piano that was imported from Russia.

Miss Ikie's is two blocks from the quaint town square, where you'll find an old-fashioned soda shop, plus antique, craft, and collectible shops. Considered the gateway to the beautiful Tri-Lakes area and midway between Dallas and Texarkana, Mount Vernon has gained fame of sorts for being the boyhood home of "Dandy" Don Meredith.

MUENSTER

Fischerhaus B&B

Host: Louise Fisher, 223 N. Oak, Muenster 76252, (817) 759-4211, 2 bedroom cottage, 1 bath, continental breakfast OYO, $–$$, no pets, no smoking, MC, V, D

Muenster prides itself on its German heritage and Texas hospitality, and you'll experience both at this B&B, which is just around the corner from Fischer's Market, also owned by the host's husband and brother. In fact, you'll make your B&B reservations through Fischer's Market, which has acquired a clientele from around the state for its hot German sausage, cheese, and apple strudel since established in 1926.

Originally located on Main Street, the Fischerhaus was used as a shoe and harness shop in the early 1890s, and more recently, a restaurant and gift shop. Cheerful and quaint, the cozy little restored cottage includes a living room, a bath with shower, and a kitchen/family area with a microwave. Rented to only one family at a time (or friends), one bedroom has a queen bed, the other, twin beds.

Located about an hour or so from the Dallas/Fort Worth Metroplex and near the Oklahoma border, Muenster celebrates its heritage with Germanfest (the last full weekend in April), while Christkindlmarkt (Thanksgiving weekend) draws thousands as well. However, because of its German food and the fact that a few of its restored buildings are now filled with antiques, Hummels, local crafts, and other collectibles,

Muenster is being "discovered" as a year-round weekend destination. Playing a round or two at Turtle Hill Golf Course eight miles from town might be an option during your stay.

Ten minutes from Muenster at 300 S. Main in **Saint Jo,** one of the historic towns on the Chisholm Trail, is a reasonably priced bed and breakfast with an entirely different ambience. Built in 1914, the stately two-story, antique-furnished **Main Street B&B** has large porches, a number of fireplaces, two suites, three rooms that share two baths, and a colorful host. Rhoda enjoys her guests, and you'll enjoy her. Call her at (817) 995-2127.

PALESTINE

"Semi-Famous" Bailey Bunkhouse

Hosts: Jan and Bill Bailey, Rt. 7, Box 7618, Palestine 75801, (903) 549-2028 or (903) 549-2059, 2 guest rooms, 1 loft, 1 bath, continental breakfast OYO, $, smoking outside, no cr

Ideal for family or friends (children are welcome; pets, too, but not encouraged), this 1,400-square-foot, two-story rustic retreat looks like an old-fashioned barn. Located on 28 acres eight miles north of Palestine off Texas Highway 155 toward Tyler, the Dutch-style cabin has two downstairs rooms with double beds and an upstairs loft that can sleep five or more comfortably. The latter has twin beds and a full-sized trundle bed, with another trundle mattress underneath, and there is even room for bedrolls. The line forms to the rear for the lone bathroom, but there is also a shower in the utility room.

With ceiling fans, a dishwasher, microwave, appliances, and TV, the Bailey Bunkhouse has every comfort you could wish for, and countless mementos of the past. Wait till you see the trophies, which include a bear, a javelina, and a wolf's head! Bill's brother, Bob (he and his wife, Carlene, are co-owners of the spread) killed the three-legged wolf in their back pasture. Both couples live nearby if needed, but privacy is the keynote.

Stay for a weekend or a week, but bring groceries. Palestine, famed for its Dogwood Trails Festival, is only minutes away, so you can go in for dinner or to ride the historic 25-mile Texas State Railroad that travels to Rusk and back. For groups of eight or more, your hosts will include a hay ride!

Wiffletree Inn

Hosts: Steve and Jan Frisch, 1001 North Sycamore, Palestine 75801, (903) 723-6793, 4 rooms, two with private baths, full breakfast, $$, no pets, no children, smoking in restricted areas, special packages need advance reservations, cr

A Victorian home built in 1911 in a town packed with the greatest number of Victorians per capita in the state, the Wiffletree Inn is a not-stuffy house. In fact, it sports a little whimsy here and there, which is bound to bring joy into your life. Example: Hostess Jan Frisch loves pansies, so you'll find them just about everywhere, including the name of their dog (Pansy Eileen Wiffle) and a room totally designed around the Eileens in the family and the pansies they love. Pansies show up in the morning during season on your breakfast plate, just for the fun and beauty of it. On a more serious side, the Frisches are renown for their murder mystery getaways, which include hors d'oeuvres, dinner, the mystery and the night with a hearty breakfast the next morning, or they can arrange a "Walk-around Palestine Murder Mystery," for four couples who want an unusual, but delightful weekend sleuthing through Palestine. For the more traditional, the porch is relaxing or you can take a train ride on the Texas State Railroad. Remember, too, Palestine is known for its dogwoods in the early Spring.

PITTSBURG

Carson House Inn and Grille

Hosts: Eileen and Clark Jesmore, 302 Mt. Pleasant St., Pittsburg 75686, (903) 856-2468, 5 guest rooms, 4 private baths, 1 shared, railroad car (2 rooms), choice of full or continental breakfast or a discounted room rate, $–$$$, children welcome, pets ok with prior approval, smoking in section of restaurant, all cr

The Tri-Lakes area is becoming increasingly popular, and why not? Its lakes are among the state's most scenic, with great fishing and recreational facilities, while towns like Pittsburg have craft and antique shops, good restaurants, historic homes, and more that draw tourists year round. Pittsburg also has a number of Christmas tree farms in the area.

One of Pittsburg's historic homes is both a restaurant and a B&B. Yellow, with burgundy and green trim, the Victorian Gothic frame house has rare curly pine wood (now extinct) on the stairs and woodwork and some chandeliers and fixtures that were original to the house. Mementos of the family who lived in the house for more than a century are on display. Over 115 years old, the Carson House Inn's Grille is on the first floor, while five guest rooms are upstairs, most with queen-sized beds, but one with a king adjoins a room with twin beds. Terry robes are provided for those who use the hall bath. TVs and coffee makers are in all the rooms; complimentary soft drinks, coffee, tea, and juice are in a special refrigerator for overnight guests.

In back of the inn is a hot tub, a patio, and a fish pond, along with a vintage railroad car with two small Victorian rooms with private baths. The railroad car was added, not because of the nearby railroad tracks, but as a historical tribute. A long-time owner of the house had a minority interest in a rail line.

Open to the public for lunch and/or dinner seven days a week, the Grille's diverse menu includes everything from chicken-fried steak and seafood to sandwiches, along with a daily salad and soup bar and an all-you-can-eat Sunday buffet. Beer, wine, and specialty drinks are also available.

Holman House

Hosts: Dan Blake and Rebecca Wolfe, 218 N. Texas St., Pittsburg 75686, (903) 856-7552, (800) 903-5033, 5 guest rooms, 5 baths, full breakfast, $$, smoking only on the balcony, no pets, MC, V

The Holman House Bed & Breakfast (formerly Texas Street B&B) was built in 1913 by a prominent merchant, John M. Holman. Six generations of his family lived in the 6,000-square-foot Greek Revival house for over 75 years. The second-floor walls are lined with pictures of early day Pittsburg and the Holman family, including one that shows Texas Street as a dirt road.

Within walking distance of downtown Pittsburg, the cheerful-looking B&B has green and peach colors on the walls and natural pine floors. On the first floor is the spacious master suite, which has a canopied king bed, a sitting area in front of the fireplace, and a bath with a claw-foot tub. A wide staircase leads up to four more handsomely appointed guest rooms, each with period furniture and private baths, some with claw-foot tubs. One room has a king-sized bed, another, a full bed, and the rest, queen.

Rebecca's souffles and quiches, homemade breads, and seasonal fruits are highlights of breakfast, which is served in the formal dining room between 8 and 10. Coffee, juice, and breads are in the guest pantry for early risers. The Holman House is available for corporate conferences and social functions.

The hosts can point the way to Bo Pilgrim's Prayer Tower, Pittsburg's famed Hot Links Restaurant, and Warrick's. The latter not only has tasty catfish and steaks, but a giant replica of the bizarre-looking Ezekiel Airship, which supposedly flew (briefly) in 1902, a year before the Wright Brothers. The Northeast Texas Rural Heritage Center Museum in the restored railroad depot and the Farm Museum are interesting, too.

Staying at the **Guest House at Lake Bob Sandlin** seven miles from Pittsburg is another inviting option where you can really enjoy some beautiful sunsets! On the banks of a quiet cove, the comfortable two-bedroom (queen beds), one bath Piney Woods retreat includes a deck overlooking the lake, a "great" room with high ceilings, a fully equipped kitchen, and a two-slip boat house, along with a pool table, dart board, and TV. Three camp cots with padded mattresses are also available, if you want to bring your children. You'll have the place to yourself, but your hosts, Tom Tinkle and his wife, Lexie McGrane, will give you a warm Texas welcome! Traveling the back country roads is easier if you arrive before dark. Phone and fax (800) 365-3899 or Bed & Breakfast Texas Style (972) 298-8586.

ROCKWALL

Barton on Boydstun

Hosts: Lindy and Edie Barton, 505 E. Boydstun, Rockwall 75087, (972) 661-4350, 3 guest cottage suites, full breakfast OYO, $$$, no children, no pets, smoking outside only, MC, V, AE

Located in the heart of Rockwall on two wooded acres, the Bartons' art center and small, but elegant art gallery long have been a magnet for those interested in art or private instruction or workshops on painting, drawing, sculpture and stone carving. (It's worth visiting just to see the magnificent pieces sculpted by Lindy.) This creative couple have added three inviting guest cottage suites for B&B buffs. Each has a tin roof, a screen porch, ten-foot ceilings, full bath, original paintings and bronzes from their fine art gallery, and an elegant decor.

Both the Avila, with its Spanish Colonial ambience, and the romantic Browning Suites, furnished with pine antiques and quilts, have a queen bed in the master bedroom and a queen sofa in the living room and a mini kitchen. Poets Harbor has a full kitchen, but only sleeps two in the master bedroom, which has a queen bed. All the suites are stocked with fresh fruit, a breakfast casserole, and assorted breads and jams, along with special coffees and herbal tea. (Stay in mid-week, and the third night is free!)

Another special place on the property is the rustic Bois d'arc Chapel, which is available for small weddings (it seats 40), retreats, and other functions.

Relax in the hammock and birdwatch or enjoy the many attractions of Rockwall, including three marinas on Lake Ray Hubbard, one of the world's premier inland sailing lakes; the Buffalo Creek Golf Club, a championship rated public fee course ranking among the top ten in Texas; and the Texas Queen, a paddle-wheeler offering live entertainment and dinner cruises, and much, much more. Only 25 miles east of Dallas, just off IH 30, Rockwall is a jewel.

Stafford House

Hosts: Kay and Michael E. Stafford, 406 Star Street, Rockwall 75087, (972) 771-2911, (888) 207-7716, fax (972) 722- 3013, 3 rooms, 2 baths, 1 suite, country breakfast, $$, MC, V, AE

Another inviting B&B that opened in 1996 in Rockwall is the Stafford House, which has a shaded lawn and patio. Built in 1850, it is older than Rockwall! All three guest rooms are on the first floor and wheelchair accessible; they have full antique beds. Rene's Room and Terry's Room share a hallway bath; Amy's Room has its own private bath.

A spiral staircase leads from the den to the suite, which has a frosted windowed door with a large rose etched in the glass, muted rose wallpaper, and lace curtains decorated with roses. Called the Rose Suite, it has a fireplace, an antique, footed tub in one corner, and a sitting room/kitchenette. An antique drop-leaf table is next to a large window that overlooks the spacious "gathering" room, which is the only room smoking is permitted. A copier and fax are available. Sausage-cheese quiche and hot brandied fruits are among specialties, but a country breakfast is still the favorite. Your bedtime snack will be special breads.

The Staffords can tell you all about Rockwall's mysterious rock wall, which you have to see, and give you a ton of tips on what to do in this recreation-oriented area. Taking one of the cruises on the *Texas Riverqueen* is an option. The Stafford House is within walking distance to Goliad Place.

ROYCE CITY

Country Lane

Hosts: James and Annie Cornelius, Blockdale Drive, Rt. 2, Box 94B, Royce City 75189, (800) 240-8757, (972) 636-2600, fax (972) 635-2300, 4 guest rooms, 4 baths, full breakfast, $–$$$, smoking outdoors only, no pets, MC, V, AE

Country Lane, eight miles east of Lake Ray Hubbard on a farm road near IH 30, is just a great place to relax, and the hosts are interesting. This '50s-style farmhouse has all the modern conveniences you could want, yet it definitely is in the country. Each guest room is decorated with antiques, art work, and memorabilia in tribute to a film star. (The dramatic Mae West Room with its mirrored ceiling fan and beaded curtains is a favorite.) Two of the rooms have whirlpool tubs (one is big enough for two people). A full breakfast is served in the Fireside Room or, if requested, in your room. Candlelight dinners, lunches, and special packages can also be arranged. No charge for children under 12.

Sit in a rocker on the porch and watch the heron and egret land on the pond, or jump in the car to go antiquing in Forney and Canton. Nearby Rockwall offers a world of shopping, particularly Goliad Place, which even has a wedding chapel, and some great places to eat, while Downtown Dallas is only 30 miles away.

RUSK

Cherokee Rose

Host: Suzann McCarty, 708 Lone Oak Street, Rusk 75785, (903) 683-6322 or (903) 683-4242, 3 rooms with baths, OYO breakfast, $$, no smoking, accommodates children, TV with cable, no phone, no cr

A reconstruction of two houses into a dogtrot cabin offers all the modern amenities with yesteryear's charm. Although the cabin's located on the road just a half a mile west of the Texas State Railroad park, it provides the quiet of almost 11 acres of whispering pines, with a chickenhouse (from which to collect morning eggs, should you wish) and a porch with rustic cedar furniture to enjoy the country evening. Handmade furniture and a cute decor inside add to the fun of this B&B. A gazebo on the lake, which is stocked with catfish you can either catch or feed, and hiking trails around the property add to its desirability. The owner lives off-premise, so you have the place to yourself. She provides sausage biscuits, sweet rolls, fresh fruit, and other goodies for breakfast. Everyone recommends eating at the Main Street Crossing, a store/restaurant on the corner of Main Street, which surprises you with its mixture of old-store decor and its superlative food. You must make reservations by 3:00 p.m. for dinner Saturdays; otherwise, stop by for lunch.

The Gables

Hosts: Jerry and Kay Jordan, 415 Main Street, Rusk (903)-683-5641, 3 suites, TV/VCR and video library, all with private baths, no smoking, full gourmet breakfast, $$–$$$, no children, no pets, no cr

Surely one of the most beautifully decorated Victorians in the state, The Gables offers you not only a huge, luxurious suite in which to stay, but also the parlor and the library and the dining room, which features a table Jerry constructed from old wall panels, among other things. Perhaps that's one of the greatest charms of the house; it contains surprises everywhere: a sewing machine that has been turned into a lamp;

antlers in a wreath, shaving brushes in Brill Cream in the bathrooms, old hats and quilts just draped over pieces of furniture, a doll house in a closet that becomes a child's playroom, collections you admire and others that make you smile. The breakfast is definitely another one of its charms: blackberry-stuffed French toast, apple dumplings, southwestern bread—just a few of the gourmet items. Hostess Kay grew up in Rusk and her love for the town is not only reflected in the care she and her husband have taken in restoring and decorating this magnificent house, it's evident in her enthusiasm about the town. She calls it a "nurturing place, with great people." You know you've met two of them when you stay at The Gables.

SHERMAN

Hart's Country Inn

Hosts: Jim and Rhay Blevins, 601 N. Grand Ave., Sherman 75090, (903) 892-2271, 4 guest rooms, 4 baths, country breakfast, $, no pets, no smoking, no cr

Though built by three doctors as a hospital—Sherman's first—in 1898, this Victorian home soon sold, first to one family, then a second, who kept it until 1988, when the Blevins bought it. Rhay, a Sherman native, and her husband restored the two-story home for a bed and breakfast.

Across the street from Austin College, Hart's Country Inn has one room with a king bed, and the rest, double beds. Full-ceiling canopied beds and hand-crafted quilts, period wallpaper and unusual fabrics, and antiques convey warmth and charm. Family photographs plus primitive art and floral oils done by Rhay are a nice touch. Guests are treated to freshly baked banana nut bread when they arrive. The aroma fills the air.

The Red River Historical Museum in the 1914 Carnegie Library, the Old Sherman Opera House, and the Heritage Row of Homes are among this North Texas town's many attractions, along with antique shops and Kelly Square. The latter includes an art museum, all kinds of shops, a bakery and restaurants. Lake Texoma and the Grayson County Frontier Village at Loy Lake are other area treasures.

STEPHENVILLE

The Oxford House

Hosts: Paula and Bill Oxford, 563 N. Graham, Stephenville 76401, (817) 965-6885, or Bed & Breakfast Texas Style, (972) 298-8586, 4 guest rooms, 4 baths, gourmet breakfast, $–$$, children 6 and over welcome, no pets, smoking in specified areas, MC, V, AE

Ever since it was built by Judge Oxford for only $3,000 over 100 years ago, the Oxford House has stayed in the same family. Framed pictures, dolls, dishes, musical instruments, and other family memorabilia are displayed in this picturesque landmark. Within walking distance of Stephenville's downtown shops and courthouse, the pale blue Victorian gem has a lot of gingerbread, spacious porches, and a cupola.

An 1890s sleigh bed, marble-top dressers, beveled glass mirrors, and antique armoires are in the inviting second-floor guest rooms. Bubble bath, special soaps, and fresh flowers are among amenities in the private baths that originally were fireplaces, then closets. The baths have claw-foot tubs and brass fixtures. The bridal suite is also referred to as Aunt Mandy's room. (She used to visit for long periods in days of old, and supposedly was a real pill who demanded to be waited on hand and foot.) A downstairs room can be used for guests as well, and cots are available for children six and over.

A welcoming glass of wine or brandy, a bedtime mint or snack, and Paula's breakfast specialties such as pears cooked in wine sauce and poppy seed muffins contribute to the Oxford House mystique. Candlelight dinners, high teas, and catered functions such as wedding receptions and reunions are available, along with honeymoon and anniversary packages.

The Oxford House even has vintage jewelry, Caswell Massey soaps, handmade items, jellies, jams, and more that you can purchase as a memento of your stay.

TEAGUE

Hubbard House Inn

Hosts: John W. Duke, 621 Cedar Street, Teague 75860, (817) 739-2629 and (817) 562-2496, 6 suites, 4 baths, country breakfast, $, smoking on porches only, all cr

The imaginative ways John has woven artificial flowers into the decor and the dining room table made from a glass-topped ornate, vintage Tiffany pool table help make the 29-room Hubbard House one of Texas' more novel B&Bs.

The three-story burgundy and white frame Georgian home's spacious guest rooms have plush burgundy carpet, king-sized beds, cable TV, and overlook gardens or a beautiful old church with lighted stained-glass windows. A second-floor balcony with old-fashioned porch swings is a relaxing retreat. "Carefully supervised children" can be accommodated at the Hubbard House, which has family suites as well as a bridal suite. The inn is handicapped accessible.

Built from 1903-1907 as the Hubbard House Hotel, the house deteriorated through the years, then was restored extensively by John in 1991. He had 12 guests his first night open, and has been busy ever since, especially hosting noon and evening banquets. (John is a jim-dandy cook and even makes great jelly.)

Located 55 miles east of Waco, Teague draws a lot of business travelers who have been discovering the Hubbard House Inn. The town also boasts a summer rodeo, the B&RI Railroad museum, and Bodine's, the world's largest junk shop.

TEXARKANA

Mansion on Main

Hosts: Inez and Lee Hayden, 802 Main, Texarkana 75501, (903) 792-1835, fax (903) 793-0878 or Book-A-Bed-Ahead Reservation Service, (903) 665-3956, 5 guest rooms, 5 baths, 1 suite, gourmet breakfast, $–$$$, no pets, smoking only on veranda and balcony, MC, V

The restored Mansion on Main is as impressive as the McKay House, one of the finest B&Bs in Jefferson, which Tom and Peggy Taylor own as well. A 1895 neoclassic/Southern colonial with 22-foot columns that were salvaged from the Saint Louis World's Fair, the Mansion on Main has period wallpapers, antique furnishings, hard pine floors, stained glass, original gas light fixtures in the kitchen—and a Texas Medallion.

The first-floor Governor's Suite (it is handicapped accessible) and the Honeymoon or Anniversary Penthouse stand out. (Wait until you see the old-fashioned footed his-and-hers tubs, which are toe to toe in the latter's bath.) Two of the five guest rooms have access to a balcony. B&B devotees who have stayed at the McKay House will recognize some of the same special touches, such as the beautiful photo albums in each room and the hall tree with vintage hats on the second floor.

The gourmet "Gentleman's Breakfast," always a treat, may include asparagus strata eggs or chicken a la Mansion. (From New Orleans, resident innkeeper Inez Hayden, who formerly taught Cajun and Creole cooking in Jefferson, also offers high teas and special dinners.)

Magnificently restored, the Perot Theatre and an Italianate Victorian house built in 1884 called the "Ace of Clubs" because of its unique shape and octagonal rotunda and rooms, are must-see attractions in Texarkana. The Art Center and the Federal Building, are also of interest. Wadley Hospital is also near The Mansion on Main.

TYLER

Charnwood Hill

Hosts: Don and Patsy Walker; Andy Walker, Innkeeper, 223 E. Charnwood, Tyler 75701, (903) 597-3980, 7 guest rooms, 7 baths, full breakfast, $$–$$$$, no children or pets, smoking outside only in designated areas, all cr

Once the palatial home of the late Texas oilman, H. L. Hunt, Charnwood Hill is now a bed and breakfast. "Common areas" for B&B guests include a formal living room, a library-TV room, the Great Hall on the first floor, a garden room, a second-floor gathering hall, front and east balconies, a screened swing porch, front porches, an arbor, and East and West gardens. Just make yourself at home!

Located in a prestigious neighborhood, noted for its red brick streets and wide variety of architectural styles, Charnwood Hill was built around 1861 as a frame house. Just after the turn of the century, it was bricked and transformed into a white Greek-revival mansion, with huge square-cut columns in front. The Hunts lived there in the mid-'30s, until they moved to Dallas.

Special pieces of interest include a great mirror of French origin that once hung in a German castle. It is in their library now. Hand-carved Italian urns, a Salvador Dali print, and an antique bronze sculpture in the Great Entrance Hall—these are a few of their favorite things. Weddings and other social and business functions are often held at Charnwood Hill as well as the other outstanding B&Bs in Tyler.

One of the more unique options is **Castle on the Lake,** a secluded retreat on a nine-acre lake on the outskirts of town, though it is easily accessible to the colleges, malls, and restaurants in town. Built in the '30s by a wealthy oilman and lovingly restored by Dr. and Mrs. J. Howard Morrison, the red brick house has unique architecture and a rustic, but elegant decor. The house, which includes two guest rooms with private baths and a fireplace in the den, juts out over the water! Relaxing on the porch swing or feeding Huey and Dewey, two friendly white geese, from the second-floor deck that overlooks the lake is fun. Flat-bottom boats and paddles are available for guests at no charge. June Morrison, who serves a great full breakfast, can tell you more about her intriguing B&B. Call (903) 566-3682.

Chilton Grand

Hosts: Jerry and Carole Glazebrook, 433 S. Chilton, Tyler 75702, phone and fax, (903) 595-3270, 5 guest rooms, 5 baths, 1 cottage, gourmet breakfast, $$–$$$$, no small children, no smokers or pets, MC, V, AE

The Chilton Grand is grand indeed! The Chilton Grand is a two-story red brick Greek Revival with six white columns and a balcony. Built around 1909, it was updated by a prominent attorney (the grandson of a former Texas Governor) in the '50s, who even added an art deco elevator.

Surrounded by stately maple, magnolia, oak, and pecan trees, the antique-filled mansion has crystal chandeliers everywhere, including the front balcony and porches. Carole has painted borders and Trompe l'oeil vines, arbors, and other designs on walls and furniture—an imaginative touch. Continuing their restoration, the ambitious couple will eventually have 12 guest rooms.

In the meantime, a two-bedroom cottage across the street has already been converted into a honeymoon retreat. Decorated in cool green and white, the **Ivy Cottage** includes formal living and dining rooms, a kitchen, sun room, and a two-person Jacuzzi bathtub.

You'd just know that anyone as talented as Carole would be a good cook, too. Mennonite breakfast pie and Swiss souffle are among her specialties.

Another beautifully done B&B, the **Bed of Roses Country Inn,** is three miles off I-20 next to Chamblee's Rose-Arama, an award-winning garden center. Mark and Sharon Chamblee have four rooms, including the Sweetheart Rose Room, with king and trundle beds, a private entrance, and large patio. A nice touch: fresh roses! And why not, Tyler is the Rose Capital of the World. Contact the Chamblees at 1 (800) 256-ROSE.

Edwards Vintage Farm

Hosts: Dee Dee and Bob Edwards, 15320 Farm Road 2767, Tyler 75705, (903) 566-1204, or contact Bed & Breakfast Texas Style, (972) 298-8586, 2 bedrooms, 2 baths, full country breakfast, $$–$$$, no children or pets, smoking only on porches, MC, V

Seeing deer come up to the house at daybreak and dusk and exploring more than 100 acres of hiking trails, especially during Dogwood season, will help make staying at Edwards Vintage Farm memorable. The old Spanish Trace Road is on the farm, which is six miles from Tyler. The circa 1836 Texas dog trot has been in the family since 1858.

Enlarged and restored through the years, the cabin has original pine floors, a country kitchen with a working antique stove, and a covered porch with a swing. Most of the furniture was in the family, too. One guest room has a king-sized bed, private bath, and a view of the hay meadow and woods. The other, a double, has an antique four-poster bed, wardrobe, and a fireplace. Hot biscuits, gravy, eggs, fresh fruit, muffins, and a breakfast casserole are samples of the hearty breakfast fare.

You'll be intrigued by the various collections—and by the host, a great story teller whose hobby is history reenactment.

Shiloh, described by Bob and Sandi Glover as a "Civil War Era bed and breakfast," is also an interesting country retreat, but it is only available from March 15 to July 1 and October 1 through December 15. The authentic double-log dog-trot house is on 43 acres ten miles west of Tyler. Fix your own breakfast, or the Glovers will pick you up and transport you through the woods to their home for a country breakfast. Since both are historians, talking to them is as much of a treat as breakfast! The Pine Cove Conference Center is only one mile away from Shiloh. For reservations, call (903) 561-4604.

Rosevine Inn

Hosts: Rebecca and Bert Powell, 415 S. Vine, Tyler 75702, (903) 592-2221, fax (903) 593-9500, 4 guest rooms, Lodge Room, Watson Cottage, all with private baths, full breakfast, $–$$$, children welcome with advance notice, no pets or smoking, all cr

Although Tyler has plenty of diversions such as the Caldwell Zoo, Tyler State Park, and Hudnall Planetarium, you'll have enough to do at the Rosevine Inn, Tyler's first B&B. A lodge-style game room with a rock floor is in the barn in back, where you can play billiards, board games, cards, darts, horseshoes, and washers. An outdoor hot tub is another amenity; robes and towels are provided. In Tyler's Brick Street Historic District, the Rosevine Inn also has a courtyard with a fountain where you can relax. Fireplaces burn regularly in the courtyard and game room. Above the latter is a quaint room with a six-foot claw-foot tub and stained-glass window. The Sherlock Holmes Suite in the Watson Cottage behind the barn has a queen-sized bed with plush linens, a corner fireplace, an antique-style bathroom, a TV, VCR, and an interesting ambience. (Find the hidden door, and you will get a bottle of champagne!) Mosquito netting helps create an out-of-Africa ambience in the second suite in the 1930's cottage.

Another wood-burning fireplace is in the two-story Georgian-Federal style home, which is even more picturesque because of the white picket fence in front. The four upstairs guest rooms are eclectically furnished with antiques and have private baths and double beds, except the Sunshine Room, which has twin beds. One of the rooms has a trundle bed, so two more could be accommodated. On the second-floor landing is a comfortable nook with a television and coffee maker for early risers. Omelets, quiche, muffins, and more are served in the dining room between 7:30 and 9:30. Business travelers can be accommodated with airport pickup, fax and copy machines, a VCR, and secretarial services.

Another Brick Street Historic District home open for B&B lodgers is **Mary's Attic Bed and Breakfast,** 413 S. College. Mary Mirsky's pretty blue unhosted 1926 Victorian bungalow has two bedrooms, a bath, and living and dining room, all furnished tastefully with antiques from her own shop next door. Period wallpaper adds to the elegance. Behind the antique shop is Mary's Attic B&B **Annex,** a garage apartment which can sleep five. Antiques and Mary's trademark—penciled decorations—make the Annex more inviting than you'd think, and children are welcome here. Contact Mary at (903) 592-5181.

The Seasons

Hosts: Jim and Myra Brown, 313 E. Charnwood, Tyler 75701, (903) 533-0803, 1 suite, 2 guest rooms, all private baths, carriage house, gourmet breakfast, $$$, no young children, no pets, no smoking, no cr

There is a room for each season at this impressive B&B. For instance, the Winter Room includes a Currier and Ives ice skating wallscape. Sheepskin rugs, streetlights, outdoor park benches, and a fireplace, along with a Victorian-style queen-sized sleigh bed, completes the distinctive decor. A garden courtyard, a gazebo, and cascading flowers are focal points of the scenic painting on the wall in the Spring Room, which has picket fence beds (a full and a twin) and a garden table and chairs. Both rooms have private baths.The rest of the accommodations are as enchanting, thanks to talented Myra's creative art and handiwork. The Brown's corporate suite in the carriage house behind their home includes two bedrooms, a kitchen, and bath. A music room, reading room, and formal parlor are among common areas where guests are welcome.

The burled wood, tiger oak floors, fireplaces, the living room chandelier, bath light fixtures, pocket French-style doors, and glass pane windows are original to the impressive home, which was built in 1911 by Samuel W. Littlejohn and his wife. Even today, it is historically known as the Littlejohn House. In 1930, the mansion was remodeled to its present Southern Colonial style. Besides a gourmet breakfast, that includes quiches and egg entrees, added treats are picnic baskets upon arrival in the summer, tea and fresh breads by the fireplace in the winter, and the Browns' warm hospitality all year long.

Woldert-Spence Manor

Hosts: Richard and Patricia Heaton, 611 W. Woldert St., Tyler 75702, (800) Woldert (800-965-3378) or (903) 533-9057, fax (903) 531-0293, 2 suites, 4 guest rooms, all private baths, full breakfast, $$–$$$, children 10 and up ok, no pets, smoking ok on porches and balconies, all cr

One of the three oldest houses in Tyler, the 4,000-square-foot Woldert-Spence Manor is on a woodsy corner with pecan trees over 100 years old and sweet gum trees in the Brick Street Historic District. The original structure was created between 1859 and 1884 when two adjacent houses were joined by John George Woldert, who was most noted for helping survey the Texas-Louisiana boundary. One of the four children born to Woldert's son became the bride of Robert Spence about 1910, and they added the second floor. Lovely stained-glass windows and doors and chandeliers original to the house, five porches, and a deck add to the charm of this B&B. Two of the five guest rooms have porches; two have a fireplace, and all have private baths, some with claw-foot tubs.

A bountiful breakfast—homemade biscuits, orange pecan French toast, fruit, baked cheese grits pie, and smoked bacon, for instance— is served on antique china, crystal, and silverware in the formal dining room. A covered spa under large shade trees in the Rear Garden, a gazebo-covered wishing well, and a fountain are among amenities. Woldert-Spence Manor is across the street from the YWCA, where you can play tennis, jog, or work out.

Another antique-filled historic B&B with wonderful hosts is **Heathwood Manor,** a two-story brick home on a wooded half-acre lot at 600 W. Rusk, which is on the edge of the Azalea District. Grady and Norma Nichols only accept B&B guests Thursday through Sunday most of the year. The four elegant Victorian guest rooms with queen beds and private baths are available daily during the Azalea Trail (usually the last two weeks of March and first week in April) and Tyler's heralded Rose Festival (held in October). Breakfast is a feast here, too, and usually even includes venison sausage from their South Texas ranch. Contact the Nichols at (903) 596-7764.

VAN ALSTYNE

The Durning House Bed and Breakfast and Restaurant

Hosts: Sherry Heath, Brenda Hix, 205 W. Stephens, P.O. Box 1173, Van Alstyne 75495, (903) 482-5188, or Bed & Breakfast Texas Style (972) 298-8586, 1 cottage (2 guest rooms, 1 shared bath), continental breakfast OYO, $$$, no children, no pets, no smoking, MC, V

The Durning House proves there is truth in that old axiom: the best things come in small packages. It's got charm galore, not only as a B&B, but as a restaurant that seats 50. Built at the turn of the century, the guest quarters of the picturesque Victorian are decorated with antiques. To appeal to men as well as women, the hosts have some novel items displayed in the restaurant and adjoining bathroom, including the hood of a 1932 Dodge 18-wheeler, a vintage gas pump, and fishing paraphernalia. This may sound a bit bizarre for a Victorian cottage, but it "works."

B&B guests have their own entrance and total privacy, even when the restaurant is open because the door that separates the two sections is locked. And since the bath must be shared, the cottage is always rented to just one couple, unless two couples are together. Sherry and Brenda, who live next door, will leave your continental breakfast in the mini-kitchen just off the parlor.

Besides its own restroom, the restaurant has its own entrance, too. Lunch hours are from 11:30 a.m. to 2 p.m. Wednesday through Friday and from 11:30 a.m. to 2 p.m on Sunday; dinner is served from 6 p.m. to 9 p.m. on Friday and Saturday. (Wine, beer, and limited cocktails are available.) If you have a sweet tooth, don't pass up the home-made pies and gourmet ice cream creations! (Remember to make a reservation or you might miss out.) The first Wednesday of every month is Hat Day; wear your own or choose one from the wall.

A lot of private parties—even weddings—are held at The Durning House. Only 30 minutes from Lake Texoma and 45 minutes North of Dallas off US 75 (take exit #51 east), Van Alstyne's attractions—besides this B&B—include a museum, a drug store with a soda fountain, and antique and specialty shops.

WAXAHACHIE

Chaska House

Hosts: Louis and Linda Brown, 716 W. Main, Waxahachie 75165, (972) 937-3390, (800) 931-3390, or Bed & Breakfast Texas Style, (972) 298-8586, 6 guest rooms, 6 baths, 1 guest house, "Texas Chic" breakfast, $$$–$$$$, older children welcome in guest house, no pets, no smoking, MC, V, AE

Built in 1900 by a prominent merchant, Edward Chaska, and his wife and on the National Register of Historic Places, the elegantly appointed Chaska House, one of Waxahachie's premiere "show" homes, has museum-quality antiques. Featured in *Texas Highways* and other magazines as well as national ads, Louis and Linda Brown's turn-of-the-century home has six rooms for guests. The Plantation Room has a queen-sized canopied bed from an antebellum plantation, while the

French Room has a private entrance to the secluded east veranda and an ornate Louis XIV double bed. Avid readers, the Browns had fun finding appropriate memorabilia and furnishings for four additional rooms that they named for favorite literary legends like Sherlock Holmes and Romeo and Juliet. (The latter room has a balcony, of course.)

Fresh flowers, afternoon tea, and bedtime turn-down service are among amenities. During the "Texas Chic" southern breakfast, which is served in the Chaska House formal dining room, the congenial hosts often tell about the town's history and attractions.

The Browns also have a contemporary unhosted 1950's B&B across the street. **Hemingway's Retreat,** an interesting salute to the author's Key West home, has two bedrooms, two baths, and spacious living area on one side (rented to one couple or friends); and one bedroom, a big Jacuzzi bathroom, living area, and galley kitchen on the other. The town square is an easy stroll from the Chaska House and Hemingway's Retreat, which are located in the heart of Waxahachie's historic district.

Rose of Sharon

Host: Sharon Frances Shawn, 205 Bryson, Waxahachie 75165, (972) 938-8833, 3 guest rooms, 3 baths, gourmet breakfast, $$–$$$, no children, pets, or smoking, MC; V

Lace curtains, stained-glass windows, fine antiques—and *Gone With the Wind* memorabilia fill this cozy, romantic inn. "Miss Sharon," as she's often called by her guests, is addicted to "All things Scarlett" (and Rhett). A music box with their likenesses, plates, pictures, and other collectibles will catch your eye—and imagination—at this country-Victorian B&B, which is surrounded by a white picket fence. Birdhouses and flowers are everywhere! Dozens of crepe myrtles, wisteria, an arbor covered with Carolina jasmine, and a myriad of other flowers frame the huge porches. Sit on the porch swings and enjoy the view.

Guest rooms include private baths with claw-foot tubs and queen-sized beds. The Honeymoon Suite bath is enormous, red, and wonderful! Breakfast is served on handsome Rosenthal china. (Wait until you sample "Miss Sharon's" apple dumplings with praline sauce!)

Scarlett would love this delightful B&B!

Seven Gables

Hosts: Jim and Helen B. Sturges Anderson, 501 N. College St., Waxahachie 75165, (214) 938-7500, 3 suites, full breakfast, $$–$$$, no children under 12, no pets, smoking only on verandas, no cr

With its seven-gable roof, a wraparound covered veranda, and gingerbread trim, this cream-colored Victorian home with the blue trim really stands out. Built in 1898, Seven Gable's South Gables Suite has a spacious living room with a spiral staircase leading to the second-floor bedroom, which has a queen-sized bed. (A more conventional stairway is available too.) In a secluded alcove, the North Gables Suite has twin cherrywood beds and a claw-foot tub and pedestal sink. Like the others, the Rose Room Suite has a TV and VCR. Victorian nightgowns and terry robes will get you in the getaway mood. Breakfast includes hearty egg and meat dishes, freshly baked breads, and blueberry-peach or strawberry crisp.

One of Seven Gable's most interesting guests, incidentally, was the daughter of the lady who was the model for the faces carved on the famed red granite and sandstone courthouse in this picturesque town. Less than 30 minutes south of Dallas and just off I-35, Waxahachie is a veritable gold mine of historic homes and buildings and antique shops, while Catfish Plantation is known far and wide for its great food and friendly ghosts!

The Bonnynook

Hosts: Vaughn and Bonnie Franks, 414 W. Main, Waxahachie 75165, (972) 938-7207, (800) 486-5936, fax (972) 937-7700, or Bed & Breakfast Texas Style, (972) 298-8586, 5 guest rooms, 5 baths, full breakfast, $$–$$$, designated smoking, all cr

The Bonnynook has been in business longer than any of the other B&Bs in Waxahachie, which has been the setting for so many movies, including *Places in the Heart* and *The Return to Bountiful.* Though still owned by Vaughn and Bonnie Franks, the Bonnynook now has an innkeeper while they are managing another impressive B&B, **Etta's Place,** in Fort Worth.

A two-story Victorian with gingerbread trim built between 1887 and 1897, The Bonnynook has a wide porch across the front with ceiling fans. Within two blocks of the downtown square, it has a cozy parlor where you can play games or talk, and a nook stocked with gourmet tea and coffee. Among amenities are a snack tray and triple sheeting, while business travelers have access to secretarial services and a computer. Guest rooms have phones and working areas, along with antique furnishings and magnificent baths. Three have two-person Jacuzzis, while the first-floor Library Room even has a mirrored ceiling and a brass chandelier. The Gavitt Room, which has a claw-foot tub in front of one of the B&B's four original tiled coal-burning fireplaces, also is a favorite. To enhance the romantic ambience, breakfast, which includes hot fruit, savory eggs, fresh crepes, and the like is by candlelight!

The Bonnynook, and other outstanding Waxahachie B&Bs like **The Harrison House,** 717 W. Main, are becoming increasingly popular for social and business functions. Built between 1912 and 1915 and boasting a Texas Historical Marker, its red brick Mission Bungalow architectural style is rare in this area. The stately home has three antique-filled guest rooms with private baths (one room has a sun porch) and a 45-foot long grand hall that is 20 feet wide. Sandee and Mark Larkin, (972) 938-1922, also have a one bedroom cottage in back with a living area.

Featured on Waxahachie's Gingerbread Trail, **Rosemary Manor,** 903 W. Main St., is a 1916 Georgian Revival home with massive statues of reclining sphinx on either side of the entry porch steps and European-style herb gardens in back. A gourmet herb-scented full breakfast is served. Judy and Dennis Cross have three suites and two guest rooms (both have private baths) named after flowers that are also herbs, representing a different period in history with appropriate antiques. Phone and fax (972) 935-9439.

WEATHERFORD

Derrick-Hoffman Farm

Host: Jean Derrick Hoffman, 7030 Thorp Springs Road, Weatherford 76087, (800) 573-9953, (817) 573-9952, 3 guest rooms, 2 full baths, 1 half bath, cottage with 3 guest rooms, 1 bath, western breakfast in host's home or continental OYO, $$, no smoking, no cr

When you see the red bandanna on the flag pole, you'll know you're at the entry gate to the 265-acre Derrick-Hoffman Farm. It's near the tiny town of Tin Top on FM 2580 (known as the Tin Top Road, if you're coming from Granbury, or Old Thorp Road, from Weatherford). A retired economics professor, Jean designed her impressive two-story cedar and field stone home, which has three guest rooms with private entrances. Two have a private bath and the third, a half bath. The most elegant room includes antique twin beds, a fireplace, a sitting area, and a few wildlife trophies on the walls. The house has an elevator, so handicapped guests can be accommodated.

Jean books only one party at a time in her little farm house nearby, because the two rooms and sun porch (one bed and a game table are in the latter) share a bath. A fully equipped kitchen/dining area and a living room has a Thurber brick fireplace, piano, TV, and a bookcase with a complete set of Dickens published in the 1800s. Browse through vintage magazines while you sit in the swing on the front porch. Not only can you bring your offspring, but your family pet as well because the backyard of the farm house is fenced. You can have a continental breakfast in the cottage or a full western breakfast in Jean's huge home at 9 a.m. It's worth the (downhill) walk.

With a fishing pond and walking paths, the Derrick-Hoffman Farm is a good place for R&R, but Granbury is only ten minutes away and Weatherford, a few minutes more. Be sure you try out Jean's four-wheel bicycle surrey!

St. Botolph Inn

Hosts: Dan and Shay Buttolph, 808 S. Lamar, Weatherford 76086, (800) 868-6520, (817) 594-1455, 1 suite, 3 guest rooms, 1 private, 2 shared baths, choice of full Victorian or continental breakfast, $–$$, no pets, smoking only on verandas, MC, V, AE

The warm and friendly host's family name is derived from a 7th-century English Monk, St. Botolph, which is how the inn's name came to be. Described by Dan and Shay as a "Victorian painted lady," their architectural gem, which has wraparound porches, gingerbread, and a turreted tower topped by the original weather vane, is painted with 12 historic colors true to turn-of the-century times.

Sloping concrete steps lead up to the restored Queen Anne-style mansion, which holds court on a hilltop amid five scenic acres. Enhanced as well by a stone archway over the steps at the landing, St. Botolph Inn's majestic entrance sets the tone for this B&B, which boasts Tudor-style wainscotting, elaborate woodwork, carved fireplace mantels, and antiques acquired on trips abroad. It even has a magnificent second-floor Victorian ballroom with a 25-foot domed ceiling and two bandstands. Three of the guest rooms are off the ballroom, including the luxurious suite, which has fabric walls and a commanding view of the Parker County Courthouse from the adjoining sitting room. Two of the guest rooms share a bath. Marking the detailed breakfast menu at night will tell the hosts whether you want a full Victorian breakfast (English coddled eggs is one option) or a continental breakfast.

Depending on the season, have Victorian tea in front of a roaring fire in the drawing room, or swim in the pool. At the St. Botolph Inn, you'll also find a children's playground, a small prayer chapel, an 1897 windmill, lawn games, and walking paths where you might glimpse some of the wildlife and birds (22 species) that find sanctuary here. The grounds or ballroom may be rented for special occasions. Parker County's Peach festival in July is a nice time to visit.

Victorian House Bed and Breakfast

Host: Candice Barnes, P.O. Box 1571, Weatherford 76086, (817) 599-9600, or Bed & Breakfast Texas Style, (972) 298-8586, 10 guest rooms, 10 baths, full breakfast, $$–$$$, only children over 6, smoking on porches, no pets, MC, V, AE

Built in 1896 by a wholesale grocer, the 23-room, 10,000-square-foot, three-story Victorian House sits on three acres on the highest point in Weatherford. You can't miss it! And you wouldn't want to. One mile from the town square, the massive Queen Anne-style showplace has become as noted for hosting special occasions, especially weddings, as bed and breakfast guests. There is a porch around the entire house, which has hardwood floors, four fireplaces, ten-foot pocket doors, lots of stained-glass windows, and three turrets (one harbors a game table).

Three first-floor guest rooms have private entrances; all exquisitely furnished rooms have king-sized beds with feather mattresses, TVs, custom bedspreads and drapes, period furnishings, and private baths, most with claw-foot tubs. Four baths have Jacuzzi tubs surrounded by six-foot mirrors and cherub candles. A marvelous cook who serves bountiful breakfasts, Candice can seat 20 comfortably in her formal dining room. Soft drinks are in a hall refrigerator; help yourself. The host has a bell outside the door to her second-floor quarters. Ring if you need something.

Thirty minutes west of Fort Worth, Weatherford's attractions include area lakes and a historic homes driving tour. The Heritage Gallery at the Weatherford Library displays costumes and memorabilia belonging to town notables such as the late Broadway star, Mary Martin, and her son, Larry Hagman, (J. R. Ewing of *Dallas*). Parker County has three wineries.

WEST

Zachary Davis House

Host: Marjorie Devlin, 400 N. Roberts Street, West 76691, (254) 826-3953, 8 guest rooms, 8 baths, full breakfast, $, no children, pets, or smoking, MC, V

Like New Braunfels' famed Wurstfest, Westfest, held Labor Day weekend, is great fun. You can waltz and polka to oompah bands, watch costumed folk dancers, and eat Czech food to your heart's content. But West has long lured I-35 motorists in-the-know into making a quick detour to stock up on kolaches (fruit-filled pastries) and sausage rolls. The tiny central Texas town has a number of outstanding bakeries and restaurants that do justice to its Czech heritage.

Located 17 miles north of Waco, West also has a bed and breakfast, the Zachary Davis House. Framed by huge pecan trees, the Colonial mansion was built in 1888 by Zachary Davis, who once owned most of the land in town. Restored by Marjorie Devlin, the mansion has six guest rooms with discreetly screened commodes, wash basins, and showers, and two with separate adjoining baths. Most have queen-sized beds, but two have twins. There is one single. Rollaways are available for a nominal fee. Marjorie had been with a major hotel chain for 28 years, so she knows what hospitality is all about.

Although the Zachary Davis House has a formal living room, you'll probably prefer relaxing in the comfortable den, where you'll find a TV, piano, and table for cards and games. A country breakfast is served buffet style in the dining room. And yes, kolaches are usually on the tempting menu.

WINNSBORO

Thee Hubbell House

Hosts: Dan and Laurel Hubbell, 307 W. Elm, Winnsboro 75494, 1 (800) 227-0639, 5 guest rooms, 5 baths, gourmet breakfast, cottage, Carriage House with six rooms and baths, continental breakfast OYO or gourmet breakfast in mansion for extra fee, $$–$$$$, children in cottage only, no pets, no smoking inside, all cr

On a two-acre landscaped estate, Thee Hubbell House is a picturesque, antique-filled Georgian colonial that is popular for formal weddings, receptions, and other functions, as well as a B&B. Special honeymoon and anniversary packages are available, along with candlelight dinners. Amenities include fresh flowers, fruit baskets, turndown service, and mints.

The dining room adjoins the formal living room and parlor, creating a nice open effect, while the entry hall is larger than rooms in some houses. Wide pine flooring with square peg nails is found throughout the home, which has a historical marker. The hand-carved stairway came from the lumber mill of Colonel J. A. Stinson, a wealthy plantation owner and Confederate Army veteran who bought the house in 1906 and converted it into its present colonial style.

Three upstairs guest rooms have queen beds, while the Rose has a double. The Master's Suite on the first floor has a fireplace and king bed, private veranda, bath, and dining room. It's a special suite for special times. The baked apple with fresh cranberry sauce and melted ice cream served at breakfast is in itself worth a visit. Six more rooms with private baths are in an adjoining Carriage House. A Jacuzzi and hot tub are nearby. One bedroom and a bath are also available in the hosts' 1906 Sears & Roebuck cottage next door, where children are welcome. It is handicapped accessible.

Winnsboro is becoming increasingly popular as a year-round destination, with antique, art, and craft shops. Its fabled Autumn Trails are held each weekend in October and the first weekend in November. Listen for the church bells that chime four times a day!

THE PANHANDLE AND WEST TEXAS

ABILENE

Bolin's Prairie House

Hosts: Ginny and Sam Bolin, 508 Mulberry, Abilene 79601, (915) 675-5855 or (800) 673-5855, 4 guest rooms, 2 private baths, 1 shared, full breakfast, $, no pets, no smoking, older children by arrangement, all cr

With three church-related colleges in town, it is not surprising that the guest rooms in this historic home in the heart of Abilene have been named Love, Peace, Joy, and Patience. One of the baths has two vanities with an oversized shower, and another, a seven-foot claw-foot tub. All the rooms have seating areas. Along with a special egg dish, you'll have homemade breads for breakfast in the dining room, where Ginny's impressive collection of cobalt depression glass and china are displayed.

Though the house had Victorian architecture when built in 1902, it's impossible to tell now, because in 1920 it was enlarged and redesigned in the Prairie style popularized by Frank Lloyd Wright. Fortunately, the covered porch was retained, and it's a great place to relax a spell. Perhaps Sam, a master cabinet maker, will tell you about his handiwork.

In Abilene, the Fine Arts Museum and several galleries and antique shops are of special interest.

ALBANY

The Ole Nail House Inn

Host: Joie Parsons, 329 South 3rd, Albany 76430, (800) 245-5163 or (915) 762-2928, 3 guest rooms, 3 baths, full breakfast, $, no children unless by prior arrangement, no pets or smokers, MC, V, D

The heralded Fort Griffin Fandangle, which has drawn so many visitors to Albany the last two weekends in June ever since it was first produced in 1938, was written by Robert Nail, who lived in this house for many years. Built in 1914, the two-story prairie-style home is across from the courthouse, and you can hear the clock chime.

Two of the guest rooms are on the second floor and have enclosed sun porches. One overlooks the courthouse, while you can see the host's two water gardens, hammock, swing, deck, and gazebo in back from the other. Robes, fruit baskets upon arrival, fresh flowers, and TV are among amenities. A telephone and computer hookup are available in the parlor downstairs. A real estate broker who offices at home, Joie's breakfasts often include broiled tomatoes stuffed with spinach and oven roasted potatoes.

You don't have to wait for the Fandangle to visit Albany, which is 35 miles northeast of Abilene. People come from all over, Joie says, just to eat at the Fort Griffin General Merchandise, which gets rave reviews. And so do the B&Bs in this West Texas town.

Virginia's Bed and Breakfast

Host: Virginia Baker, 310 Breckenridge, Albany 76430,
(915) 762-2013, 3 guest rooms, 3 baths, 1 suite, 1 guest house,
country or continental breakfast, $$, no pets, smoking, no alcohol,
no cr

West Texas is full of surprises, like Albany's Old Jail Art Center,
which not only has Western art, but 37 magnificent Chinese tomb fig-
ures from the Han Dynasty to the T'ang Dynasty, works by Picasso,
and an extensive collection of pre-Columbian art. At one time, the his-
toric landmark was going to be demolished, but Robert Nail bought
it so it could be preserved, leaving another legacy besides the Fandangle.
He used it for a studio. About a decade after he died, it was converted
into an art center.

Another anachronism out on the plains is Virginia's, an ivy-covered
English Tudor rock home that should be nestled in Stratford-Upon-Avon
rather than West Texas. Guests are invited to share the cheery sun room
with its yellow antique wicker and plants, relax in the hot tub or the
snug den with its huge fireplace, or watch TV (play a tune on the piano,
if you wish) in the music room. Family heirlooms and needlework are
of interest in this 1926 B&B. Several of the guest rooms have twin beds,
while the guest house has a full kitchen.

Virginia invites you to picnic on her spacious back patio, and even
has a trampoline your children will enjoy. And hunters, she has facil-
ities for cleaning and freezing game. Now that's a B&B first!

ALPINE

Holland Hotel

Host: Carla McFarland, 209 W. Holland Ave., Alpine 79830, (915)
837-3844 or (800) 535-8040, 10 guest rooms, 10 baths, penthouse,
continental plus breakfast OYO, children welcome, pets okay by
prior arrangement, smoking in two guest rooms, $-$$, MC, V, AE

A major gateway to Big Bend National Park and at the edge of the
Chihuahuan Desert, Alpine is surrounded on three sides by mountains.
McDonald Observatory (don't miss a Star Party), Balmorhea (the

world's largest spring-fed pool) and Fort Davis are other sidetrips possible from the Holland Hotel. Built in 1912, it is the only three-story building in town—and now a bed and breakfast.

Carla has owned it for quite a while, and now that she is once again manager as well, it has regained the look and ambience of old. The colorful proprietor invites everyone to come see her homey West Texas treasure.

The peach-colored lobby with original terracotta Spanish colonial tile floor and antique church pews sets the tone of welcome and warmth. The guest rooms have different decors with antiques here and there to give each a touch of character, and upholstered walls that lend a touch of class. Each room also has a mini-kitchen, TV, and ceiling fan. The little fridge is well-stocked for a continental breakfast. The third-floor penthouse is small, though it has a double bed, TV, kitchen, and best of all, a large deck where you can sit and enjoy the view of Alpine. AMTRAK is right across from this B&B.

The Corner House

Host: Jim Glendinning, 801 East Ave. E, Alpine 79830, (800) 585-7795 or (915) 837-7161, fax (915) 837-3638, 6 guest rooms, 4 private baths, 1 shared bath, country or continental breakfast, $, Smoking only on porch, MC, V, AE, D

Your host, Jim Glendinning, is a native of Scotland, and keeps his homeland's flag flying on his brick B&B year round. (He even dons kilts on special occasions.) This isn't a fancy B&B, but the host is interesting. Built in 1937, The Corner House has a herb garden and flowers in front. The attic has been converted to a spacious Tree House Room, with a king-sized bed and couch, while The Loft has a double bed. One of the first-floor rooms has a fireplace, and another a desk and TV. In the carpeted cellar are three twin beds, which are ideal for children and available at a nominal charge. Pets are welcome, too, in this informal B&B. Breakfast is served in his Cafe, which takes up part of the first floor.

The Corner House is two blocks from Sul Ross State University, where you'll find the Museum of the Big Bend, which includes a reconstructed frontier general store, a stagecoach, and blacksmith shop. If you have a question about the area, just ask Jim, who has written a comprehensive insider's paperback guide to the region.

The White House Inn

Host: Anita Bradney, 2003 Fort Davis Hwy., Alpine 79830, (888) 774-7171 or (915) 837-1401, fax (915) 837-2197, 6 guest rooms, 6 baths, 1 guest house, gourmet breakfast, $$, children over 12 welcome, no pets, no smoking MC, V, D

When the weather is nice (and it is more often than not), a gourmet breakfast is served on the patio at The White House Inn, a stately white brick B&B that was built in the '30s on the outskirts of Alpine near the Municipal Airport. (If you'd like lunch or a picnic box, let Anita know.) Because of the lovely, landscaped grounds and distinctive decor, the inn is also used for special occasions and business meetings and retreats. Set off the highway on two acres, the impressive house has a wide veranda in front and two patios in back where guests like to sit, especially when Anita's wildflowers are in bloom (from spring into fall).

Anita has rooms to suit every preference, whether a king, queen, double or twin beds, while a hair dryer, robe, TV, and phone are among amenities. Three guest rooms are in her home and three more in a recently constructed, smaller two-story, white brick building in back. A spacious, first-floor guest room in the latter is wheelchair accessible.

Continue north from The White House Inn, and you'll be in historic Fort Davis, which is 26 miles away. Travel south from Alpine to Marfa, and maybe you'll see the mysterious ghost lights!

AMARILLO

Auntie's House

Hosts: Skip and Corliss Burroughs, 1712 S. Polk St., Amarillo 79102, (806) 371-8054, 3 guest rooms, 3 private baths, 1 guest house, full breakfast, $$$–$$$$, children over 12 welcome, no pets, no smoking inside, MC, V, AE, D

Amarillo has long been one of the state's most popular destinations, primarily because of nearby Palo Duro Canyon, but it has lots of other attractions, too, like an exquisitely furnished mansion that may be toured by reservation, The Harrington House, 1600 S. Polk.

The latter is not far from Auntie's House, one of the growing number of historic properties now open to B&B guests in town. On the National Register of Historic Places, the two-story, antique-filled Craftsman-style 1912 home has been nicely restored and furnished. Fresh flowers and a hot tub are among amenities, along with TV and VCRs. Phone jacks are in all the rooms. The hosts have named their one-bedroom guest house in back, The Enchanted Cottage, and hope you will be enchanted, too. Designed for romance, it has a two-person Jacuzzi and two shower heads, along with a sitting area, Victorian furnishings, and 10- and 12-foot ceilings.

Corliss can tell you all about Amarillo, especially the neat antique shops and eateries that continually crop up in a ten-block area along 6th street (formerly historic Route 66).

Galbraith House

Hosts: Mary Jane and David Johnson, Innkeeper: Martha Shaw, 1710 S. Polk St., Amarillo 79102, (806) 374-0237, 5 guest rooms, 5 baths, full breakfast weekends, continental weekdays, $$, no pets, no smoking, all cr

If you are an opera buff, you will be especially impressed with this inviting B&B, which is next door to Auntie's House. Mary Jane Johnson has posters on display from her many performances as an internationally known soprano, plus photographs and autographs of Pavarotti. The two-story Galbraith House also has some marvelous art pieces and fine antiques.

Built in the early 1900s with the finest woods by a wealthy Amarillo lumberman, this Prairie-style mansion is a showplace. Located in the heart of town, the Galbraith House is yours to enjoy, including a handsome parlor, library, two TV areas, porches, a big backyard and garden.

This Panhandle town is a long way from most everywhere in Texas, but the drive is worth it because there are so many unique things to do in the area! Options include a Goodnight Jeep Tour of recently accessible parts of Palo Duro Canyon, or visit the museum and Boothill Cemetery at Cal Farley's Boys' Ranch.

Parkview House

Hosts: Nabil and Carol Dia, 1311 S. Jefferson, Amarillo 79101, (806) 373-9464, fax (806) 373-9464 (but call first), or Bed & Breakfast Texas Style (972) 298-8586, 4 rooms, 4 baths, 1 suite, 1 cottage, continental plus breakfast, $$, no pets, no smoking, MC, V, AE

Amarillo's first B&B, Parkview House, was built in 1908 by former Mayor J. H. Patton, who moved his Victorian manse to its present location in the mid-20s. The Dias (Nabil is from Jordan) restored and modernized the home, but retained its historic ambience. Carol has added antiques, lace curtains, and lots of Victorian charm. The guest rooms and cottage have queen-sized beds, radio/alarm clocks, and different decors. The cottage also has a TV and fax.

Breakfast is served in the cozy country kitchen or formal dining room, and Nabil will be delighted to brew you a special cup of blended American/Arabic coffee to start your day. You may even sip a cup of this exotic mixture from a wicker chair on the front porch or retreat to the hot tub under the stars.

The Harrison House

Hosts: David Horsley and Michele Fortunato, 1710 S. Harrison Street, Amarillo 79102, (806) 374-1710, 1 guest room, 1 bath, full breakfast, $$, pets and children are welcome ($10 extra per child), smoking only on porches, MC, V

Blueberry pancakes are the speciality of the house—The Harrison House. Light snacks are served between 5 and 6 each afternoon to guests, whose spacious first-floor room has a queen-sized bed. Relax by the fireplace in the winter or drink ice tea on the porch swings in summer. In the music room, imagine how it must have been in days of old when "Granny" Storm, who remained in her home until her 90s, played her grand piano for guests.

Built in 1931, The Harrison House was acquired by the hosts in 1990 and then modernized, but the '30s-era character of the house was preserved, in keeping with the neighborhood. It is centrally located in Amarillo's Plemon's Eakle Historic District, which has one of the best collections of bungalow-style homes in the country, tree-lined brick streets, and an old-fashioned ambience.

The heralded Harrington House Museum is only three blocks away from this B&B, while two parks with jogging trails are within easy walking distance. Walking around the Eakle-Plemons Historic District is a treat, too.

BALLINGER

Miz Virginia's B&B in the Olde Park Hotel

Hosts: S. C. and Juanita Chrisco, 107 S. 6th St., Ballinger 76821, (800) 344-0781, 4 guest rooms, 4 private baths, 4 rooms share 2 baths, $–$$, country breakfast, children and pets ok with advanced notice, smoking in downstairs rooms, MC, V, AE, D

Homey and unpretentious, Miz Virginia's B&B is on the square across from the courthouse, and consists of seven rooms in what was once the historic Olde Park Hotel. Built before the turn of the century, the 111-year-old building had been in Juanita's family since 1922, but was under different ownership for many years. Juanita and S. C. bought the building back in 1988 when it was going to be torn down and turned part of it into a bed and breakfast two years later.

Furnished with antiques and collectibles from her own shop on the first floor, the guest rooms and suites have canopy and half canopy beds, hardwood floors, sitting rooms or porches. Smoking is allowed in two bedrooms on the first floor. B&B guests usually are served a full breakfast in the smallest—and nicest—of two dining rooms, but you can have a continental breakfast on request, which those who get up early to fish or hunt often do.

Juanita's daughter, Jeanette Findlay, manages the B&B and lives on the premises with her family. Jeanette was instrumental in starting the heralded Christmas in Olde Ballinger.

The huge, new O.H. Ivie Reservoir and Lake 20 miles southeast of Ballinger, along with the nearby Indian pictographs, are among area attractions.

CANYON

Country Home Bed and Breakfast and Mom's Place

Host: Tammy Money-Brooks, Rt. 1, Box 447, Canyon 79015, (800) 664-7636 or (806) 655-7636, 4 rooms, 3½ baths, 1 guest house, full breakfast, $–$$$, no pets, no smoking, MC, V, AE, D

Palo Duro Canyon and its internationally acclaimed outdoor summer musical, *Texas,* have literally put Canyon on the map, along with the wonderful Panhandle–Plains Museum. In recent years, the Country Home, which has a long front porch and a two-story living room with a fireplace, has been a magnet, too, especially for folks seeking a quiet, but picturesque getaway and genuine hospitality. (It's popular for weddings and parties, too.)

Furnished in antiques and vintage memorabilia, including Great Grandma Money's 1907 wedding dress, family portraits, and quilts, Country Home also offers some wonderful amenities, like fluffy robes, cheesecake in the evening, and a gazebo. Sit on the porch swing and take in a West Texas sunset or in the hot tub under the stars. Besides two guest rooms in her home, Tammy also has two more rooms with private baths in a second B&B across the road and can sleep up to 10. Children are welcome here; her mother is the host. No wonder it's called **Mom's Place.** There is a hot tub there as well. Spending time on this 200-acre ranch will be time remembered!

At Palo Duro Canyon, don't miss the two-mile, narrated scenic tour on the Sad Monkey Railroad, the Amarillo Gunfighters at the Rusty Spur Outpost, or the Cowboy Dinner on the Canyon's rim at Figure 3 Ranch.

The Hudspeth House

Hosts: Mark and Mary Clark, 1905 4th Ave., Canyon 79015, (800) 655-9809, (806) 655-9800, fax (806) 655-7457, 8 guest rooms, 8 baths, full breakfast, $–$$$, MC, V, AE, D

A number of bed and breakfasts offer candlelight dinners for two (for an additional fee), but we doubt if another has a host who will play the guitar and serenade you with a ballad like Mark Clark does at the Hudspeth House.

Giving newlyweds who start their honeymoon at the Hudspeth House a ride to the International Airport in Amarillo (16 miles away) at no charge is another service the amiable hosts provide.

Since acquiring the 8,200-square-foot Hudspeth House in 1994, the Clarks have created three more oversized period bathrooms, restored the beautiful oak floors, and done extensive remodeling. They even added a hot tub and furnished the house with antiques from the Panhandle area, in keeping with its Prairie-style architecture.

One of the guest rooms has a king-sized and double bed; the rest, queen. All also now have a phone, cable TV, and a separate telephone jack for a modem. The computerized phone system can accommodate most business needs, including speed-dialing.

The three-story Hudspeth House has a Texas Historical Marker, 12-foot ceilings, lots of original millwork and stained glass, more than 90 windows—and an interesting history. Ordered from Sears & Roebuck as a boarding house for female students and faculty at what is now known as West Texas State University, it was given to Mary Elizabeth Hudspeth by the owners, the Turks, four years later to pay a debt. She soon moved it to its present site near the college.

Canyon has become one of Texas' better known small towns, primarily because of Palo Duro Canyon's dramatic production, *Texas*. Seeing the rider on the white horse racing across the ridge of the canyon carrying the Texas flag as lightning lights up the sky is a scene few forget. You won't forget your stay at the Hudspeth House, either.

CROSBYTON

Smith House

Hosts: Sandy and Terry Cash, 306 W. Aspen, Crosbyton 79322, (806) 675-2178, fax (806) 675-2619, 10 rooms, 8 baths, 2 suites, full breakfast, $–$$$, MC, V

About 35 miles east of Lubbock, near the Caprock of Texas, is the small town of Crosbyton that has been getting increased acclaim for its outdoor musical, *God's Country*. The 1921 Smith House has been attracting additional acclaim, too, not only as a B&B, but for being ideal for reunions, receptions, and special events, just as in days of yore.

A reflection of its rich and colorful heritage, the Smith House still has most of the momentos and furniture left behind by the Smiths, who were the original owners. Her china plate collection still lines the walls of the large dining room, and the original player piano adorns the gorgeous parlor. In a way, it seems the Smiths never left. Yet, Sandy and Terry have added their own special touch.

DEL RIO

The 1890 House

Hosts: Alberto and Laura Galvan, 609 Griner Street, Del Rio 78840, (800) 282-1360 or (210) 775-8061, fax (210) 775-4667, 3 rooms, 1 suite, gourmet breakfast, $$–$$$$, no pets MC, V

Located in the heart of downtown Del Rio, this Victorian B&B is in a great location! Area attractions not only include the Judge Roy Bean Historic Site at Langtry, Alamo Village, Lake Amistad, and the Val Verde Winery, but Ciudad-Acuna, one of Mexico's most popular border towns, is only minutes away.

If you prefer to just relax and enjoy yourself at The 1890 House, that's just fine with the delightful hosts. Built around 1890 by the town's first doctor as a gift for his wife, the house has huge pecan trees, beautiful gardens, a veranda and period furnishings that include a turn-of-the-century player piano in the parlor. (Guests often congregate for a sing-a-long.)

Some of the guest rooms have oversized tubs big enough for two, while the romantic Victorian Suite has a king-sized four-poster bed, a fireplace, a love seat, and Jacuzzi. Linens and towels from England are examples of Laura's quest for the best for her guests. Crab enchiladas and tortillas española are among breakfast specialties.

Del Rio has another notable B&B, **The Inn on the Creek,** (210) 774-6198. Near San Felipe Springs and of special appeal to those who like to hunt or fish, the secluded inn's amenities include a sauna, Jacuzzi, and pool. Surrounded by horse farms and on 40 acres, the inn's four guest rooms overlook the creek and waterfall in back.

FLOYDADA

Lamplighter Inn

Hosts: Evelyn Branch and Roxanna Cummings, 102 S. 5th, Floydada 79235, (806) 983-3035, 20 guest rooms, 6 private baths, 3 shared baths, full breakfast, $, no children, no pets, no smoking, no cr

Since Floydada is the "Pumpkin Capital of the USA," Roxanna and her Mom serve homemade pumpkin butter—and the best biscuits you've ever tasted—with their huge country breakfasts. You'll find pumpkin butter on the menu if you join the line for the delicious luncheon buffet that is available to the public, too, during the week at the Lamplighter Inn, which was built in 1912 when Floydada was a bustling railroad town.

As a special surprise, there's at least one pumpkin included in the decor of each guest room at the Lamplighter Inn, which is just west of the Courthouse Square. All of the rooms have special themes relating to the area's history, from pre-pioneer days (Coronado and the Comancheros) to the tent show era (performers stayed at the Lamplighter) to the mercantile and soda fountain era. The Garden Room will give you a feeling of the outdoors and peace. The ceiling is sky blue, with clouds and thousands of tiny dots of starlight to lull you to sleep, while fireworks "light up the sky" in the Patriotic Room.

Avid antique lovers, the two women may have bought the old Lamplighter Inn just to show off their huge collection! Their biggest prize, of course, is the inn itself.

FORT DAVIS

Neill Museum B&B

Host: Shirley Neill Vickers, P. O. Box 1034, Fort Davis 79734, (915) 426-3838 or (915) 426-3969, 2 rooms, 2 baths, continental breakfast OYO, $–$$$, no children, pets, or smoking, no cr

What could be more historic than spending the night in a museum? Located seven blocks west of the courthouse at the end of Court

Street in Fort Davis, the Neill Museum is probably the only museum in Texas open to B&B guests. Filled with hundreds of antique dolls and toys dating back to the 1880s, as well as quilts and bottles, it's delightful. You'll even find dolls and buggies in your room.

Although the museum is open to the public June 1 through Labor Day, as well as by appointment or chance the rest of the year, B&B guests are welcome anytime.

The restored Queen Anne-style house was built in 1898 as a summer home by a Galveston family, and is also known as the Trueheart House. You'll be intrigued by the huge volcanic boulders on the north and west sides of the historic house. Some are higher than the house—and thousands of years old.

Two porches, two gazebos, and patios with picnic areas add to the charm of the Neill Museum B&B. A bird haven, deer and wildlife are sometimes spotted on the grounds.

The Veranda Country Inn

Hosts: Kathie and Paul Woods, 210 Court Avenue, Fort Davis 79734, (888) 383-2847, 3 guest rooms, 5 suites, 1 guest house, private baths, full breakfast, $–$$$$, no pets, no smoking, MC, V, D, S

One block west of the Court House, The Veranda Country Inn is surrounded by walled courtyards and gardens. Built in 1883, this adobe building has two-inch thick walls, 12-foot ceilings, and polished oak or pine floors. It's aptly named, too! Wait until you see the front porch, which has 12 rockers! You won't find many empty seats at night when guests stargaze.

Furnished with antiques and collectibles, the Veranda's eight rooms and suites are spacious; most have king-sized beds, but two have double beds. Behind the gardens, under the shade of a large pecan tree, is the 1,400-square-foot Carriage House, which has two rooms with king-sized beds, a bath, kitchen, and living room.

You won't go hungry here! Hearty breakfast highlights may include everything from freshly baked biscuits or coffee cake to soufflés, omelets, crepes, or French toast made from homemade French bread, and fresh fruit salad. A lot of the herbs, produce, and fruit come from the Veranda's gardens and orchard.

Minutes away from renowned astronomy and historic sites, and scenic hiking and biking trails, this charming B&B is perfect for small conferences and retreats as well as those seeking a change in pace.

LUBBOCK

Woodrow House

Hosts: Dawn and David Fleming, 2629 19th St., Lubbock 79410, (806) 793-3330, fax (806) 793-7676, 7 guest rooms, 7 private baths, breakfast buffet, $$, children welcome, no pets, no smoking, MC, V, AE

You can walk across to the Texas Tech campus if you stay at this B&B, which is named for David's paternal grandfather. The hosts themselves are graduates of the University, so naturally, one guest room has a red and black decor and Red Raider memorabilia. Items of interest in other guest rooms include a shadow box in the President's Room containing David's father's ticket to the luncheon planned for Kennedy and Johnson in Dallas on November 22, 1963, and Buddy Holly posters and '57 toy Chevys in the 50s Room. Almost all guest rooms have a claw-foot tub with a ring shower, a phone, and alarm clock. The couple paid as much attention to detail in decorating as in designing their dream house—a three-story, Greek Revival-style structure, which they built in 1995 after four years of research.

David is the chef, and guests gobble up biscuits and gravy and other dishes on the bountiful buffet either at the big bar in the kitchen or the formal dining room. There is a vintage Coke machine on the back porch, videos games in the basement, and cable TV in the Gathering Room. With four children of their own, the couple have plenty of toys for young visitors on hand, too. Hospitality abounds, and Dawn doesn't need much coaxing to play the harp for guests!

Lubbock has a number of other appealing B&Bs, which David and Dawn can tell you about if the Woodrow House is full.

MARATHON

Captain Shepard's Inn

Co-managers: Bill and Laurie Stevens, P. O. Box 46, Marathon 79842, (800) 884-4243, fax (915) 386-4510, 5 guest rooms, 6 baths, full breakfast, $$$, children welcome, but no pets, smoking in one sitting room, all cr

Captain Shepard would be pleased that the spacious, two-story adobe home he built in 1899 has become an appealing bed and breakfast inn that bears his name. The former sea captain, who came to this area as a surveyor in 1881, got a headstart on immortality when he decided the terrain reminded him of the Plains of Marathon in Greece, which is how this West Texas town's name came to be. Not content to rest on his laurels, the good Captain helped lay out the town lots in 1885, established the first post office, and served as the first postmaster.

Captain Shepard's Inn has hardwood floors and an eclectic ambience that reflects Western, Spanish Colonial, and Mexican influences. All the guest rooms have private baths and porches. One also has a Jacuzzi and a queen-sized antique brass bed, while another has two double beds and a porch with a view of the Glass Mountains. Two sitting rooms, a dining room, kitchen, a TV, and phone are also available.

Breakfast is served at Captain Shepard's Inn between 7 a.m. and 9 a.m. B&B guests also can use the pool and other facilities at the nearby historic Gage Hotel, which now manages and takes reservations for Captain Shepard's Inn as well for Russ Tidwell who owns both. Marathon is the major gateway to Big Bend National Park.

QUITAQUE

Quitaque Quail Lodge

Hosts: Vinita Floye and Guss Hrncir, Highway 86 (Box 36), Quitaque 79255, (806) 455-1261, (800) 299-1261, 3 guest rooms, 3 baths, 2 suites, 1 carriage house, country breakfast, $$–$$$$, smoking areas provided, mature children welcome, smoking in designated areas, no pets, no cr

First of all, pronounce it Kitty-Kway! It means "End of the Trail." This is a retreat that you hunters will especially enjoy, but the hospitable hosts and scenic ambience should appeal to most everyone. The Quitaque Quail Lodge is on 36 acres at the base of the Caprock. This contemporary country ranch-style lodge has a lot of amenities, such as a really nice-sized swimming pool (don't forget your bathing suit), as well as courts for tennis, basketball, volleyball, and croquet. Play to your heart's content!

You might find it more exciting, however, to go exploring. It's an interesting area, with hike and bike trails. The wildlife in Caprock Canyon State Park six miles away will present some great photo opportunities. Fish in Lake Theo or hunt. Quail, turkey, pheasant, mule deer, aoudad sheep, and wild hog are all fair game in season.

Quitaque Lodge has an inviting room with a 20-foot fireplace and imported rock pillars, a dining room with a mirrored ceiling (this is where you'll eat breakfast), and seven lovely guest rooms. You have a choice of king, queen, or twin beds in the guest rooms; two rooms have a private veranda. There is also a separate carriage house. Three miles away in Quitaque is a Sidewalk Museum, and you're only 13 miles from Turkey.

SHAMROCK

Ye Olde Home Place

Host: Anaruth Pendleton, 311 E. 2nd St., Shamrock 79079, (806) 256-2295, 5 guest rooms, 3 shared baths, full breakfast, $, no pets, no smoking inside, MC, V

Don't be deceived by this B&B's name. It is *not* a rustic getaway, but the showplace of Shamrock with a terraced lawn and garden. Known as the Pendleton Manor and filled with family treasures and Persian carpets, it has hand-painted ceiling designs, mahogany beams and doors, and leaded windows. Built in 1904, it was enlarged considerably and remodeled in 1933 as a 5,000-square-foot, red brick English Tudor home.

Two huge bathrooms downstairs have an art-deco look: pink and lavender tile, green fixtures and stained-glass windows in the shower and in the ceiling above the tub. The upstairs bath is striking, too, with black and white tile flooring.

Between the two first-floor rooms, which have double beds, is a sunroom with a day bed and a trundle, so a family can have a suite. There are twin beds in one of the upstairs guest rooms and double beds in the other two. A second floor sitting area has a TV, a small frig with complimentary soft drinks, and a coffee pot. An evening snack is another hospitable touch. Breakfast is served in the formal dining room.

Shamrock, a town of about 2,500 that has a celebrated St. Patrick's Day parade plus an outstanding museum, is about 90 miles east of Amarillo.

SWEETWATER

Mulberry Mansion

Hosts: Beverly and Raymond Stone, 1400 Sam Houston St., Sweetwater 79556, (800) 235-3811, (915) 235-3811, fax (915) 235-3811, or contact Bed & Breakfast Texas Style (972) 298-8586, 2 suites, 2 rooms, 4 baths, 1 two-bedroom suite in the Annex, a four-course gourmet breakfast, $–$$$$, no restrictions, all cr

Spending the night at this incredible B&B is something to savor. Just inside the front door of the 9,200-square-foot, open, California-style home is an elevated, glass-roofed atrium that is about 24-feet high, 20-feet wide and full of palm trees and tropical plants! For an additional price, you can enjoy a lavish, candlelight dinner for two in the beautiful atrium. At Mulberry Mansion, romance is in the air!

Built in 1913 by Thomas Trammel, the Father of Sweetwater, the luxurious mansion opened to the public as a B&B in 1993, the year after it was acquired and restored by the Stones. Furnished with elegant French antiques, the white stucco house has a Texas Historical Marker and gets its name from the large mulberry tree on the spacious grounds.

A bottle of wine or champagne or drink of your choice (the B&B has an extensive wine cellar) and a generous-sized tray of chicken strips, shrimp, and croissant sandwiches and other snacks are welcoming treats, while amenities include plush robes and turned-down sheets. You'll enjoy the bar room with the big screen TV and tabletop shuffleboard, too.

The richly appointed Royal Suite, which takes up the entire second floor, has a king-sized bed, a sitting area, a sound system, refrigerator, a private dining room, and a deck, which wraps around three sides of the house. And wait until you see the huge bathroom with a glass-enclosed marble shower, window seat, and a 90-gallon Roman marble tub. Bubble bath, oils, candles, and special soaps are furnished for added pleasure. There is also an oversized marble tub in the Victorian Splendor suite on the first floor, which includes a glass-enclosed porch and fireplace. The other two guest rooms—one has a king-sized bed, and the second, a queen—are smaller than the suites, but charming. TVs, stereos, and telephones are in all guest rooms, which are handicapped accessible.

In the morning, juice, coffee, a fresh fruit compote, and the newspaper are brought to all the guest rooms. Then comes a four-course gourmet breakfast, which many prefer to eat in the atrium or their room.

The Stones also have a 2,400-square-foot, elegantly furnished, two-bedroom suite available in a 1915 house across the street they call the Annex. It includes a living room with a fireplace, formal dining room, breakfast nook and kitchen, glassed-in porch, and bath.

Surprisingly, there are no restrictions, and children, pets, and smokers are all welcome in the marvelous Mulberry Mansion or the Annex.

TURKEY

Hotel Turkey

Innkeepers: Gary L. and Suzie Johnson, P. O. Box 37, Turkey 79261, (800) 657-7110, (806) 423-1151, 15 guest rooms, 10 baths, full breakfast, $$, no pets, no smoking, MC, V, AE

Yes, there really is a Turkey, Texas! A Panhandle town of about 500, Turkey's population increases considerably the last weekend of April when thousands come for Bob Wills Day, one of Texas' best festivals, and to see the Bob Wills Monument. (He was the town barber before he made millions with "San Antonio Rose.")

Listed on the National Register of Historic Places, Hotel Turkey, which was built in 1927, has attracted quite a few fans of its own since Jane and Scott Johnson acquired and restored it in 1988. Thanks to their clever marketing and management and offbeat 1927 country decor,

Hotel Turkey has become a living museum. Jane's cooking, especially her sweet potato pancakes, helped put it on the "must visit" map, too. Since everyone was clamoring for her sweet potato pancake mix, Jane and Scott are marketing that now, so Gary (his cousin) and Suzie are keeping Hotel Turkey on track. On five acres that include tennis courts and chuck wagons for catered dinners, Hotel Turkey attracts a lot of group tours as well as B&B buffs.

VERNON

Victorian Rose

Host: Jan Bergman, 2929 Texas Street, Vernon 76384, (800) 805-8066, ph/fax (817) 552-5354, or contact Bed & Breakfast Texas Style (972) 298-8586, 2 guest rooms, 2 suites, 4 baths, continental breakfast OYO, $, outdoor smoking, "well-behaved" children and pets welcome, MC, V

Located midway between Dallas and Amarillo on US 287, Vernon originally was called Eagle Flats because of the large number of eagles nesting in the area. The name was changed when the town became the county seat in 1880 in honor of George Washington's Virginia home. (Since there are no mountains, "Mount" was dropped.)

The front porch of this 1920 three-story Victorian house overlooks landscaped grounds. On the first floor is a tea room with lace tablecloths and hardwood floors where lunch is served during the week. Popcorn is a pleasant surprise in the second-floor guest rooms, which have a Victorian decor, a TV, phone, microwave, refrigerator, and coffee/tea pot. One suite overlooks the pool, while the L-shaped Swing Room has a porch swing where you can read or watch TV. Pets are welcome in the backyard, which is fenced. The reasonable room rates bring business travelers back time and again, as well as vacationing B&B buffs. The Victorian Rose B&B is unhosted, but Jan lives a few doors away.

She can point the way to a number of antique shops and The Red River Valley Museum, which includes memorabilia and records of jazz artist Jack Teagarden, a Vernon native. Just north of town is Doan's Crossing, where more than six million cattle crossed the Red River.

HOUSTON, THE GULF COAST, EAST, SOUTHEAST, AND SOUTH TEXAS

BELLVILLE

High Cotton Inn

Hosts: George and Anna Horton, 214 S. Live Oak, Bellville 77418, (800) 321-9796, (409) 865-9796, 4 guest rooms, 2½ baths, full breakfast, $, no pets, children allowed depending on age, no smoking, MC, V, D

Bellville, the "belle of bluebonnet country," has within its midst a stately Victorian B&B, the High Cotton Inn. Merchant Charles W. Hellmuth, son of one of Stephen F. Austin's original 300 settlers, built the 4,000-square-foot cypress homestead in 1906 for his wife, Emma Anna, and their eight children. Today the historic home, characterized by large, accommodating rooms, balconies, giant windows and transoms, is presided over by owners George and Anna Horton, who enjoy visiting with guests on the back porch or poolside.

205

High Cotton Inn

Spacious second-floor guest rooms are decorated in honor of Horton relatives and friends. Uncle Buster's Room, for example, is dedicated to Cleveland Sewall, George's great-uncle, a respected name at Rice University. The room contains many of Sewall's possessions. For the ladies, the Hortons have put on display the delicate white beaded ball gown worn by grandmother Sallie Sewall when she attended Houston's Notsuoh Ball ("Notsuoh" spells "Houston" backward), held at the turn-of-the-century to commemorate "cotton as king."

While you're here in Horton "high cotton," forget the diet. The couple offers six varieties of their famous "High Cotton Cookie," distributed nationwide. Anna explains how they got the idea to market their goodies. "Our guests kept stealing our cookies out of the cookie jar, so we decided they must be good enough to sell." Other dietary pitfalls include Anna's Christmas rum cake and tours conducted by the Blue Bell Creamery and Bellville Potato Chip Factory. Great attractions, these companies give visitors two excellent chances to take in a few more calories.

BRENHAM

Historic Brenham, the county seat of Washington County and the birthplace of Texas, is best known for its bluebonnets and Blue Bell Ice Cream. Tourists here can tour the ice cream creameries, the nearby Antique Rose Emporium, the Monastery of St. Clare, known for its miniature horses, and the Star of the Republic Museum at Washington-on-the-Brazos State Park. But the most spectacular time to visit Brenham is in late March and early April, when the entire county is ablaze with bluebonnets and Indian paintbrush. But whatever time of year, Texas is at its country best in Washington County.

Ant Street Inn Bed and Breakfast

Hosts: Tommy and Pam Traylor, 107 West Commerce, Brenham 77833, (800) 481-1951, (409) 836-7393, fax (409) 836-7595, 14 rooms with private baths, gourmet breakfast, $$$–$$$$, children over 12 welcome, no pets, smoking in designated areas only, most cr

From the outside, the Ant Street Inn doesn't look like a B&B but more like a historic downtown building. Built in the late 1800s, the imposing two-story structure covers a full city block. However, there's no doubt this is a "traditional" B&B when hosts Tommy and Pam Traylor greet guests at the door. Like proud parents, they lead their guests through their luxurious accommodation to guest rooms that reflect Pam's gift for decorating and Tommy's knowledge of antiques. In the morning, this hospitable couple serves a gourmet fare fit for the pages of *Southern Living Magazine.* And no wonder, as Pam worked for the publication's prestigious cooking school for more than seven years as it toured the South. An average breakfast here includes such delights as Brie and Bacon Quiche, Strawberry Popovers with Romanoff Sauce, and lowfat blueberry and yogurt parfaits.

Guest rooms here are named after each southern city Pam toured, and furnishings differ depending upon the style indicative of that state's theme. Most pieces, including valuable antique bedroom suites (one is a magnificent chestnut plantation bed and dresser), stained-glass windows, and artwork, were purchased on a whirlwind tour of the United States. Pam has used her knowledge of decoration, probably learned from her connection with the magazine, to add color and flair with her choice of fabrics and wall coverings. Correct choices regarding antiques stem from the couple's knowledge of the field as Tommy is a dealer, and both are licensed auctioneers who occasionally host local auctions in their grand ballroom.

Little touches here and there hint to the hosts' humor. Humorous old family photos, a stuffed squirrel and weasel, an umbrella lamp, and a dentist chair mix with elegant furniture to add variety. For a chuckle, ask to see the restored 100-year-old freight elevator, which is the focal point of the Memphis Room. A huge place that can accommodate up to 250, this B&B, with its smoke-free bar and massive stained-glass chandelier, is a great spot to enjoy a microbrewery beer. The ballroom is also available for business meetings and receptions. Businessmen also have access to work tables and in-room phones with computer jacks.

And for you history buffs—an old-time gambler lost his life over a poker game upstairs over 100 years ago.

Captain Tacitus T. Clay House

Hosts: Thelma M. Zwiener, Fieldstone Farm, 9445 FM 390 E. Independence, Brenham 77833, (409) 836-1916, 5 guest rooms, 4 baths, full breakfast, $–$$, children welcome, no pets, smoking in designated areas, no cr

Before Captain Tacitus T. Clay left Washington County to defend the Confederacy, he talked of converting his home's upper floor into a ballroom. That all changed once he returned from bitter battle minus a leg. The war hero would waltz no more, his dreams of building a ballroom abandoned.

Today, Captain Clay's home, now owned by Thelma Zwiener, presides over the serene Fieldstone Farm in Independence on the outskirts of Brenham. The front veranda of this 1852 Greek Revival house looks out over verdant fields, shaded in the distance by trees that must have been there during the captain's day. Guests here really get a sense of Confederate life before Reconstruction. The house is a history lesson itself, whispering secrets about the past with markings made on the porch by a whittler 150 years ago. As was the custom, rooms were built around a "dog run," a grand hall dividing the house symmetrically. Many of the furnishings are original to the home, as well as a family quilt, adorned with the Clay family star and brought to Texas by wagon.

If you love horses, you'll really like the Captain Clay House, where Thelma raises quarter horses and thoroughbreds as well as curious miniature horses that share the surrounding pastures. Breakfast with Thelma is southern style with focus on eggs from the barnyard. Wine and cheese are served in the evening on the veranda, and the morning sun brings a fresh fruit basket to each guest room. A hot tub enclosed in a gazebo is also a relaxing treat, and recently Thelma has added a room to the Gate House, perfect for families.

Far View—A Bed and Breakfast

Hosts: David and Tonya Meyer, 1804 South Park Street, Brenham 77833, (409) 836-1672, 5 bedrooms, 4 with private baths, gourmet breakfast, $$$—$$$$, children over 12 welcome, no pets, smoking permitted in designated areas, MC, V, AE

In the late twenties and early thirties when Brenham residents celebrated Mayfest, the porch landing of the gracious Far View provided a stage for the crowning of the event's king and queen. In 1936, Texas governor James V. Allred and Governor Phillip La Follette of Wisconsin stayed here when they visited Washington-on-the-Brazos for the annual centennial celebration. The Brenham National Guard Honor Team stood at attention as the governors walked up the driveway.

High-ranking among the best B&Bs in Texas, Far View, originally built by a respected Brenham resident, is a must if you're staying in Brenham. A true B&B in that hosts are on the grounds and serve an elegant breakfast that varies from potato, egg, and cheese casserole with hot homemade bread to French Toast Estrada, complemented by fruits and vegetables straight from the garden. Morning sunlight changes color as it comes through six original stained-glass windows of the dining room, furnished with 1930 Chippendale. Recently restored by David and Tonya Meyer, the mansion with its surrounding two acres offers elegant "rooms with a view" that look out onto the antique rose garden or the ancient oak trees, or the gardens that mix herbs, flowers, fruits, and vegetables. Guest room decor ranges from modernized Victorian to intimate and canopied to masculine and rustic. Some open to private balconies that give visitors a northward view of Brenham—a great shady place to have a glass of wine.

Nothing is musty here, and these great hosts share warmth for true hospitality and yet a nose for business that makes a stay here one without want. The outside matches the inside. Stone walkways lined with violets, impatiens, and caladiums invite guests to stroll under towering trees. English ivy and fountain with bird feeders projects a coolness even on hot Texas days.

Schuerenberg House

Host: Kay Gregory, 503 West Alamo, Brenham 77833, (409) 830-7054, (800) 321-6234, 3 bedrooms (2 with private baths), 1 double suite, third-floor grand attic suite with private bath, gourmet breakfast, $$$–$$$$, children over 12 welcome, no pets, smoking permitted in designated areas, MC, V

A National Register of Historic Places listing that also sports a Texas Historical Marker, the Schuerenberg House sits majestically amid the 4,428-acre land grant awarded to widow Arabella Harrington by Mexico in 1831. Drawn up for Stephen F. Austin's second colony, this parcel of land is now home for Washington County, including the city of Brenham. What Mrs. Harrington had to do to get a small part of Texas must be a story in itself, but this newly restored three-story B&B, with its pale yellow Queen Anne and Eastlake exterior trimmed in burgundy and dark green, has a history that goes back over 100 years.

Family and marriage counselor Kay Gregory is understandably proud of her Victorian jewel that still contains original fixtures, stained-glass windows, curly pine staircase, long leaf pine floors, and original furniture, all just restored. If you stay here, ask Kay to tell you the amazing story of how she purchased the home and all its furnishings and family memorabilia. All was in dire disrepair down to caved in roof and decaying furniture. Now, the home stands as testimony to Kay's diligence and hard work as she has saved a masterpiece and filled it with period wallpapers, elegant fabrics, and tasteful carpets to bring out the shining original woods.

Built by the son of an exiled Prussian military man, Captain Johan Frederick William Von Schuerenberg, who later trained Confederate soldiers, the house contains two parlors, one for gentlemen and one for ladies, a dining room with a "hunt" motif, and space enough to accommodate a family network in town for a reunion, a wedding, or a tour of the bluebonnets. The third floor, however, a huge grand attic room, houses two double beds, a little balcony, a turret toy room, and a "sleeping porch," used in the old days when it was too hot to sleep indoors.

The fare here is gourmet and varied from Eggs a la Schuerenberg, an egg and cheese, ham, and mushroom dish to ham and basil quiche. Historic tours can also be arranged here.

James Walker Homestead

Hosts: John & Jane Barnhill, Route 7, Box 7176, Brenham 77833, (409) 836-6717, fax (409) 836-6922, 1 bedroom, 1 loft, 1 daybed, 1 bath, full breakfast, $$$$, OYO, no pets, no children, no smoking, no cr

When the Barnhills bought a parcel of hilly pastureland 20 years ago, they didn't know that the log hay barn was one of the oldest existing buildings in Texas. Today the fully restored cabin that was covered in tin and thus preserved in its own "skin," is a tribute to builder James Walker, one of Stephen F. Austin's original 300 colonists. Located downhill from the Barnhill residence, this Texas treasure is characterized by original pine floors, cedar logs, half dove-tailed construction, a huge fireplace, and loft. If you like Texas antiques, you'll appreciate the way Jane and John, vice-president of sales/advertising for Blue Bell Creamery, have used Fayette County pieces to lend even more charm to this unique B&B.

A listing of the National Register of Historic Places, the cabin, which in John's words is painted "homemade vanilla," sleeps four people and is surrounded in the spring by wildflowers that add brilliance to rolling pastures. Enjoy wine and cheese in the evening as you watch the sun descend on the resident 60 acres with stocked pond. Of course, you'll find the refrigerator stocked with Texas' favorite ice cream. As for the Barnhills, they call their treasure a BB&BB—bed and breakfast and Blue Bell. James Walker never had it so good.

BRYAN/COLLEGE STATION

Angelsgate Bed and Breakfast

Hosts: Gary and Beth Goyen, 615 East 29th St., Bryan 77803, (409) 779-1231 or (888) 779-1231, 2 suites with private baths, gourmet breakfast, $$$–$$$$, children 10 and over welcome, no pets, smoking permitted outside only, MC, V

You'll certainly feel protected here under the sheltering arms of two stone angel statues that guard the front door of Angelsgate Bed and Breakfast. Apparently their guardianship has been steadfast as this pretty B&B has had staying power enough to last through a century of progress. Built in 1909 by Allister M. Waldrop, Angelgate has held the lofty distinction of being listed as a national historic landmark and past residence for one of Bryan's most respected early families. Allister, in fact, established the first exclusive retail mercantile business in the city and held the presidencies of the Chamber of Commerce and the Bryan City School Board. Mrs. Waldrop, however, would stand in no man's shadow for she also served as president of the United Daughters of the Confederacy, the Bryan Garden Club, and was a charter member of the Daughters of the American Revolution. Both Waldrop and his patriotic wife would be proud of what the Goyens have done to their beloved home.

Furnished with antiques, the most romantic accommodation is Lady Margaret's Suite, a nostalgic Victorian room with private bath and sitting room. All decorated in pinks, whites, and beige, the lace canopied bed surrounded by a rose garland motif is the focus of a room that looks out over the gazebo. Lord Garrett's Room, shaded in aristocratic emerald and gold leaf, also features a four-poster queen-sized bed with an adjacent fireside sitting area with art deco bath accent.

Also a great place for Aggies, no one goes home hungry here. The fare is gourmet and lots of it. An historic carriage house and backyard cottage is also available to guests who wish to stay for a weekend or longer.

Bonnie Gambrel (Bryan)

Hosts: Blocker and Dorothy Trant, 600 East 27th St., Bryan 77803, (409) 779-1022, fax (409) 779-1040, 1 suite with private bath, 2 guest rooms, 1 bath, gourmet breakfast or brunch, $$$–$$$$, children 12 and over (facilities for one infant), no pets, smoking permitted in designated areas, MC, V, D

Located in the original township of Bryan, Bonnie Gambrel was the first home in the city to be placed on the National Register of Historic Places. Built by a Scottish widow in 1913, the deep red two-story barnlike 15-room structure with white columns, porches, and facia presents a stately American picture, particularly with the American flags flying at the entrance. And no wonder, as the Trants have deep political feelings rooted in their love of America's diverse history. Blocker, in fact, is an avid Texas historian and has acted as a precinct judge. He also is an equestrian, who is affiliated with the Larkspur Hunt.

As for Dorothy, she is known as an hostess *extraordinaire* who has acted in that capacity for many notables, including one First Lady, who visit A&M on a regular basis. However, you don't have to be Texas "royalty" to stay here. In fact, Aggie fans are treated like kings and enjoy the many amenities such as the swimming pool, spa, and exercise room, wraparound porches with wicker furniture, and wet bar. A significant antique collection here makes those in the know truly envious. The impressive cherry oak dining room table, which is canopied by a rose-painted ceiling and surrounded by chairs decorated with delicate needlepoint hummingbirds, has provided surface for a very famous

Texan indeed. According to Blocker, General Sam Houston plotted his strategies of war against Santa Anna at this very table.

Messina Hof Vineyard/Vintner's Loft Bed & Breakfast (Bryan)

Hosts: Paul & Merrill Bonarrigo, 4545 Old Reliance Rd., Bryan 77802, (409) 778-9463, fax (409) 778-1729, 1 bedroom, 1 bath, continental breakfast, $$$, no pets, no children, no smoking, MC, V, AE

Now, award-winning wine is not the only thing you can enjoy at the Messina Hof Wine Cellars and Winery. Paul and Merrill Bonarrigo have converted the loft of their romantic Visitor's Center for B&B guests. Reconstructed from Brazos Valley's first grand estate owned by a past ambassador of Uruguay, the Visitor's Center with its intriguing architecture, governs the 40-acre vineyard that has made Messina Hof a wine to be reckoned with among competitors.

As they approach, guests to Messina Hof are always charmed by a pretty rose garden, filled with 360 pink floribunda and planted in honor of the ambassador's wife who oversaw 3,500 of her own rose bushes. In the downstairs cellars, guests browse through racks filled with a variety of vintages and learn as hostesses explain how to choose, savor, and store good wine. As you walk along the vineyard, note the rose bushes that stand guard at each row's end. They not only add color to the crop's geometric climb over the Bryan hills, they also fall victim first to bugs who prefer grape leaves second only to roses. This gives sprayers fair warning.

The Vintner's Loft, though small, is a great place for a couple to be alone. It has a private bath and is decorated with antiques and pretty fabrics of harvest gold. Morning fare is continental and served in B&B quarters.

For lunch or dinner, guests can now enjoy authentic Sicilian meals at the winery's Trattoria Restaurant with its patio nestled in the vineyard itself. And, by mid 1997, a 12-suite B&B should be standing among Messina Hof vineyards.

The Flippen Place (College Station)

Hosts: Flip and Susan Flippen, 1199 Haywood Dr., College Station 77845, (409) 693-7660, fax (409) 693-8458, 3 guest rooms, 3 private baths, gourmet breakfast, $$$-$$$$, no children, no pets, no smokers, MC, V, AE

Aggie fans, this one's for you. The Flippen Place, surrounded by breathtaking natural beauty, provides the tired visitor with a place of refuge. Once an Amish barn transported from Ohio to the Flippen 40-acre property, this understated elegant abode is unhosted; although, Susan arrives in the morning to prepare a gourmet breakfast or brunch for her guests, who enjoy sipping coffee as they gaze from the spacious living area out onto the lush greenery of surrounding woods and graceful English gardens that surround The Flippen Place. Anything but "country cute," the decor here is fashionably simple, a hint of the Flippen's taste for elegance.

Some 30 feet overhead, 170-year-old beams remind us of the staying power of nature and are testimony to the craftsmanship of old masters. Hiking trails lure even the most sedate visitor, and two fish ponds are full of bass and catfish that await your bait. Susan greets guests with arrival snack baskets, says good-bye with a check-out gift, and provides conversation if asked. Flip, her husband, is a psychiatrist, so she has been schooled in the art of knowing when her company is wanted. Oh! An added fact for A&M fans—both Flippens are avid Aggies!

BURTON

The Knittel Homestead

Hosts: Steve and Cindy Miller, P.O. Box 132, 520 Main, Burton 77835, (409) 289-5102, 3 bedrooms, 3 baths, gourmet breakfast, $$-$$$, no pets, children over 12 welcome, no smoking, no cr

In 19th-century Burton, cotton was king. When the crop lost its prominence in Texas in the 1920s, most local farmers moved on. Today, only remnants of that prosperity remain, but visitors can get a sampling here of what the good life was like for Burton's leading citizen, Herman Knittel, whose Main Street house is now a B&B.

A Prussian immigrant, a true Confederate, and later a state senator, Knittel saw the importance of cotton in Texas and fought to keep it productive. He established the post office and mercantile store, and in 1870 built his family a 4,000-square-foot Queen Anne home, shaped like a Mississippi River steamboat. Upper and lower galleries, wraparound porches and a magnificent turret grace the exterior while inside an Old World winding staircase transported by ship from Germany is testimony to exquisite workmanship.

Monday through Saturday mornings experience a delicious all-you-can-eat country breakfast across the street at the Miller's Burton Cafe. Also owned by the innkeepers, this historic cafe was built in the 1930s and is the hub of community activities as well as a favorite of tourists. Sunday morning you will enjoy a full breakfast in the inn's formal dining room. Savor offerings such as French Toast Royale, buttermilk pecan pancakes, and fresh Burton sausage and bacon.

The Long Point Inn

Hosts: Bill and Jeannine Neinast, Route 1, Box 86-A, Burton 77835, (409) 289-3171, 3 bedrooms, 2 baths, 1 log cabin, full breakfast, $$–$$$$, no pets, children welcome, smoking designated areas, no cr

If you've ever dreamed of sitting in bluebonnet fields while cattle graze languidly nearby or if you're in the mood to fish in a private flowing stream, make haste to Burton. Col. William Neinast and his schoolteacher wife, Jeannine, preside over their German-style B&B, patterned after the old hunting lodges and located within a stone's throw of Lake Somerville. A 175-acre working Beefmaster ranch, this accommodation provides a view unspoiled by advancing progress.

The land, in fact, has always stayed the same. A part of the historic Stephen F. and Henry Austin leagues, the hilly ranch land was patented by the Mexican government to the Austin family and the Original Three Hundred. The Neinast family has owned the property for well over a century.

Guests may come alone or bring a party of ten, children included. The Neinasts have also restored an 1840s log cabin that was on the property when Bill's grandfather bought it after the Civil War. Equipped with all the modern conveniences, it has a perfect distant view of Lake

Somerville. Six fish-stocked ponds, flowing streams and a spring-fed waterfall share this land that is full of shady nature trails, perfect for biking and hiking. A particularly beautiful time to visit here is March through May when bluebonnets and Indian paintbrush flourish. Featured in the Texas Highway Department slide presentation on wildflowers for LBJ State Park visitors, the grounds of the Long Point Inn are shown blanketed with bluebonnets.

CHAPPELL HILL

Browning Plantation

Hosts: Richard and Mildred Ganchan, Route 1, Box 8, Chappell Hill 77426, (409) 836-6144, (713) 661-6761, 4 guest bedrooms, 2 private baths, 2 shared half baths, gourmet breakfast, $$$$, no pets, no children, no smoking, no cr

On the outskirts of Chappell Hill, hidden from the present by ageless cedar, pecan, and bois d'arc trees, stands the Browning Plantation, a listing on the National Register of Historic Places. Once the social center for area society, the Greek Revival-style residence is today, as it was then, a monument to its builder, Colonel W. W. Browning. The colonel loved his land, his family, and the South, but he was also a man of learning who became president of two local colleges.

In 1857, he built a graceful plantation home with porches, verandas, and a spectacular rooftop widow's walk, amid his 2,000 cotton- and corn-yielding acres. The good life prevailed here until 1860 when the Civil War broke out—a war that would eventually put an end to Browning's prosperity and bring the death of his only son. Then by purchasing worthless Confederate war bonds during the final days of the war, he lost his entire fortune to a lost cause.

The hollow remains of the old mansion were all that was left of the Brownings until Richard and Mildred Ganchan bought the shell ten years ago. The broken windows and doors became avenues for every woodsy creature, and generations of raccoons and bees had for years lived in the old chimneys. The new owners, however, saw it as a gold mine of history about to be lost. They spent a fortune and performed a miracle, and today the Browning Plantation stands as a tribute to the love of a man for his country and his son.

Browning Plantation

The Ganchans also offer guests another accommodation, located behind the plantation. The Depot, designed to resemble a Santa Fe Railroad station, provides overnighters with two bedrooms, each with its own private bath. There's also a garage full of steam trains, once the property of an amusement park. When the Ganchan son-in-law, an engineer, is present, he takes visitors on the little train that spits and sputters down a one-mile track.

The Mulberry House

Host: Katie Cron, P.O. Box 5, Chappell Hill 77426, (409) 830-1311, 5 bedrooms, 5 baths, gourmet breakfast, $$–$$$, no pets, no children, no smoking, no cr

The John Sterling Smith, Jr. home, known affectionately as The Mulberry House because of the profusion of mulberry trees on Chestnut Street, has been painstakingly restored to its original 1855 condition with all the conveniences of modern day added. Almost as old as Chappell Hill itself, it looks as though it was built yesterday, the result of efforts by Houstonians Myrv and Katie Cron.

In 1873, John Sterling Smith purchased the home that was passed down to his descendants for the next 110 years. In 1983, Marie Ward Smith, a teacher and Chappell Hill's first lady postmaster, sold the homestead to the Crons. The only surviving example of Queen Anne architecture in this area, this listing on the National Register of Historic Places and Texas Historical Landmark recipient reminds guests of a storybook setting with wraparound porches, Doric columns, and impressive octagonal cupola with high tent roof. You won't find a dark corner in this romantic B&B where country light streams through large windows and transoms. Twelve-foot ceilings add a sense of space, while light colors, antiques, and over-stuffed sofas and chairs project a homey ambience. Guest rooms are inside, while the carriage house provides additional quarters on the grounds to accommodate larger groups.

The Stagecoach Inn

Hosts: Mr. and Mrs. H. Moore, Main at Chestnut, P.O. Box 339,
Chappell Hill 77426, (409) 836-9515, 6 bedrooms, 4 baths,
gourmet breakfast, $$$–$$$$, no pets, no children, no smoking,
no cr

If a real Scarlett O'Hara would have existed in Chappell Hill, she and strong-willed Mary Hargrove Haller would have been great friends. In 1847 the 18-year-old Mary, barely a bride of three months, founded Chappell Hill without consulting a soul, not even her husband. Imagine the poor groom's surprise when she told him she had used his money to buy the townsite. Apparently the marriage survived the blow as three years later they opened the Stagecoach Inn together. Before long, it became a favorite stop for many noted Texans riding the westbound stage from Houston.

The accommodations at the Stagecoach Inn were (and still are) nothing short of luxurious. A fine Texas example of early Greek Revival architecture, its 14-room two-story structure, built sturdily of stone and cedar, reveals a Texas eye for beauty, even in Mary's day. Gracious lines also go indoors beginning with the entry's beautifully curved oak stairway and walnut handrail.

Today, the Stagecoach Inn stands tall, thanks to Houstonians Harvin and Elizabeth Moore. Harvin, a Fellow in the American Institute of Architects, is well-known for his work in historic preservation. Elizabeth, an antiques dealer who has dedicated her life to preserving Texas history, has filled the inn with quality pieces, oriental rugs, and period fabrics. The Stagecoach Inn is open for tours by appointment only. Overnighters have their choice of staying in the inn or in Elizabeth's antique shop, the Hackberry Tree, also historic.

Chappell Hill is in the heart of bluebonnet country, where wildflowers are in full bloom the latter part of March and early April.

COLUMBUS

When Columbus celebrated its 150th anniversary in 1973, playwright I. E. Clark wrote of the town that had commissioned him to write an historical pageant: "Out of the most gripping episode in Texas history has grown an independent community with a personality all its own.

I think this symbolizes the story of America. I'm glad Columbus discovered America so that America could discover Columbus."

Today, Columbus, known as the "city of live oaks" with its tree-lined streets and low crime rate, seems unaffected by the ever-changing world. But for the explorer in search of land with a past, this old town is well steeped in Texas history. Local archives tell of the town being burned by Sam Houston in an attempt to stifle the advancement of Santa Anna and his men on their way to the Battle of San Jacinto.

Visit here and see the beautiful 1886 Stafford Opera House, which once hosted such celebrities as Lillian Russell and Houdini. See also the United Daughters of the Confederacy Museum, the Nesbitt Memorial Library with Texas Room, and the Santa Claus museum, and in May, residents open their doors to tourists for the annual Magnolia Homes Tour.

The Gant House

Host: Laura A. Rau, 936 Bowie St., Columbus 78934,
(409) 732-5135, 2 bedrooms, 1 bath, continental, OYO, $$–$$$,
no pets, no children, no smoking, V, MC

The interior walls of the Gant House provided an excellent canvas for some unknown 19th-century German artist who loved to stencil. He would have been happy to know that Laura Ann Rau has gone to a considerable amount of trouble to immortalize him by preserving his work for the modern world.

Laura Ann discovered the rustic home in deep woods near Alleyton. She struck a deal with the Gants who had lived in it for a century and then moved it to Columbus. She realized as time went on that what she found had historic significance, for not only did the structure represent primitive Texas but the interior also still displayed the original pattern box stenciling executed with buttermilk-based paint. So authentic were the colors and designs that they were later copied for the Texas Room of the DAR Museum in Washington D.C.

Laura Ann, proprietor of Atascosita Antiques and direct descendant of the Alleys who helped Stephen F. Austin settle this land, has furnished the two-guest home with quality period pieces, including sturdy "Texas" beds. Other rooms include a hall-sitting room, bath, and a modern kitchen with steep German staircase and original cabinetry displaying tin star panels, a popular 19th-century feature.

Magnolia Homes Tour participants visit the Gant House every year during the first full weekend in May.

Magnolia Oaks Bed and Breakfast

Hosts: Bob and Nancy Stiles, 634 Spring, Columbus 78934, (409) 732-2726, 6 guest rooms, 6 baths, full breakfast, $$$–$$$$, no small children, no pets, smoking in designated areas, no cr

The Magnolia Oaks B&B has Texas royalty in its lineage as it was built in 1890 by Marcus Harvey Townsend, a Texas state representative and senator. A splendid example of Eastlake Victorian gingerbread, this striking home was built in the shape of a cross, thus a feeling of closeness to nature on all sides. In fact, massive magnolia and oak trees shade the decorated porches with their delicate laces of wood. Ten-foot-tall walk-through windows, intricately carved doors and woodwork, and stained-glass windows paint colorful designs through the many rooms that emit peace and solitude. Robert Frost would have loved it here.

Owners Bob and Nancy Stiles (Nancy is an elementary school principal) are great hosts who serve a banquet for breakfast including quiches, biscuits, muffins, bacon, and sausages, for starters. Bob sometimes entertains guests with his guitar and a song. Guests testify that his tribute tune to the Sweetwater rattlesnake roundup is really funny. If you love the Lone Star state, you must stay in the Texas Room with its covered wagon lamps, boots resting near the fireplace, Texana books, and a Texas-sized cedar-log bed.

Raumonda House

Host: R. F. (Buddy) Rau, 1100 Bowie—P.O. Box 112, Columbus 78934, (409) 732-5135 (daytime), (409) 732-2190 (evenings), 3 bedrooms, 3 baths, continental plus, $$$, no pets, children (12 and over), smoking in designated areas, no cr

In 1965, R. F. (Buddy) Rau's dream of "always wanting to live in the shadow of the courthouse" came true. He and his mother, Hope Heller Rau, bought the 5,000-square-foot cypress mansion of 19th-century cattleman, Henry Ilse, and opened its spacious rooms, graceful verandas, and glassed galleries to the B&B traveler. The back porch looks out onto the formal Victorian garden with heated pool area, alive with blooming roses, camellias, jasmine, red bud, and bridal wreath. Crepe myrtle and crab apples accent an always occupied birdhouse near the flowing fountain and statue of a young woman, the personification of summer.

Buddy, owner of Atascosita Antiques, has filled this nine-room B&B with antiques and complements them with soft gold hues, muted green fabrics, and oriental rugs. The double parlor with original marble fireplace adds balance to the downstairs with matching chandeliers from Houston's old Majestic Theatre. Of particular interest is a striking painting created by artist David Crowley of a young boy frozen in thought. Other interesting accents include a massive brass lamp in the shape of a hawk and a baby grand piano for the musically inclined.

Buddy, who seconds as Columbus' tourism director *extraordinaire,* explains that his town sports 71 historic markers, many included in the self-guided walking tour. Plan also to see one of the monthly performances staged at the magnificently restored 1886 Stafford Opera House, the largest "flat floor" opera house in the state. Call (409) 732-8385 for a listing of the many Columbus events sponsored by the Chamber of Commerce.

CONROE

Heather's Glen

Hosts: Edward and Jamie George, 200 E. Phillips, Conroe 77301, (409) 441-6611 or (800) 66-JAMIE, fax (409) 441-6603, 5 guest rooms with private baths, gourmet breakfast, $$–$$$, call about children, no pets, smoking outside in designated areas only, V, MC, DC, AE

This turn-of-the-century Victorian mansion, located in downtown Conroe, is a tribute to its creator, John Wahrenberger, Conroe's wealthiest resident who owned everything from the general store to the town's funeral parlor. Today, known as Heather's Glen, the grand manor stands newly restored and a testament to the diligence of Ed and Jamie George, realtors who have saved their share of homes almost claimed by time.

Circled by its stately verandas and porches that are open for guest enjoyment, the 8,000-square-foot estate sits amid an acre grove of pecan and fruit trees. Grand old oaks add their shade as well as ambience to a home that was once the hubbub of Conroe society. Inside, Jamie has added soft greens and hues of rose with white accents for her rich fabrics and wallcoverings. Antiques here come from worldly corners yet furnishings are comfortable and inviting. One guest room is canopied with dusty rose coverlets. Goose down comforters and Ralph Lauren linens add quality to this stay, while fresh flowers adorn silver-and-crystal-set dining table and parlor. Soft music plays while guests enjoy a candlelit gourmet breakfast of Belgian waffles with nuts, and gourmet coffee. An industrious hostess, Jamie explains without hesitation that she can seat as many as 50 people for special occasions. All rooms, two with double Jacuzzis, have phones and an e-mail address is frequently used. Those handicapped have use of the motorized chair that glides up and down one of the two staircases.

As for Conroe, shoppers delight as they visit the wealth of antique shops, the Conroe Outlet Center, and the many golf resorts nearby. For fishermen, Lake Conroe is only a cast away, and for a romantic dinner and sight-seeing cruise, the Southern Empress, a 250-passenger stern-wheel paddle boat is a phone call away. For hikers, the Sam Houston National Forest is here as well as the Lone Star Hiking Trail, Jones State Forest, and Sweetleaf Nature Trail.

CORPUS CHRISTI

Bay Breeze Bed and Breakfast

Hosts: Perry and Frank Tompkins, (512) 882-4123 or contact Sand Dollar Hospitality, (512) 853-1222, 3 rooms with private baths, 1 cottage with private bath, kitchen, TV and porch, full breakfast, $$–$$$, no pets, no children, smoking in restricted areas, no cr

On the corner of the old, affluent Louisiana Boulevard, overlooking Corpus Christi Bay, the Bay Breeze Bed and Breakfast is hosted by a charming hostess, a model, and host, a real estate investor, who love to entertain and take pride in the home in which they or their family have lived since it was built in 1935. The house is chock-full of fascinating things, from the mahogany Steinway that belonged to Ohio

Corpus Christi

Barber, the man who invented the striking match, to an antique pool table from Brunswick. There are also smaller pieces such as Grandfather's hand-carved chairs and whatnots or Grandmother's collections of just about everything, including beaded purses, books, plates, tablecloths, paperweights, and children's clothes. Well, you name it and it's probably here in a tasteful array, lovingly cherished. The breakfast, served on china with crystal and silver, is spectacular to say the least (for example, a shrimp omelet for a non-meat eater in our party and a frittata, an egg with cream cheese and chives, with sauteed mushrooms on the side).

Colleyhouse B and B

Hosts: Evie and Tom Bookout, 211 Indiana, Corpus Christi 78404, (512) 887-7514 or Sand Dollar Hospitality, (512) 853-1222, 2 rooms with private baths and central entertainment room, $–$$, accepts older children, no pets, smoking in designated areas, older dog and cat in residence, no cr

Just off Ocean Drive in Corpus, this house—which is named for the architect who designed it and the Texas Instruments complex in Dallas—is deceptive from the outside because it looks like, well, a bunkhouse (but, we hasten to add, a well-designed bunkhouse!). The interior is more elaborate, primarily because your hosts have traveled extensively, which is reflected in their many sets of dishes from Japan, several Oriental pieces, and the various antiques. Rosemary from the garden on the veranda is added to the spinach omelet in the morning, and fresh-baked bread and muffins are standard fare. The core character of Colleyhouse, however, is found in the philosophy of its owners: they haven't met anybody who isn't interesting, and they're in the B&B business "for the fun of it." They truly want people to have a good time, so they stash the fridge in the entertainment center room with all kinds of things to drink, have a pile of peanuts no one could possibly eat in one night, and can arrange anything from a night sailboat ride (only one sailor, Captain Vic Laragione, goes out at night and it's well worth the ride) to a night of music, should you want to join them playing (they're learning the dulcimer).

La Maison du Soleil

Hosts: Peg and Pete Braswell, (512) 992-0115. Contact Sand Dollar Hospitality (512) 853-1222, 1 room with bath, full breakfast, $$–$$$, no children, smoking in designated areas outside, cats in residence, pool, tennis court in subdivision, TV in room, no cr

The name of the B&B should give you a hint that your hosts are Francophiles, which means you'll be treated to some wonderful dishes for breakfast, such as Quiche Lorraine in puff pastry. Peg designs art glass, pottery, and jewelry, which you'll see displayed throughout the house located in a very nice subdivision in Corpus. Pete is a retired history professor, with a library and historical games (on computer) to die for, if you're into that sort of thing. The pool is heated, so you can enjoy it year-round, and your hosts go to great extent to facilitate your comfort.

Manitou Cottage

Contact Sand Dollar Hospitality (512) 853-1222, 1 bedroom cottage with living room, full breakfast, $$–$$$, no children (because of pool), restricted smoking, fax on property, pet accepted in enclosure, dog in residence, no cr

Three blocks from the Corpus Christi Bay, your B&B accommodations are a converted pool cottage, behind a restored 60-year-old New England-style farm house. The cottage is full of "special things," from your hosts' son's (6'5") brass bed to a restored barber chair to old signs that make you smile because they bring back fond memories of earlier times. A little wine, homemade cookies, fresh flowers, and candles add to the delight of Manitou Cottage (along with a huge breakfast with newspaper delivered to your door in the morning). But your hosts surpass all the details with their all-out charm and concern for your comforts. The fact that they have a lumbering dog who adopts everyone as his own adds to the impression that you've settled into a delightful place, thank you, and maybe all those activities you thought you'd do in Corpus and Padre just don't have the appeal you thought they might before you arrived, because you're so happily ensconced.

Smith Place

Hosts: Cissy and Sid Smith, 420 Grant Place, Corpus Christi 78411, (512) 854-6564, or Sand Dollar Hospitality, (512) 853-1222, $$–$$$, children with approval (because of pool accessible from B&B cottage), smoking in restricted area, well-behaved small pets, private off-street parking, no cr

A delightful cottage nestled in an incredibly beautiful, landscaped pool area, with vines covering a deck so you can enjoy the outside in the warmest weather is just blocks from the bay and the compelling Ocean Drive. The Smiths accommodate everything from afternoon snacks (pico de gallo, peach ice tea) to extra towels, beach chairs, and coolers to touring bikes (should you want to bike around), and flexible check-out times so you can get a little more time in at Padre, if you chose to cross over the bridge to go to the beach. A refreshing pool awaits your return. The cottage is accented with Georgia O'Keeffe prints and Michelangelo's angels overlooking your queen-sized bed. A fridge packed with all kinds of goodies is just one of the many amenities, not the least of which are hosts who can get you tickets to practically anything in Corpus (their son is in the ballet)—something not to take lightly because Corpus is making waves in the arts as well as in its natural terrain.

CROCKETT

Warfield House Bed & Breakfast

Hosts: James and Judy Ostler, 712 East Houston Avenue, Crockett 75835, (409) 544-4037, 1-888-988-8800, 4 bedrooms, 4 baths, full breakfast, $$$–$$$$, no pets, children over 12, smoking designated areas, AE, V, MC

When Davy Crockett crossed East Texas on his fateful way to the Alamo, little did he know that the tiny beginnings of a nearby town would take his name as it rose to prominence among the piney woods. Southwest of Nacogdoches and the Davy Crockett National Forest, Crockett, known as oldest of the old towns in the state, flourished in the 19th century first as a stagecoach stop on the El Camino Real, the old Spanish "royal road," and then as a bustling lumber and mining town.

This elegant Victorian inn revolves around the 1890's formal dining room decorated with turn-of-the-century antiques. Judy, a seventh-generation East Texan, is proud to add her decorating talents and gourmet cooking to the many extras offered by the Warfield House. The lovely four bedrooms are lavishly decorated for those who seek the "great escape" from city life in this wonderful small town atmosphere.

The Warfield House is also available for special occasions such as rehearsal dinners, weddings, brunches, lunches, teas, coffees, business seminars, and theme parties. There's also a sparkling pool with deck and private hot tub on the premises. You'll be within walking distance to the shop-filled town square.

EAGLE LAKE

Eagle Hill Inn & Retreat

Hosts: Linda Ferguson, 307 E. State St., Eagle Lake 77434, (800) 324-3551 or (409) 234-3551, fax (409) 234-3553, 15 bedrooms, most with private baths, full breakfast, $$$–$$$$, no pets, children over 12, smoking designated areas, V, M

Known as the "Goose Hunting Capital of the World," Eagle Lake is part of the great Central Flyway, where geese and ducks come to feast on acres of rice fields. Scores of hunters also flock here to claim their limits in farmland where three major vegetational zones and three sub-zones bring rare wildlife.

Today, sportsmen and tourists cannot only hear the "call of the wild," but they can also rest for the hunt in the 9,000-square-foot mansion of Houstonians Philip and Linda Ferguson. The three-story Georgian B&B was originally built in 1936 by banker Hayes Stevens, proprietor of so many businesses he minted his own money. Though his empire has long since "gone with the wind," his house still stands as a tribute to his fortune.

B&B goers certainly don't feel cramped here. The massive living area, library, two dining areas (Linda can seat 65), and a solarium are open to guests who stay upstairs. They are also free to use the third-floor game room with regulation pool table, TV, stereo system, computer, and fax and can use the elevator to get there. And, of course, there's an elevator. Outdoors, there are lighted tennis courts, a trampoline, and a heated Olympic-sized pool with steam and sauna bath house that seconds as additional sleeping quarters. A third house, part of the complex, adds even more space for large groups.

When you make reservations, ask Linda about the murder mystery weekends and hunting packages. Church and family groups are welcome.

FREEPORT

Anchor Bed and Breakfast

Hosts: Elliot and Kathy Loy, 342 Anchor Drive (Treasure Island), Freeport 77541, (409) 239-3543, 3 guest rooms, 2 private baths, third-floor door with 8 single beds, full breakfast, $$, children 10 or over, no pets, one smoking room available downstairs, handicapped facilities, M, V, D, AE, DC

Located in southern Brazoria County 50 miles southwest of Houston, Freeport is the place to go if you love to fish, crab, birdwatch, beachcomb, deep-sea fish, or scuba dive. A haven for red fish, flounder, and specked trout, fishermen here marvel as brown pelicans crisscross each other as they divebomb mullet that innocently meander just under the surface.

To experience this prolific coastline firsthand, the Anchor Bed and Breakfast, situated east of Surfside Beach at Cold Pass, is the place to be. The luxurious waterfront accommodation offers not only a restful stay but its own private 50-foot lit pier that connects with a boat dock, deep channel access, and screened pier house complete with refrigerator for bait and storage room for tackle. The Loys also sometimes use the little house for crab boils and steak cookouts. They have also outfitted the pier with stationary swivel chairs for anglers who want to cast from the pier for red fish, or birders who enjoy the melodies of the songbirds who fly through Freeport on their way south for the winter. Naturalists also marvel at the dolphins who regularly play here, and the sea horses who skim the water's surface. Fishermen will be happy to know that the Loys will have their fish dressed and stored in their freezers until it's time to go home.

As for the Loys, they are of a unique breed. Once avid hunters, they still are able, in spite of their handicaps, to cast a line and spin a good yarn. Guests don't suffer because of host limitations, however. A B&B staff meets every need, and even provides lunch and dinner that ranges from soup and gumbo (the cook is Cajun) to fried fish to steak to shrimp and crab boils. Those handicapped have access to elevator, Even smokers have it good. One downstairs guest room accommodates them as well.

The Anchor Bed and Breakfast was featured in an accommodation guidebook just for birders so, anglers, call early.

FRIENDSWOOD

Brown House

Host: Sky Lyn Minkoff, 312 South Friendswood Dr., Friendswood 77546, (800) 959-2802 or (713) 482-2802, 6 bedrooms, 5 baths, full breakfast, \$\$–\$\$\$, no pets, children (12 or over), smoking in designated outside areas, MC, V, AE

In 1895 Frank J. Brown, a buffalo hunter and free spirit until he joined the fold, founded Friendswood, a small Quaker settlement in a woods near Galveston Bay. Pioneers of a growing fig industry, the Quakers who also farmed satsumas, could have never guessed that they would someday neighbor the famous Johnson Space Center.

Today, Friendswood is a quiet community where guests can rest between visits to NASA, the new Gulf Greyhound Park, and Houston and Galveston, both within 45 minutes of the Brown House, which was built in 1935 by Frank's son Cecil, owner of the community's one industry, a fig preserving plant. The three-story, 5,000-plus-square-foot B&B with basement was constructed by River Oaks' architect, Henry A. M. Stubbe, whose plans called for walls to be from eight to eleven inches thick to weather any storm, and equipped the house with the first central air and heat system in the area. The B&B also features large windows draped with French lace curtains that let in the sunlight and each room is decorated with tasteful furnishings. The grounds cover a two-and-a-half acre lawn with huge old oaks and a rose garden.

GALVESTON

1890 Trube Castle Inn

Host: Nonette O'Donnell, 1627 Sealy Ave., Galveston 77550, (800) 662-9647, 2 suites with private baths, continental plus, $$$$, no pets, children over 12, smoking designated areas, V, MC, AE

In 1840 a small Danish boy, along with his two older brothers, stowed away on a ship heading for the New World. He could not have known that they were destined to make their fortunes on Galveston Island. The Trube brothers reached this promised land by the sea, grew up to learn the principles of good business, and made wise investments in real estate and merchandise.

The youngest, J. Clements, built a magnificent home for his wife and nine children the likes of which islanders had never seen. As Galveston has been dubbed "a city of strange houses," the white stone and green-shuttered Trube home, with 27 rooms in all, is called the "strangest" of all. Patterned after a Dane castle, its architecture reflects a Gothic and Moorish blend with nine gables and 40 stained-glass windows.

Opened in 1991, this formal yet comfortable B&B features an entire third floor for guests who may choose the King or Queen Suites. One features a Jacuzzi, while the other a "tree-house bathroom," located in a tree-surrounded turret. The standing library replicates a Danish guard chamber, where soldiers stood ready to defend sleeping royalty.

One of the most unique characteristics of this home, though, is the tower, a rooftop open air perch. The view is spectacular with the Sacred Heart Catholic Co-cathedral, the Bishop's Palace, the Hotel Galvez, and the Gulf of Mexico in the distance.

Gilded Thistle

Host: Helen Hanemann, 1805 Broadway, Galveston 77550, (409) 763-0194, (800) 654-9380, fax (409) 763-3941, 3 guest rooms, 2 baths, gourmet breakfast, $$$$, no pets or children, smoking designated areas only, M, V, D

If phrases like "treetop nursery" and "stairway to nowhere" tickle your curiosity, or if you've always wanted to know more about the

Texas Rangers than the history books reveal, then the Gilded Thistle on Galveston Island is for you. Built in 1893 and known historically as the Baily-Phillips home, this B&B was named by owner Helen Hanemann and son Pat after the hearty prickly plant that sheds its ugliness when it blooms along Gulf Coast seashores.

Once the part-time residence of John E. Baily, general manager of the bustling port, and later shipping magnate William Parr, the home has weathered every hurricane for the past 100 years. Today, this gorgeous Queen Anne example with its porches, balconies, transoms, and spacious upstairs guest rooms has been beautifully restored and filled with quality antiques and collectibles. Helen's own dried flower creations appeal to the senses, their fragrances calling to mind long forgotten memories. And in every niche, she has placed a teddy bear, each with its own name and personality.

Amenities here abound at this five-star B&B. They include an evening glass of wine, soft drinks, candy, filtered water, a nighttime snack, and a morning coffee tray.

Each room is also equipped with a color TV, a VCR, a collection of movies, and a telephone. The Gilded Thistle also provides the businessman with everything in the way of office equipment from fax to computer hookups to an on-line computer. And, if you feel like being nurtured, Helen, who'll also respect your privacy, is the perfect grandmother and a true southern lady. Without a doubt, you'll get an abundance of food and drink here as well as quality care. A personal favorite of this traveler.

For more information, feel free to visit the Thistle's Web site at http://www.houston.–TX.NET/lodging/Gilded Thistle/. The e-mail address is gilded@houston–TX.Net.

Madame Dyer's Bed and Breakfast

Host: Larry and Linda Bonnin, 1720 Postoffice St., Galveston 77550, (409) 765-5692, 3 guest rooms with private baths, hosted, full breakfast, $$$–$$$$, children over 12, no pets, smoking outside in designated area only, M, V

In 1889 the noted Galveston architect Nicholas Clayton, creator of many island structures such as the Bishop's Palace, Grace Episcopal Church, and the W. L. Moody Building, built a grand residence for Dr.

Arthur F. Sampson. Both builder and buyer had worked hard to make names for themselves in the growing city still feeling the effect of the Galveston Fire of 1885. Little did anyone know that they were about to encounter a catastrophe that would change the financial health of Galveston forever—the Great Storm of 1900. Dr. Sampson, a respected physician and surgeon, must have seen too much after the storm, whose massive tidal wave claimed 6,000 lives, for he and his family moved from Galveston forever. He left behind him his beloved two-story home with its double, wrap-around galleries characterized by Stick-style balustrades.

Happily for island visitors, however, the Sampson home not only survived the forces of nature but also of time. Today known as Madame Dyer's Bed and Breakfast, it has been brought back to its original luster by owners Larry and Linda Bonnin. The Victorian "raised" beauty is walking distance of the Strand, dubbed before the storm as the Wall Street of the Southwest.

Filled with a combination of period and eclectic furnishings, this B&B features rich wall coverings and fabrics. Great natural light and arty dried flower arrangements call to the visitor to sit down and stay awhile. Guest rooms are romantic from Ashten's Room, a large accommodation with queen-sized carved oak bed and adjoining bath, to Blake's Room with its grand bay window as a backdrop for its antique English furnishings to Corbin's Room with its king-sized four-poster bed, tiled fireplace, and mirrored oak mantel. Spacious balconies look down onto butterfly-laden gardens that remind one of Europe.

Guests here enjoy morning coffee (gourmet or regular) or tea at the buffet bar on the landing. They also have use of plush robes and quality linens and towels. Turn-down service, along with a bedtime chocolate and lemon water, is given here. Breakfast consists of meat, potato and egg dishes, fruit, breakfast spreads, muffins, and traditional morning beverages. The city's horse-drawn carriages pass here regularly, and, for a fee, passengers can hop a ride into Galveston's past.

Michael's Bed & Breakfast Inn
Hans Guldmann Mansion

Hosts: Allen and Mikey Isbell, 1715 35th St., Galveston 77550, (409) 763-3760, 4 bedrooms, 2 baths, continental plus, $$$–$$$$, no pets, children over 12, no smoking, no cr

Hans Guldmann, Galveston's one-time Danish vice-consul and director of the South Texas Cotton Oil Company, bought what he wanted and didn't mind the price. In fact, he and his wife were the epitome of that golden era when America was roaring headfirst into the twenties. Together they made their 5,000-square-foot home a Galveston showplace.

The 1915 construction of the mansion had a rocky beginning, however. When a hurricane caused damage to the unfinished structure, Hans had the existing three-story house torn down and rebuilt. This time, he ordered the foundation reinforced with concrete bags and he chose thick, sturdy window and door glass for the strongest gale-force winds. For blue skies, he orchestrated elaborate verandas, sun porches, swivel-glass windows, and transoms.

Owners, Houston attorney Allen Isbell and his wife Mikey, have over a ten-year period succeeded in bringing the mansion back to its original luster and are now restoring the spacious grounds. When you're there, be sure to see the basement shooting gallery and wine cellar where a few dusty bottles of Guldmann stock still remain.

The Coppersmith Inn

Host: Lisa Hering, 1914 Avenue M, Galveston 77550, (409) 763-7004, hosted, 4 rooms with private baths, gourmet breakfast, $$$–$$$$, children over 12 in main house/over 6 in cottage, no pets, smoking outside in designated area only, M, V, D, AE

The noted Galveston architect Alfred Muller completed the elegant Victorian Howard Carnes home in 1887. Now known as the Coppersmith Inn, its name comes from the second owner who made his living working with metals. Today the romantic residence is open to tourists and business people who appreciate those architectural creations with staying power. Graceful archways and keystones mark the home's

Michael's—Hans Guldmann Mansion

interior as truly Muller, while the exterior two-story structure is best known for its triple-arched porches that add balance and frame to its tall shuttered windows.

Hostess Lisa Hering has taken pains to maintain the home's historic significance, while making her guests feel quite at ease. Working fireplaces, private balconies, and windows that open floor-to-ceiling give this B&B a personality all its own. Of particular interest are the many examples of *faux painting*, a rage during the Victorian era. Be sure to see the "red leopard" faux marble on the parlor's fireplace. Houston artist Virginia Page created delicate stenciled art in tasteful places, giving added touches of warmth to the period furniture of this historic B&B.

Early morning coffee is served upstairs. A formal breakfast that varies is served in the dining room. Lisa says she knows 365 ways to serve French toast. On certain days she also prepares Eggs Benedict, along with bread pudding and quiches. Wine and other refreshments such as cheese and banana bread are also available at certain times. Wassail greets guests who come in from the winter cold. A comfy cottage is also available behind the main house.

Queen Anne Bed and Breakfast
The Davis/Tucker Home

Hosts: John McWilliams and Earl French, 1915 Sealy Ave., Galveston 77550, 800-472-0930 or (409) 763-7088, 4 bedrooms, 2 baths, full breakfast, $$$–$$$$, no pets, no children, no smoking, MC, V

This classic example of a four-story Queen Anne design, recently restored by John McWilliams and Earl French, is conveniently located just off Broadway, only six blocks from the Strand. Guests climb the impressive front steps that lead to a flower-adorned porch. The exterior is freshly scrubbed and painted white, and the interior filled with an attractive combination of old and new furnishings.

Built in 1905 for $8,000 by Banker J. J. Davis, a Galveston Wharves board member, the home stayed in the Davis family until 1928 when Davis's widow sold it to the North Methodist Episcopal Church. Today B&B guests lounge in tastefully decorated rooms of pastel shades. Amenities include guest bathrobes and a complimentary evening snack tray with wine. Breakfast fare ranges from egg dishes, potato casserole, quiche, fresh fruit, ham, bacon or sausage, and coffee or tea. You'll find John, a Houston hairdresser and Earl, a computer operator, conscientious hosts who will keep their company smiling.

Victorian Inn

Host: Don and Nancy Mafridge, 511 17th St., Galveston 77550, (409) 762-3235, 6 bedrooms, 3½ baths, continental, $$$–$$$$, no pets, no children under 12, smoking designated areas, V, MC, AE

A survivor of the Great Storm of 1900, the Victorian Inn lasted through an era when a giant tidal wave flattened the island, killing 6,000 residents. Since that time the pretty red and white three-story structure has witnessed two world wars, the Great Depression, and at least one big hurricane every five years.

A National Register of Historic Places listing, the home was built in 1899 by cement contractor Issac Hefron, who spared no expense. He hired the best artisans who constructed Belgian tiled fireplaces and private wraparound balconies along with huge walk-through windows to ensure good Gulf breeze circulation. Original hardwood pegged floors and carved intricate scrollwork on staircases make a stay here a walk back to a time when craft was art. Featured on the Galveston Historical Foundation's Tour of Homes, this B&B is within walking distance of the Strand.

HOUSTON

Angel Arbor Bed and Breakfast Inn

Host: Marguerite Swanson, 848 Heights Blvd., Houston 77007, (713) 868-4654, fax (713) 861-3189, 3 guest rooms, 1 suite, private baths, full breakfast, $$$$, no children, no pets, no smoking, MC, V, DC, AE

A seasoned bed and breakfast hostess who is well-known for her Houston murder mystery and dinner parties, Marguerite Swanson knows the secret of sweet success. She entered the hospitality business 14 years ago and has graduated from a Spring Branch residential home to an angelic Georgian-style residence on Heights Boulevard called Angel Arbor Bed and Breakfast Inn. Built in 1923 for John and Katherine McTighe, this was later the home of Jay L. Durham, a prominent Heights family who earlier built another area landmark that Marguerite purchased and also opened as an inn. Houston B&B goers knew it as the stately Durham House Bed and Breakfast.

Today, Angel Arbor stands tall, elegantly surrounded by flowering manicured gardens that feature an artfully placed angel statue as a focal point. As this hostess is an antiques dealer, each room is filled with priceless pieces and complemented by luscious draperies and rich carpets. Some rooms are feminine with lace and canopied beds, while others have a strong atmosphere with deep hues that appeal to men as well as women.

Breakfast here is not only tasty but filling with an abundant table of Marguerite's specialties. And, if you are a game player, you must catch one of Angel Arbor's murder mystery dinner parties. Each guest is given a dossier and comes dressed as an assigned character. It is only at the end of the evening that the true murderer is revealed, and it might be you. Located five minutes from downtown, business people and tourists alike find the Heights very convenient to not only the professional sector but also to the Medical Center, the museum district, Saint Thomas University, and Rice.

Sara's Bed and Breakfast

Host: Donna and Tillman Arledge, 941 Heights Blvd., Houston 77008, 800-593-1130, (713) 868-1130, fax (713) 868-1160, 10 bedrooms, 9½ baths, continental, $–$$, no pets, children in carriage house, smoking designated areas, all cr

A one-story Victorian cottage probably built around the turn-of-the-century, Sara's Bed and Breakfast has grown. Today it is three stories, and according to innkeepers Donna and Tillman Arledge, Sara's is the city's only "public" B&B inn able to sleep a host of folks.

Antiques, lace curtains, floral fabrics of blue, rose, and gray add to the romance as do the scores of silk flowers that bloom among wreaths of baby's breath and ribbon. An upstairs sitting room opens to the balcony that looks on to Heights Boulevard. Throughout the inn, guests have an abundance of seating areas from the upstairs sitting room with balcony to a huge deck in the back. For the private-minded, the carriage house has two bedrooms, two baths, full kitchen, living area, and balcony ideal for families or wedding parties.

HUNTSVILLE

Longhorn House Bed and Breakfast/Jordan Ranch

Hosts: Claire and Bill Jordan, Rt. 1, Box 681, Huntsville 77340, (888) 295-1774, (409) 295-1774, fax (409) 295-1768, 1 duplex and 1 house, full breakfast, $$–$$$, children welcome, no pets, smoking in designated area only, cash or check only

Members of the Texas Longhorn Breeders Gulf Coast Association, the Jordans are Texas proud of their breathtaking 1,040-acre ranch. Located in the East Texas piney woods, Sam Houston country, guests are always amazed as they clear the trees to get a first look at the family ranch house with detached grandmother and guest wing. Made of Austin stone and trimmed in rich rustic wood, the home sits guard over the private 40-acre lake stocked with catfish, sun perch, and bass. Obviously a great place to fish, families may cook their catches on barbecue pits and afterward enjoy a campfire. Those with keen eyes will also see a variety of wildlife from raccoons to skunks to armadillos to wild hogs.

Hunters are close to deer grounds, while scuba divers may go to the Blue Lagoon, an open-water facility only 16 miles from the ranch. As the Jordans are avid certified divers, they are available to provide training and, for an extra charge, will accompany you on a dive. For the kids, there's horse shoe pitch, tether ball, a watering tank filled with goldfish, and walking sticks for hikers. Breakfast varies from blueberry pancakes to Tex-Mex egg burritos, the Jordan specialty. Other favorites here are the Texas-sized French toast and homemade venison sausage. Assorted teas and coffees are also available.

The Jordans advertise a modest 1898 house that is near the ranch's front gate. The no-frills facility is adequate, but this writer's favorite is the duplex accommodation adjoining the house. New and furnished with a Texas motif, it looks out over the lake. This would also put you closer to Bill, a Houston lawyer who commutes, and Claire, a permitted Texas Parks and Wildlife rehabitat volunteer. Perhaps you'll be there when Claire is nursing a fawn back to health. A word of advice: be sure to get clear instructions to the ranch and, once inside the gate, to the ranch house—or you may find yourself as this traveler did—lost on a dirt road and nose-to-nose with a Texas Longhorn.

The Whistler

Host: Mary Clegg, 906 Avenue M, Huntsville 77340, (409) 295-2834, (713) 965-0311, (800) 404-2834, (800) 432-1288, 5 bedrooms, 4 baths, full breakfast, $$$, no pets, children 12 and over, no smoking, no cr

The Whistler, named in honor of an ancestor who loved to whistle, stands in Huntsville as it did when it was completed in 1859. Owned by Mary Thomason Clegg, the two-story Victorian mansion, built by Mary's great-great uncle, J. Thomason, has been in her family for 130 years. No wonder Mary Clegg is proud of the Whistler with its grand facade and wrapped porches, which she has filled with family antiques. The most memorable piece is a piano spared by Gen. Sherman's men at the persuasion of Mary's great aunt. Guests here are encouraged to enjoy the parlor, the formal reception, music and dining rooms, and the gigantic kitchen-family area. An elegant breakfast is served on the east terrace or in the formal dining room, weather permitting. And, if you hear wedding bells, The Whistler's impressive front lawn makes a pretty backdrop for that big day.

As for the Whistler, he was Mary's grandfather. And, if you listen close enough, you just may hear his melodious song coming from somewhere in the home that gave him so much happiness.

KEMAH AND SEABROOK

Seabrook, an art and antique seaside colony that neighbors Kemah, is flanked by both Galveston Bay and Clear Lake. Both seaside retreats are a sailor's paradise with three major marinas and the Lakewood Yacht Club, one of the top ten yacht clubs in America. Land lovers, though, also love the area, not only for the constant parade of vessels that travel the channel that undercuts the Kemah/Seabrook Bridge, but also for the colorful enclave of restaurants, shops, and seafood markets that make these coastal towns so picturesque. Visit here, and you're 20 miles from the Gulf Greyhound Racing Park and the Lone Star Outlet Mall. The Nasa Space Center and Space Center Houston is only three miles away.

1874 Kipp House (Kemah)

Host: Matt Wiggins, P. O. Box 975, Kemah 77565, (281) 334-3474, 2 suites, unhosted, gourmet breakfast at Captain's Quarters, $$$$, no children, no pets, smoking outside in designated areas only, all cr

Built by John Kipp, a sea captain and the founder of Kemah, this exceptionally kept bay home whispers of affluence, seafaring strength, and good taste. Now owned by businessman Matt Wiggins, also grandson to Kemah's famous restaurateur Jimmy Walker, this bed and breakfast with richly varnished walls, oriental carpeted floors, and comfortable, yet elegant furnishings, provides a panoramic view of Galveston Bay—one fit for a man who loved the sea.

Matt has added personal touches, however, that reveal his wide range of interests. Visitors here can't decide what to admire first—his original Audubon prints, his nautical memorabilia, or his collection of gaming tables and other items taken from Galveston and Kemah gambling houses once alive but illegal during a time long gone. Be sure to note the European roulette wheel with the absent "double O," so indicative of the American ones. Also inspect the original "floating" Galveston County crap table, designed to make quick getaways from gun-toting Texas Rangers.

This unhosted B&B doesn't lack for a gourmet breakfast either. Guests walk just across the street to Mary Patterson's Captain's Quarters, where everyone sits at a crystal- and china-laden dining table for fruit, scrambled eggs, and sausage-filled rolls.

The Ark (Kemah)

Host: Suzanne Silver for owner Paul Strizek, 705 6th Street, Kemah 77565, (713) 474-5295, fax (713) 474-7840, unhosted, gourmet continental, $$$–$$$$ (depending on number of rooms or whole house rental), children over 10, no pets, smoking outside in designated area only, M, V, D, AE

The Ark is a three-bedroom, two-bath bay house that overlooks Galveston Bay. Decorated with a nautical theme in foam greens, pale tans, sea blues, and warm reds, the furnishings definitely have a decorator's touch. But the most impressive feature of this house is its deck that reaches toward the beautiful Galveston Bay. In fact, from the side windows, one can see the distant sailboats as they make their way into the channel that leads to the Kemah/Seabrook Bridge.

Under the house is a ten-person hot tub, stereo speakers, a patio area, and access to the water via a small pier where crabs and speckled trout await your bait. On the lot, guests can sit under ancient Texas pines— a great place for a watermelon party. The gourmet continental breakfast includes granola yogurt, fresh pastries, fruit from the local market, coffee, and juice. The table here sits a "small" family of twelve!

Captain's Quarters (Kemah)

Hosts: Mary Patterson and Pat Patterson, 701 Bay Ave., Kemah 77565, phone and fax (713) 334-4141, 4 guest rooms with private baths, gourmet breakfast, $$$$, no children, no pets, no smoking, AE

Featured in *Southern Living* and *Texas Highways,* this five-star waterside B&B, the Captain's Quarters is a stately New England-styled sea captain's home with a spectacular view of Galveston Bay. Nothing short of magnificent, the five-level 19th-century-styled structure topped with widow's walk, encompasses 8,500 square feet. Here guests, captains for a stay, linger in rooms each named after a famous ship. Outdoors, a grand stairway leads from upper levels to the grounds that open to a private pier. Owned by architect Royston and wife Mary, a tour guide, this luxurious B&B, filled with quality furnishings, sits only 30 feet from water's edge.

The house, with its numerous fireplaces, is suitable for winter use. In fact, the Honeymoon Suite, with its king-sized bed and fireplace, will seal a union forever. Guests can use the pier, the Yacht Club pool and tennis courts, and moor at the nearby basin. You're 20 minutes from Galveston, 30 minutes from San Jacinto Monument and 40 minutes from the Astrodome.

Crew's Quarters (Seabrook)

**Host: Mary & Pat Patterson, 114 Waterfront Dr., Seabrook,
(mailing address: 701 Bay Ave., Kemah 77565), phone and fax
(713) 334-4141, 3 bedrooms, 3 baths, gourmet breakfast, $–$$,
no pets, children over six, no smoking, MC, V**

Seabrook is a quaint seaside retreat on Galveston Bay. Kemah, its salty sister port, is in viewing distance, just across the channel that plays host to scores of sea lovers who like to fish or sail. Mary Patterson invites you to see the sailing regalia from the deck of the Crew's Quarters, located where the channel and the bay join. Perched on pilings, the summer place, turned B&B, has been in Mary's family for 50 years.

Inside, every nautical room is painted a cheery color, in keeping with the sea motif. Outside, wind socks catch salty breezes as you shout "Ahoy" to passing captains and crew. Breakfast specialties include Scotch eggs, fried shredded wheat, rolls, Canadian cereal, freshly squeezed orange juice, and special cinnamon coffee. Be sure to seek touring advice from Mary, a tour guide, while she serves you. But, if you would rather sit on the deck and play bridge, then your hosts will join you in a hand. Guests may also use the pool at the nearby yacht club or enjoy a platter of steaming boiled shrimp at one of the many local restaurants.

The Pelican House Bed and Breakfast

**Host: Suzanne Silver, 1302 First St., Seabrook 77586,
(713) 474-5295, fax (713) 474-7840, unhosted but full breakfast is
served, $$–$$$$ (depending on number of rooms or whole house
rental), children over 10, no pets, smoking outside in designated
area only, M, V, D, AE**

Just footsteps away from Seabrook's Back Bay Lagoon, a charming little yellow house has made a local name for itself as one of the most endearing spots in town. The Pelican House, a 90-year-old one-story home owned by the first area school teacher, sits on more than an acre shaded with pecan and live oak trees. City-wearied guests race for the white rockers that move by themselves when sea breezes pick up strength. Others prefer the tree swing for two that faces the lazy bay, home of herons, pelicans, and the hawk-like osprey. Hours seem like minutes as one watches the waterbirds dive for their breakfast. In the distance, a rooster crows "Good morning!" and Schooner, a neighbor's parrot, giggles "Help me!"

The decor is arty, with sea murals painted by local artists and clay pieces, created by the potter who lives in the garage apartment out back. The main motif is the gangly old pelican. You can't miss the interesting pelican mailbox that greets everybody that walks through the lantana-and-rose-lined picket fence.

Suzanne Silver, a hostess with personality-plus, comes in for breakfast and prepares such specialties as a Sunday Stuffed French toast with pepper bacon and apricot glaze or morning crepes. Wine, ice tea, or champagne welcomes guests. Oh! While scanning the bay from your bedroom windows, look for the neighbor's pig who loves water. Fishing and crabbing is in walking distance. Bring your gear.

KINGSVILLE

B Bar B Ranch Inn

Hosts: Luther and Patti Young, Road 2215 East (eight miles south of Kingsville off Highway 77, (512) 296-3331, 6 bedrooms with private baths, 2 hot tubs, swimming pool, TV, pet kennels, full breakfast, $$

There's too much to see, do, and experience at the B Bar B Ranch Inn in Kingsville to just spend one day and night. "Variety" is the key word for this working ranch owned by Luther and Patti Young. Originally a part of the King Ranch, The B Bar B retains the rustic look in some of its furnishings, but the ranch house has been completely restored to a well-appointed lodge with modern conveniences. Behind the main lodge is the swimming pool, hot tub, lush picnic grounds, and a gazebo for large parties. The inn's meeting room holds up to 60 persons, with catering available for all meals. Luther will even roast a pig. Hunters flock to the B Bar B during hunting seasons because dove can be hunted on the ranch's acreage and quail and deer are available on the adjacent King Ranch. All hunts are with professional guide services (package start at $125). Fishing in nearby Baffin Bay packages are also available ($275).

LOVELADY

Log Cabin Bed and Breakfast

Host: Greta P. Hicks, P.O. Box 485, Lovelady 75851, (409) 632-2002 or (409) 632-9016, 3 guest rooms, 2 baths, full breakfast, $$$, children welcome, no pets, smokers outside, MC, V

In 1853, Alfred and Susan Bitner and four of their children moved from Tennessee to make a new life in Texas. They settled just east of the 1893 Shiloh Church, a nearby landmark that was used as a Civil War recruiting station and the site of campground meetings during that historic time. It was here in the Piney Woods that the Bitners carved out an existence for themselves and more than 100 years later, that host and rancher, Greta Hicks decided to spend her free time.

Recently featured on the *Eyes of Texas,* Greta and her Log Cabin Bed and Breakfast provide an experience that's truly Texas. An accountant by profession and a rancher by heart, Greta represents all that's good about the human spirit. She makes up her mind to do something, and before her neighbors know it, it's done. As for the Log Cabin B&B, it lies hidden down a narrow dirt road somewhere in the woods between Crockett and Lovelady. There is plenty of room here, though, not only in the sanctuary of the landscape but also in the homey rambling accommodation that acts as Greta's headquarters for her ranch with its 24 head of longhorns.

To guests, Greta offers three rooms—all named after the Texas heroes—Sam Houston, Davy Crockett, and Stephen F. Austin. Sam's Room, the largest accommodation, features two lodge pole-pine beds and a bathroom complete with a whirlpool tub. Davy's Room is furnished with a futon couch that opens to a queen size, and Stephen's Room, decorated with Texas keepsakes and done in red, white, and blue, has exposed log walls that give it a primitive look. An upstairs loft, perfect for an older child, holds a sofa. Everywhere there is evidence of Greta's love of garage sale collectibles.

Breakfast here is family-style and tailor-made. Picnic baskets for other meals are also available.

NACOGDOCHES

John M. Sparks House and the Barret House

Hosts: Captain Charles and Ann Phillips, Rt. 4, Box 9400, Nacogdoches 75961, (409) 569-1249, 2 houses, each accommodating four, with private bath, OYO breakfast in your own quarters including homemade bread and fresh venison sausage, $$, no pets, no children, no smoking, no cr

Deep in an 800-acre pine tree forest plantation, Captain Charles and Ann Phillips host two of the most unique bed and breakfasts in the state. Both houses are so well-restored, researched, and decorated, they are like stepping back in time to the 1840s. Rope beds with feather mattresses are standard fare. The rooms are cozily situated under the sweet gum eves and filled with lovingly collected antiques (many from the families who built the houses so many years ago). If you appreciate history and restoration, you will love the Phillips, who have spent nearly 25 years restoring every board, fiber and object you routinely use in these "museum houses." The Phillips deservedly were made recipients of the Texas Medallion. Should you request, they will give you a personal tour of the houses or their project in progress (Rosewild) or share their stories over some afternoon refreshment when you arrive. The John M. Sparks home, in which the Phillips live downstairs, was built by a pioneer doctor in 1831. Down the path, past a quiet lake, the Tol Barret house, named after the first man to strike oil in Texas, consists of the original cabin, now a museum filled with period antiques, and a cabin behind the original, a replica of the detached Barret kitchen. Even the table you breakfast upon is the original Sparks table, and the roses you enjoy while rocking on the porch are the wild roses originally planted by Angelina Martha, the mistress of the house over 150 years ago. It's an incredible journey into the past, with the most gracious and knowledgeable hosts.

Mound Street Bed and Breakfast

Mound Street Bed and Breakfast

Hosts: Chappell and Mary Elizabeth Jordan, 408 Mound Street, Nacogdoches, (409) 569-2211, 4 bedrooms, 3 baths, full breakfast, $$–$$$, no pets, children 12 and over welcome, no smoking, cr

The stately Mound Street 1899 Victorian features columns on pedestals, rambling galleries and sun porches, spacious rooms, and a house chock-full of historic clocks, and other interesting objects. Hosts Chappell and Mary Elizabeth have turned off the chimes upstairs, so guests can enjoy the beauty of their huge collection without being concerned about the impact of approximately 200 clocks bonging on the hour. Chappell's avocation is furniture making; the challenge is to discover what he's carved and what are antiques because you can't tell the difference. Needless to say, your hosts are experts on clocks and can charm you for hours, if you choose, telling their tales. Guests may enjoy breakfast in the dining room or take a tray to the sun porch or their rooms, whichever they prefer. Their home is located in the old Washington Square Historic District, three lots away from the city's last remaining Caddo Indian historic ceremonial mound. Within walking distant from downtown and the old Stephen F. Austin State University, Mound Street B&B is perfect for an escape from a hectic lifestyle.

Pine Creek Lodge B&B Country Inn

Hosts: The Pitts Family (two generations at least), Pine Creek Road (off FM 2782), Rt. 3, Nacogdoches 75961, (409) 560-6282 or toll free (888)714-1414, 7 rooms with private baths, 3 common rooms and dining room, dinner available, $$$, no pets, smoking in restricted area, children by arrangement

Pine Creek Lodge B&B is indicative of the newest trend in B&Bs, which is reflected in their name. In some ways, they are more like an inn, with the efficiency and pristine decorum of a hotel/inn, but, in other ways—most obviously, they serve a full breakfast—they're a B&B. The location is enticing if you want a getaway because the two rustic buildings are situated on a peaceful wooded hill in the middle of a 140-acre farm. Two buildings about 150 feet apart on the bend of a flowing creek contain seven room, each with a king-sized bed, ceiling fans,

TV/VCR, individual air conditioning, telephones for outgoing calls, and refrigerators. Some of the rooms have private decks, while others front the large wraparound porch. A fishing pond, swing, rockers, hammock, hot tub, pool, and gardens of over 200 rose bushes and other flowers beckon the visitor to slow down and enjoy the rustic beauty. All of the bedrooms have additional bed capacity, which makes the Pine Creek a great place for business meetings and retreats of all kinds.

NAVASOTA

The Castle Inn

Hosts: Eugene and Joyce Daniel, 1403 E. Washington, Navasota 77868, (800) 661-4346, 4 bedrooms, 4 baths, gourmet breakfast, $$$–$$$$, no pets, children over 13, smoking designated areas, no cr

In 1893 Robert Templeman, who dabbled in everything from cotton and oil to ownership of Navasota's mercantile store, gave the ultimate wedding present to his son, Ward. That was 100 years ago, and since that time Robert and Ward have gone the way of all flesh. But the gift, a 7,000-square-foot prairie-styled mansion remains, testimony to a father's love for his son.

Known today as the Castle Inn, the refurbished two-acre turreted estate supremely governs over Navasota's E. Washington St. Owners Eugene Daniel, a retired two-star Army general, and his wife, Joyce, have decorated with antiques, collected over 30 years, to maintain the mansion's time period. As you walk up the steps, you'll enter the glazed wraparound porch with 110 beveled panes. The library and living room are to the right, while a giant dining room is to the left. Note the pine cone, the symbol of wealth, stenciled above. Ask Joyce to also show you the "jealous husband" icebox with its outside door and the ultimate in opulence—a fuse box with beveled glass cover.

The furnishings here incidentally come from all parts of the world and are remembrances of all the places the Daniels have lived. As for the hosts themselves, they have brought the Castle full circle—Eugene gave it to his wife as a Valentine gift and as a sign of one person's love for another.

Castle Inn Bed and Breakfast

NORTH PADRE ISLAND

Fortuna Bay Bed and Breakfast

Hosts: John and Jackie Fisher, 15405 Fortuna Bay Drive, (512) 387-5666, or contact Sand Dollar Hospitality, (512) 853-1222, 2 suites including living room, full bath, kitchen overlooking the inland waterway, OYO breakfast, $$$, TV, phone, no pets, no children over 5, smokers in restricted area

This hideaway, in a three-story, red-tiled-roof inn, is quite simply incredible because of its location on the intersection of five canals, with the main canal leading to the Laguna Padre five minutes away. The Gulf of Mexico and its white sand beaches are, likewise, five minutes away. The view of the sunset off the huge deck, complete with swimming pool, in front of your condominium is breathtaking. Your host will take you for a pontoon ride down the canal (so you can see the fabulous houses and boats on the water side, as well as the birds for which the area is known) or you can play golf at the Padre Island Country Club (on his membership) or fish off the deck. You may want to go birding at the national seashore, 15 minutes away, or hop over to Corpus (although the seafood and entertainment on North Padre is quite wonderful and, strangely enough, more reasonable). John has a delicious snack waiting for you when you arrive and he has stocked the refrigerator with a basketful of goodies. Although it's Texas in all the attractions (Texas State Aquarium, Columbus Fleet, Corpus Christi Art Museum, Corpus Museum of Natural Science, Greyhound racing, Lexington Aircraft Carrier Floating Museum), Fortuna Bay B&B captures the feel of the Caribbean with its picturesque charm and color.

PALACIOS

Moonlight Bay B&B

Host: Gaye Rogers, 506 South Bay Blvd., Palacios 77465, (512) 972-2232, 4 guest rooms, 4 baths, full breakfast, $$–$$$$, no children, no pets, no smoking, AM, V, DC, DIS, AE

Palacios, a seaside town on Tres Palacios Bay in Matagorda County, can only be described as picturesque with its lighted fishing piers, public boat ramps, seawall walking course, fleets of shrimp boats, and its seven miles of shoreline. For B&B goers, however, this little Gulf of Mexico retreat holds a gem accommodation reminiscent of pineapple plantations in the Hawaiian Islands. It's the Moonlight Bay B&B, a grand old dame constructed in 1910 by Palacios socialite Opal Price, a gifted hostess whose parties were known for their elegant flair and impressive guest lists. Old-timers remember melodious evenings when bandstand music from the landmark Pavilion drifted over the surf as guests, dressed in white and sporting straw hats, strolled along Mrs. Price's breezy porches.

Today, Opal Price would be proud that Miss Gaye Rogers has taken over where she left off. An accomplished pianist, gourmet cook, and talented interior designer, Gaye welcomes guests with genuine gladness. As for her accommodations, they are elegant with wallpapers, fabrics, and carpets that reflect her taste. The living room of the Moonlight Bay B&B, though, is the best spot in the home as it offers a spectacular window revealing a clear view of the Palacios Bay.

Breakfast is Gay Rogers' style with *Huevos de Rita,* the house specialty, or *Quiche Lorraine.* Her mother's homemade jams and jellies and her own great granola are complemented by seasonal fresh fruits. Upon request, biscuits with gravy can also be brought steaming from the kitchen. Other packets are available as well. Just call Gay.

PORT ARANSAS

Harbor View B&B

Hosts: Marlene and Jim Urban, 340 Cotter Street, Port Aransas 78373, (512) 749-4294, or Sand Dollar Hospitality, (512) 853-1222, 4 bedrooms with 2 shared baths, full on-site mooring facilities for crafts up to 50 foot in length, full breakfast, $$–$$$, children welcome, no pets, smoking outside, no cr

If you come in from Aransas Pass, renown for its bird sanctuary, you take a ferry over to Port Aransas, renown for its small fishing village atmosphere and its fabulous seafood. Home to Bertha's, the only four-star restaurant on the coast, and artist Steve Vaughn (who paints in his studio on Roberts Street), Port Aransas has been a popular getaway for years for urbanites who want to avoid crowds. Port Aransas offers great music on the weekends, excellent restaurants, ten miles of well-manicured beach, and access to boating and fishing that some say is unparalleled.

Located immediately after you come on-island, Harbor View B&B is a three-story Mediterranean style home, located on the Port Aransas Municipal Harbor. On each of the three levels, the decks and balconies afford a beautiful, unobstructed view, where you can see the dolphins follow behind passing sailboats, yachts, and shrimpers. You can moor your own boat at the B&B, but don't expect a full breakfast at 5 a.m.! If you can wait until a little later, you're in for a treat. The attractive decor of this B&B is bright and breezy, befitting its character. Your hosts are fierce conservationists who know where to crab and catch flounder and find an unspoiled marsh in and around St. Joe's Island. They share it all with you.

RAYMONDVILLE

The Inn at El Canelo

Hosts: Monica and Ray Burdette, P.O. Box 487, Raymondville 78580, (210) 689-5042, 4 bedrooms (2 in the main house, 2 in the guest house), 4 private baths, continental plus and one evening meal, $$$$, no pets, children by special arrangement, smoking designated areas, no cr

In the late 1800s, Don Francisco Yturria, a pioneer banker and contemporary of Captain Richard King, bought 81,000 acres of South Texas ranch land. Today, the name "Yturria" is well known in these parts, and the land he passed down to his descendants remains intact. The Inn at El Canelo, a five-star B&B and a working cattle ranch, sits on 3,200 acres of the original holdings. Under the auspices of retired Army Lieutenant Colonel Ray Burdette and his wife Monica, great-great-granddaughter of Don Francisco, the sprawling hacienda reflects a mix of Texana and European, the result of the host couple's worldly experiences. Warm earthy fabrics add color to rich woods and wide-paned windows and doors that afford a great countryside view.

Guests here play tennis, hike, bird watch, stargaze, and go hunting by special arrangement. The grounds are dotted with bougainvillea and palm trees that sway in the gentle breezes that originate from the Gulf, 20 short miles away. Antique lampposts, the ancient ranch school bell mounted in the yard, and a grotto add serenity to the secluded environment. Original corrals keep exotic goats and sheep safe nearby, and there is the 60-year-old guest house, additional B&B space, making this inn a great place for groups.

When you make reservations, ask about hunting and cooking class packages. Monica is a gourmet cook, having studied cuisine in Europe and California. By the way, the El Canelo's signature is "Champagne Margaritas."

ROCKPORT

Anthony's by the Sea, A Bed and Breakfast

Hosts: Tony Borghi and Dennis Barsness, 732 S. Pearl Street, Rockport 78382, (512) 729-6100 or 1 (800) 460-2557 or Sand Dollar Hospitality, (512) 853-1222, 1 suite with full bath and wet bar, 2 rooms with shared bath, 2 guest houses with kitchen facilities, gourmet breakfast, $$–$$$, smoking allowed, children accepted, no cats, TV/VCR in rooms, V, MC

Anthony's by the Sea offers one thing few B&Bs allow: smoking (except in the inside common area). Two things are striking when you arrive: the B&B is an oasis of plants—huge tropicals that totally disguise the '50s-style beach house; further, you enter through a lanai (outdoor-style patio) that is covered, carpeted, contains a chandelier and more plants, barbecue pit and fountain, with a backdrop of even more plants, pool and hot tub (with a special germ-killing purifier). Host Tony, formerly in charge of banquets at Caesar's in Las Vegas, is properly proud of his breakfast cuisine (Eggs Benedict, Apple French toast, among other delicacies). While eating, you might see hummingbirds (the house is on the Hummingbird Tour, something birders shouldn't miss), butterflies, squirrels, or geckoes. Both Tony and Dennis, a retired school teacher, are actively involved in community politics, environmental and educational programs, so, at the least, conversation at Anthony's by the Sea is never dull.

The Blue Heron Inn Bed and Breakfast

Hosts: Nancy and Gary Cooper, 801 Patton Street, Rockport 78382, (512) 729-7526, 2 rooms with private baths, 2 rooms with private ½ bath and shared shower/tub, full breakfast, $$$, no children, no pets, no smoking, V, MC

If you come to Rockport, you can't miss The Blue Heron. It resides majestically overlooking the glistening waters of Little Bay. Although the original house dates to 1890, the Federal-style home has been gorgeously updated, retaining its external grandeur, including its veranda and huge palm and live oak trees, but accommodating the most discriminating of guests with large, light, airy rooms punctuated by spectacular art. Most of the art is from local artists (although small, Rockport has a huge number of working artists in residence). Some of the art is from your hosts' stint in the Peace Corps in Africa (Zaire) or South America (Brazil), after they retired from their executive jobs. The gourmet breakfast, with herbs from the garden, is legendary (their version of Eggs Benedict with smoked roasted red pepper sauce is incredible), and guests can request dinner by special arrangement. You are greeted with homemade snacks and drinks upon your arrival, and they provide bikes and beach towels (gratis) and almost anything else (including a picnic lunch for an extra fee) you might need to make your stay memorable.

Chandler House Bed and Breakfast

**Hosts: Michelle Barnes and sister Mary Burney, 801 Church Street, Rockport 78382, (800) 843-1808 or (512) 729-2285, 3 rooms,
1 with private bath and fireplace, the others with shared bath, full breakfast, $$–$$$, children over 12 accepted, smoking in restricted areas, turn-down service, public tearoom downstairs, verandas up and downstairs, no pets, V, MC**

The Chandler House, named after the ship chandler who sold ship goods in the 1870s, is a traditional Cape Cod Victorian, with large verandas both up and downstairs. The knickknacks and china are pieces from the hosts' aunts', mother's and grandmother's families, giving the house a family feel often associated with big, old homes. The common area offers a fireplace and parlor games for guests' enjoyment. Located in the center of Rockport, just four blocks from Aransas Bay and 30 minutes from Padre, visitors can enjoy beachcombing, golfing, boating, water sports, fishing, and bird watching (which is a BIG sport in Rockport). The quaint main street in town offers numerous art treasures—another big reason people visit Rockport, which until rather recently, was primarily known as a fishing town. Great breakfasts are a given here and, if you'd like, you can come back for lunch in the tearoom that occupies part of the downstairs.

Hummingbird Lodge and Educational Center

Hosts: Rod and Kim Rylander, HCO 1 Box 245, Rockport 78382, (888) 827-7555 or (512) 729-7555, e-mail: rodkimry@aol.com, 6 rooms with private baths, full breakfast, $$–$$$, smoking in restricted areas only, no pets

A mecca for birdwatchers and naturalists, this jewel of a B&B is set in a natural wonderland, among twisting live oaks and wildflowers of the wetlands and Copano Bay. The porch view of the hummingbirds and coastal birds is captivating for anyone but, for birders, you might as well feel you've died and gone to heaven. Adding to the beautiful gardens (especially attractive to hummingbirds), workshops for artists and craftspeople (such as basketry, pottery, and watercoloring) are also available on some weekends, primarily in the fall. Nearby attractions include the Aransas Wildlife Refuge, Goose Island State Park, Copano Fishing Pier, the Texas State Aquarium, Matagorda and Mustang Islands and thousands of acres of wetlands, rookery islands, and of course, beaches. A large swimming pool and bathhouse are also available, along with a naturalist on staff to answer questions about the birds, plants, and animals you might see.

ROMAYOR

Chain-O-Lakes Resort/Hilltop Herb Farm

Hosts: Dr. and Mrs. Jimmy Smith, P.O. Box 218, Romayor 77368, (713) 592-2150, cabins with 2 and 3 bedrooms and private baths, full gourmet breakfast, $$$–$$$$, no pets, children welcome, no smoking, MC, V, AE, D

At last, here is a B&B that caters to children as well as adults. Hidden just within the borders of the Big Thicket, Chain-O-Lakes has everything from riding stables to fish and swim lakes to an impressive 14,000-square-foot lodge with dormitories and Texas-sized dance hall. The resort itself covers 300 acres of unspoiled woods with 13 spring-fed lakes dotted among cabins, primitive sites, and RV hookups. Breakfast served at the Hilltop Country Inn Restaurant is scrumptious, flavored with herbs that replace harmful seasonings.

Guests stay in one of the resort log cabins, each with its own front porch, deck, and private lake. Accommodations vary from two to three bedrooms with one being a second-story loft, perfect for the kids. Each cabin, decorated in country blue and named after a Texas hero, has living and fully equipped kitchen areas with a stone fireplace (firewood included). As an added treat, owners Jimmy and Beverly Smith give guests a morning horse-and-buggy ride to the restaurant. Guests may also rent golf carts, pedal boats, and canoes, or go horseback riding with the resort's trail boss. Lakes are stocked with bass, croppie, perch, and coppernose bluegill. Bring your rod and boat, but leave noisy motors at home. Also, special gourmet dinner packages are available.

ROUND TOP

Round Top, population 81 and the smallest incorporated town in Texas, holds treasures discovered long ago by Texans of Fayette and Washington counties. Believed to have gotten its name from an early stagecoach mileage designation, Round Top is home of the prestigious Festival Hill, headquarters of the James Dick Foundation for the Performing Arts and for the past 26 years a place where aspiring musicians come to perfect their skills. Henkel Square, a German museum village sponsored by the Texas Pioneer Arts Foundation, is also here as well as the Winedale Historical Center just four miles away. Festivals, holiday celebrations, and antique fairs also occur regularly including Winedale's Shakespeare Festival that happens in the spring and summer. Bluebonnets grow profusely here in late March and early April.

As for food, it's worth a trip to Round Top just to taste Bud Royer's gourmet fare at his well-known Royers' Round Top Cafe. Cuisine ranges from country to continental, but Bud's pies (nine varieties in all) are his specialty. As for Bud and his "creative" wife, Karen, be sure to greet them and experience Round Top hospitality at its best.

Broomfields Bed and Breakfast

Hosts: Julia and Bill Bishop, 419 N. Nassau Rd., Round Top 78954, (409) 249-3706, fax (409) 249-3852, 5 bedrooms, 4 baths, full breakfast, $$$–$$$$, no pets, no children, smoking in designated areas only, no cr

Broomfields, named for the broomweed that once filled the pastures that surround this B&B, is the pride of geologist Bill Bishop and his wife Julia, an interior decorator. Though the Texas-styled residence is new, the cypress exterior has weathered so that the home looks as if it has always belonged to this 40-acre meadowland, shaded by oak and cedar trees and ablaze with wildflowers.

The house, with center cupola and large front and back porches features a large upstairs suite, the Blue Mountain Room. An extensive balcony library surrounds the living room with 28-foot ceiling. Also upstairs is the Kairouan Suite and the downstairs Gwynedd Room. And, if you like to shop, you'll find Julia is a wealth of information on local spring and fall antique shows. In fact, the Bishops have their own Broomfields Gallery located next to the house that is full of antiques, collectibles, and decorative arts.

As for furnishings, the pieces here represent the Old and New World as the hostess has mixed European antiques with American. And, as only a decorator can do well, she has added a variety of conversation pieces from cowhide rugs to a collection of contemporary and traditional art. All is light and airy, with hand-hewn walnut beams from an Ohio barn overhead and bleached pine floors.

Heart of My Heart Ranch Bed and Breakfast

Hosts: Bill and Frances Harris, Fayette Co. Rd. 217, P.O. Box 106, Round Top 78954, Office/fax (409) 249-3171 or (800) 327-1242, 17 bedrooms, 17 baths, full country breakfast, $$$$, no pets, children in log cabin, smoking (porches only), MC, V

A Santa Gertrudis cattle ranch, Heart of My Heart Ranch, owned by Bill and Frances Harris, is "the stuff of which dreams are made."

The spacious ranch house, with carriage quarters, two cottages, and historic log cabin, seems picture-perfect with the lake and lighted pier as a backdrop. The property is secluded with wooded trails that Stephen F. Austin knew well. In fact, you can see the remnants of Gaucher Trace, a wagon trail cleared in 1828 to the colony at San Felipe.

Guests here can picnic anywhere on the ranch if they don't mind the family dog or Shetland pony tagging along. Fruit trees and live oaks shade the main house and the lake, and there is an English rose garden near the porch where breakfast is served. The house is lavishly furnished with many pieces traceable to Bill's pioneer doctor lineage. As for the first meal of the day, no one here goes hungry with Frances' Dutch babies, sourdough blueberry pancakes, smoked meats, and strawberry smoothies that taste great served in the country air. Guests may stay in the main house, carriage quarters, or the authentic settler cabin.

There's horseback riding, biking, tennis, and golf nearby. Swedish massages are also available here as well as a conference center, pool, fishing, driving range, boats—everything you could want and more. Great for large groups.

The Settlement House

Hosts: Larry and Karen Beever, 313 Bauer-Rummel Road and 2218 Hartfield Road, P.O. Box 176, Round Top 78954, (409) 249-5015, 3 separate cottages with private baths, gourmet continental, $$$–$$$$, no children, no pets, smoking permitted in designated outside areas, M, V, AE, D, DC

For an authentic taste of life during the 19th century, the Beevers of Round Top offer three unique cottages, each with its own history and each with its own set of accommodations. The Townplace (Stadt-plaz), a composite of two structures, one a barn, and one a residence, is an Italian Renaissance B&B that dates back to 1880. Located only four blocks from the Town Square, the front of the house is a remarkable little shop filled with artistic pieces, so reflective of the Beevers themselves, both artists with a flair for beauty.

Three guest rooms connect with the shop via a relaxing side porch that looks out onto a pair of magnificent oak trees that were probably there during Stephen F. Austin's time. One accommodation, the Cowboy Room, takes visitors back to wrangler days with its antique brass queen-sized bed, old claw-foot tin tub, and Old West motif that runs through fabrics, wall hangings, and old saloon pieces. The second guest quarters, The Garden Room, provides an interesting contrast with pastel down comforters, old quilts, and dainty wisteria vine stenciling. The Country Room, brilliant with original milk painted walls, is pretty amazing and a discovery yet to be uncovered by Smithsonian historians. There's a pleasant feel here in all of the rooms, with duvet covers and stained-glass windows.

Two miles away on the Beever farm, two other cabins (1830 and 1860), small but well-decorated, are open to guests. A fourth accommodation, the Santa Fe House, is also here. The Settlement House Farm is historic land, by the way. Confederate soldiers helped raise the rafters for the main house. If you like art, history, or just plain good conversation, you'll love the Beevers. They make everybody feel at home with their breakfast baskets of bakery goods.

Note: Other "B&B" accommodations, all unhosted, are provided by the Texas Pioneer Arts Foundation (409) 249-3308. Their historic houses, one of which belonged to the noted benefactor Faith Bybee, are scattered throughout town. Guests here don't see hosts but are served breakfast at local cafes. Former Houstonian Roland Nester and his sister Mary Nester Stanhope also run Briarfield (409) 249-3973 a small complex of accommodations, where they serve a simple continental breakfast.

SILSBEE

Sherwood Train Depot Bed and Breakfast

Host: Jerry Allen, P.O. Box 2281, Silsbee 77656, (409) 385-0188, 2 guest rooms, private bath, full breakfast, $$, children 5 and older welcome, no pets, no alcohol, smoking outside in designated areas only, no cr

Located about 30 minutes northwest of Beaumont, this host home is among neighboring homes, each on at least an acre of land, clustered in a wooded subdivision. Actually a two-story cypress home that resembles the depots of the Old West, resident trees are actually part of the Big Thicket.

Hosted by Jerry Allen, who seconds as an artist who loves crafts, this B&B features an attraction that is offered by no other—an "LGB" model train runs throughout the home. Built by Jerry's husband, the cypress ceiling-hung track, with 12 or more switching spurs, runs 350 feet through the parlor, the dining area, and then the sprawling kitchen, then makes a spiral loop upstairs to the loft where it turns through a miniature replica of the town of Silsbee with its Santa Fe Freight Station and the Kirby Lumber Mill. This site is pretty when the tracks are lit with twinkling lights.

Accommodations are nice. One guest room has a hot tub and shower. For those who like an occasional glass of wine, however, these folks are teetotalers.

SOUTH PADRE

Brown Pelican, A Bayside Bed and Breakfast

Innkeeper: Vicky Conway, 207 West Arles, South Padre Island 78597, (210) 761-2722, 8 rooms with private baths (1 for mobility impaired and 1 with kitchen facilities), continental plus, $$$$, children over 12, no pets, smoking in restricted areas

Comfortably furnished with European and American antiques, the Brown Pelican Inn is located on the Laguna Madre Bay. With its large wraparound porches, "island time" mandates slowing down and soaking up the relaxed ambience. The vista is spectacular, to say the least. Within a five-minute walk to the Gulf beach, the Inn is convenient to swimming, sunbathing, birding, fly fishing, windsurfing, beachcombing, bicycling, or a trip to Old Mexico, which is a must for shoppers. Most rooms have incredible bay views, so the only concern you should have is your choice of the many dining options that await you on South Padre.

SPRING

McLachlan Farm Bed and Breakfast

Hosts: Jim & Joycelyn McLachlan Clairmonte, 24907 Hardy Road, (mailing address) P.O. Box 538, Spring 77383, (800) 382-3988, (713) 350-2400, 3 bedrooms, 2 baths, gourmet breakfast, $$–$$$$,

no pets, no children, no smoking, no alcoholic beverages, please,
no cr

Only 20 minutes from Houston's Intercontinental Airport, Old
Town Spring is a little country hamlet leftover from pioneer days. Today
it is filled with 150 quaint shops and restaurants, including the historic
Wuenche Brothers Cafe. Four annual festivals take place here, which
give tourists insight into small Texas town life.

The McLachlans settled a 160-acre plot of land during the Civil War.
A school superintendent and railroad man, the original McLachlan
farmed the then sparse prairie that today is dense with trees. The
farm house, built by Joycelyn's grandfather in 1911, is circled by 50
acres of sycamore, pecan, pear, and crepe myrtle. The pretty yellow-
and-white farm house beckons you with a warmth that makes you think
you have been there before. White wood, accented with blue and yellow decor, brings out the best in the old house by accenting its unique
ceilings lines. The Great Room, patterned after the New England
kind, is the very best place in the house with its "great" fireplace and
view of Joycelyn as she prepares homemade muffins and banana pancakes. Windows open the great room to the outside on two sides and
invite morning rays.

If you are in need of a romantic weekend, the upstairs bedrooms with
bath, porch, and swing await. Everybody loves the color-coordinated
claw-foot bathtub. Be sure to ask about the Honeymoon Package, which
includes gourmet cider, bubble bath, candlelight, and truffles.

UVALDE

Casa de Leona

**Hosts: Ben and Carolyn Durr, FM 140, Box 1829, Uvalde 78802,
(210) 278-8550, fax (210) 278-8550, 5 guest rooms, 5 baths,
1 guest cottage, continental plus breakfast, $–$$, no children,
no pets, smoking only outside, MC, V, AE**

Welcome to Casa de Leona, where your hosts will greet you with
a thirst quencher!

On 17 acres of wilderness on the Leona River, Casa de Leona is in
an area with an intriguing history. What makes this Spanish hacienda

unique is that it sits near a volcanic blister formed millions of years ago when Southwest Texas was part of the sea. The entire area served as a gathering place for various Indian tribes, then became the site of Fort Inge, built in 1849. Now most of the land is a park for fishing, hiking, camping, and picnics. The Durr's house and property is on part of this historic land, too. (Carolyn enjoys telling guests about the area!)

Casa de Leona has a lushly landscaped courtyard with flowing fountains and a gazebo—and a spectacular view of the river. Inside, you'll find a pleasing Spanish-style decor accented by paintings and wall hangings. It has formal areas, a music room, an art studio/gift shop, sun deck, balcony, and wood-burning fireplaces. You can try your luck on the fishing pier, but hunting isn't allowed on the property. However, it's fun to watch the deer.

About an hour-and-a-half west of San Antonio, Uvalde has a museum in tribute to one of its most famous—and colorful—"sons," John Nance Garner. Crusty "Cactus Jack" was FDR's vice president.

WOODVILLE

Antique Rose Bed and Breakfast

Hosts: Jerry and Denice Morrison, 612 Nellius, Woodville 75979, (409) 283-8926, (800) 386-8926, 3 guest rooms, 3 baths, full breakfast, $$–$$$, children 13 and over, no pets, smoking in designated areas, no cr

Built in 1862 during the Civil War, the Antique Rose Bed and Breakfast was once known as "The Old Female Academy." Today it reigns as a showplace in Woodville, a shady little town in dogwood-dotted East Texas that has long carried the title of Gateway of the Big Thicket. One of the few B&Bs in this area, the Antique Rose Bed and Breakfast is a Federal-style plantation house that has gone through extensive renovation by owners Jerry and Denice Morrison. Named for Jerry's love of growing antique roses, the home offers three guest rooms, each nicely furnished with period antiques, lace, and country decor. Each room has its own bath with claw-foot bathtubs. Predominant colors here are powdered blue and shades of pink and violet.

The Morrisons serve a full breakfast in the dining room. They begin with a fruit frappé made from apple juice, strawberries, and bananas, followed by quiche and homemade cinnamon rolls. Guests are also provided tea, hot chocolate, homemade breads, soft drinks, and lemonade. For Java lovers, each room has its own coffee pot. As for the roses, they are the pride of Jerry who is happy to show you all of his 150 lace and nostalgic varieties.

INDEX